Criminal

Criminal

How Our Prisons Are Failing Us All

ANGELA KIRWIN

First published in Great Britain in 2022 by Trapeze
an imprint of The Orion Publishing Group Ltd
Carmelite House, 50 Victoria Embankment
London EC4Y 0DZ

An Hachette UK Company

1 3 5 7 9 10 8 6 4 2

ISBN (Hardback) 978 1 3987 0583 8
ISBN (Export Trade Paperback) 978 1 3987 0584 5
ISBN (eBook) 978 1 3987 0586 9
ISBN (Audio) 978 1 3987 0587 6

Typeset by Input Data Services Ltd, Somerset

Printed and bound in Great Britain by Clays Ltd, Elcograf S.p.A.

www.orionbooks.co.uk

'It is said that no one truly knows a nation until one has been inside its jails. A nation should not be judged by how it treats its highest citizens, but its lowest ones.'

– Nelson Mandela

criminal

Noun
A person who has committed a crime.
'*these men are dangerous criminals*'

Adjective
(of an action or situation) deplorable and shocking.
'*the state of our prison system is criminal*'

For Mickey, and all the others

CONTENTS

AUTHOR'S NOTE

The language of prison is vulgar: it's derogatory and discriminatory and dehumanising. Words like 'con', 'crim' and 'inmate' tick all three boxes. While I've avoided every expletive uttered – the book would have doubled in length if I'd included them all – it would be disingenuous to ignore the everyday words used inside to refer to people with criminal convictions. Language matters, and I'm not using any of these words lightly. Where they are used, it's to highlight that these men are defined by their crimes: any other characteristic is secondary to their incarceration. To juxtapose this language with the human stories of these men, I hope to highlight that how we think and talk about people in prison has a real-world impact. As we start to understand a little more about the humanity of these people, maybe the way we identify and describe them can shift, too.

CHAPTER 1

What Are You in For?

'I've gone straight, miss,' the scrawny, sweating con opposite me says with a smile so sincere even I almost believe him.

Deano has landed back on the induction wing for the third time this year. He's dressed in the tracksuit of an inmate, remnants of unidentifiable prison food crusting into the collar. He's even donned a set of the plastic rosary beads that are the accessory of choice of the incarcerated. It does not appear, by any measure, that Deano has gone straight.

I usher him to take a seat at one of the bolted-down picnic benches that line the landing, circled by the noise and chaos of ninety other unlocked crims rushing around for showers, medication, drug deals and phone calls. It's only 10 a.m. I got in at 8 a.m. and have already completed a group therapy session. I've got three more assessments to finish before bang-up for lunch at 11.30 a.m., but Deano is telling me he needs to talk, so we talk.

There's a special sort of social worker body language they teach you at university. Be open, nod empathetically. Then once you start working in prison, there's another sort of body language you learn. Safe distances, no sudden movements, keep your eyes on the whole landing while listening intently to the man in front of you. I'm well practised in both. With notepad open and neutral expression fixed, Deano starts talking.

'I'm just really addicted to smoking crack,' he says.

I nod back at him knowingly, biting away the smile.

'It does certainly seem that way.'

'I know, right, miss. It's like I can't stop or something. Weird, innit?'

I can't decide if Deano has actually forgotten that he's now had six custodial sentences, all directly related to his drug use.

'I just fucking love crack,' he says, slamming his palms onto the table for emphasis.

But, Deano tells me, he also loves his mum and his girl-friend and has noticed that carrying on smoking might be causing them some pain.

'My mum cries every time she comes up to visit me. That' – he puts his hands on his hips and puffs his chest out with pride – 'is why I've gone straight.'

Deano doesn't elaborate. Smiling, he closes his eyes briefly to bask in the glory that comes with being a reformed member of society.

I stare blankly at him, wondering if these delusions are symptomatic of a serious problem. I reach for my file, surrep-titiously leafing through for the mental health team referral form.

'Can you tell me where we are right now?' I ask gently, my pen poised over the question that asks: Oriented to time and place?

'On A wing, miss.' He looks at me with concern, wonder-ing why I'm confused about our location.

'And can you tell me why you're on A wing, Deano?' I continue.

'Because of going straight.' He slaps the table in frustra-tion. 'Are you not listening to me?' His face reddens, screws up tight like a toddler's.

'I'm sorry. I am listening.'

'I decided I don't want it no more. I don't want to be having to just do things because the drugs want me to do things, do you get me? I've had enough.'

I nod slowly in agreement.

'Go on,' I prompt. 'You mean you don't want to be committing crime any more to score drugs?'

'Yeah, exactly!' he replies excitedly. 'Now you're getting it, miss.'

I slap my forehead at my own stupidity and the loose skin on his sunken cheeks wobbles as he laughs.

It transpires that Deano has set up his own business.

'What's the business?' I ask.

Surely it can't be dealing. Tell me it's not dealing. Deano won't last a month. He'll smoke half his stash and then the other crims will rob him of the rest. He's too gullible, not menacing enough.

'Well,' he says theatrically, 'I'm gonna be Dan – Dan the Bagel Man. Seriously, you can make a killing.'

I've worked with Deano on and off for two years, but I still glance down at his file just to double-check it's him who has got his own name wrong, not me.

'So, I'm gonna sell sandwiches. Well, bagels.'

He's on a roll now, speaking rapidly, only pausing for breath when he clearly expects me to add some 'oohs' and 'ahhs'.

'Get one of those trailers and pull it on my bike, cycle up to the big office blocks every morning and sell them for a fiver each. Me and my girlfriend have set up a . . . what do you call it? A production line. Making the bagels. Cut them up first.'

He makes a slashing movement, trying to demonstrate cutting up a bagel, which on the CCTV cameras will look like he's role playing a violent crime.

'Don't wave your arms around like that, Deano. The

officers will be piling on you, you look like a fucking maniac,'
I say while slyly giving a thumbs up to Officer Owen at the
far end of the landing, who glances over, concerned.

In exhaustive detail, he takes me through how they make
the bagels.

'Then off I cycle. I love it. Those guys in the suits up there
will spend a fortune on a bagel. Imma be rich, miss.'

He sits back, folding his arms across his ribcage as if he's
just made a successful pitch on *Dragons' Den*.

I hadn't realised Deano had it in him.

'This sounds really positive. This sounds great, Deano. Do
you reckon it'll keep you busy while you get off the crack?
Keep you focused on something else, instead?'

'Yeah, miss, definitely. I mean, I accidentally had a little
dabble and smoked the first profits.'

He grins and hums a weird laugh, clearly hoping I'll
indulge him and say something like 'Ah, but what's a little
dabble between friends, hey?'. I don't.

Deano keeps talking to fill the silence.

'But since that first time I've been good. I've not picked up
the pipe in two weeks. It's hard work, it's an early start. But
once I get rolling properly, I can probably get someone else to
do the morning shift and I'll just be the face of the business.
The salesman,' he says emphatically as he points at himself.

'So, how have you landed back here?' I ask casually.
'Because this plan sounds pretty solid.'

'Business teething problems, innit. They came to get the
bike back and then found the freezer full of salmon and
bagels and stitched me up for it. They ended up doing me for
criminal damage, too.'

'What bike, Deano? What criminal damage? Who found
the freezer full?'

'The Boris bike. I took a Boris bike. I didn't realise they had
a tracking system on them. I was keeping it on my balcony.

They're well heavy to carry up three flights of stairs too, but there I was, carting it up and down every day. Didn't know that you have to pay for them. Found it outside the corner shop. Good business move. It's not even stealing if no one owns it, you get me, miss?'

It's harder to bite back the smile now.

'I thought it was the proper police who turned up at mine. It wasn't. Just the bike police, you know? Those fake police in the high-vis vests. I didn't know that. They look official. I panicked when I saw them pull up. I chucked the Boris bike off the balcony. Didn't realise they could track them down. And now' – he shrugs his shoulders as if none of this is his fault – 'I've been done for criminal damage because it landed on the neighbour's shed.'

I continue to stare in silence.

'Then the real police did show up and they came and bust down my door. And they found all the bagels and salmon, too, and I've been done for them as well.'

'Where did the bagels and salmon come from, Deano?' I ask slowly.

'Brick Lane for the bagels and Billingsgate for the salmon.' He doesn't offer any more information.

'So what? You went down there in the mornings and bought them off the traders?' I ask, suspecting I know the answer already.

'Nah, miss. I didn't have enough money to start off with, so I cycled on the Boris bike up and down Brick Lane at 5 a.m. and they always leave their vans open. I climbed in and took a bag of bagels. Same with the salmon. The trucks are always open, so you can just take it out of the back. Cycle home to my girlfriend, get the production line up and running and then be ready to sell them for 8 a.m.'

'Deano,' I ask, 'you do know that "going straight" means you stop committing crimes?'

He screws his face up again.

'But I have, miss. I've got the business and everything,' he replies, visibly upset.

'Do you understand why you've been arrested and charged?'

Deano stares around the landing, considering the question for a while.

'I got no idea, miss.'

It's easy to find the story of Deano and his bagels hilarious. Light relief in an otherwise dark and depressing environment. We laugh at him, knowing that we'd never end up in his situation. Because we're different from him, with different morals and logic and values. Because he's wired to be a crim and we're good upstanding members of society who would never find ourselves in the criminal justice system, let alone stuck in its endless cycle.

But when you've sat on wings watching hundreds of men enter prison and leave and return again and again, trapped in the system, the joke quickly wears thin. Deano had been inside most of his adult life and still hadn't learned, at any level, what it meant to be a law-abiding citizen. And he's not alone.

Of the 62,000 people released every year,[1] 48 per cent will reoffend within twelve months. If a doctor told you that your open-heart surgery only had a 52 per cent chance of success, you'd hardly be offering your organs up to the scalpel. Or imagine boarding a plane that had a 52 per cent chance of landing. You wouldn't even order from a takeaway with a 52 per cent rating. Yet prison keeps churning out reoffenders year after year and somehow this is acceptable.

At a certain point you start to ask yourself, if every year thousands of Deanos are leaving prison so utterly unequipped to re-enter society that they bounce straight back onto the wings, then what, precisely, is any of this for?

Asking just what it is for in the first place is probably a good place to start. Because most people have been lucky enough to avoid prison altogether. And therefore, most people haven't ever had to give much thought as to why we build them and then stack them to the rafters with men, women and children. But if they did, they'd usually pause for a moment and then say that it's the place you put the bad people. And if you were to press a little further, you'd likely hear that it's to keep society safe. Or maybe it's a punishment for breaking society's codes. Or a deterrent to stop them from breaking the rules in the first place. Or – and this is always the suggestion that comes last – there's the vague idea that it could be for rehabilitation. That a crim can somehow learn the error of his ways if we bang him up for long enough.

But even way back in 1993 when Michael Howard MP famously stood up in the House of Commons and said, 'Prison works,' anyone who had experience of the system knew that he was chatting shit. We now have evidence that confirms it's utterly untrue. Whether for deterrent, punishment, public protection or rehabilitation, prisons are failing on every metric.

Incarceration is the least successful punishment available to us, particularly when sentences are short. It's proven to create and perpetuate more crime, costs an absolute fortune, and traumatises both staff and inmates. But each government remains desperate to maintain the myth that the only way to safety is prison bars and walls topped with barbed wire. Even when the Ministry of Justice (MOJ) publishes its own data stating that released prisoners are at a higher risk of reoffending than those serving non-custodial sentences, community treatment and supervision remains underfunded and underutilised. Even with clear statistics that demonstrate the success of non-custodial punishments,[3] the use of such sentences has more than halved in the decade from 2008 to 2018.[4] Politicians want to be tough on crime and, to them, the only way to do that is to throw more crims in prison on even longer sentences. From 2006 to 2018 there has been a 250 per cent increase in the number of prisoners sentenced to ten years or more. The average sentence length in 2006 was 35.7 months. By 2018, it had reached 58.3 months.[5]

There is another way. But if we are to seriously consider any alternative to the current system then the next inevitable questions need to be answered. And I know these questions will be asked, because I've heard them a thousand times over the years. What about the rapists, the paedophiles? What if someone killed your nan? How do we keep society safe? You think we should just let them all go? You don't believe there should be consequences?

They've made their own beds, dug their own graves, lain down with dogs. And these comments are often bound up with the media narrative that 'prisons these days are holiday camps'. Or with reporting on the early release of a murderer after a woefully short sentence. Or a newspaper's outrage at the taxpayer footing the bill for the legal defence of the crim. For many people, the instinct is that we need more prisons and more sentences, not less. The notion of prison reform has become antithetical to the idea of a safer society.

This is because there's often a fundamental misunderstanding of who is in prison. It's true, prison houses some really dangerous people and while they're inside we can all sleep more soundly. But they don't stay inside. Almost every one of them, except for around sixty to sixty-five whole life licence cons, will become one of the 62,000 people released every year.[6]

At any one time, there are around 82,000 men, women and children incarcerated.[7] Yet it's only a minority who are in for serious offences: 12,500 of them are in for sexual offences; 7,000 will be serving life sentences;[8] over 3,000 of them are on the highly controversial Imprisonment for Public Protection (IPP) sentences.[9] You can make a very strong argument that it's necessary to keep society safe from this lot.*

But on any given day, there are also around 12,000 people on remand, not yet found guilty of any crime. And half of them will be acquitted or receive a non-custodial sentence when their case finally reaches court. Almost half of the 59,000 sentenced each year will receive a sentence of six months or less and 69 per cent didn't commit a violent crime.[10] These are the people who make up the vast majority of the prison population. Those on remand and with short sentences for non-violent crimes are the ones who overcrowd the wings and lead to Scotland, England and Wales having the highest per capita incarceration rate in the whole of Western Europe.

Yet even as we fill our wings with more inmates than anywhere else, crime hasn't reduced. The National Audit Office can draw no link between increased incarceration and a reduction in crime.[11] And this fact is hard to swallow, because it's the opposite of what we've been led to believe. Most of us

---

* The make-up of the prison population in the UK changed in a number of ways during the pandemic. The prison population has reduced, mainly due to the police arresting fewer people and less crime being reported. The number of people being recalled to prison on licence also fell. Fewer people were sent to prison on remand, although those already inside when the pandemic hit were waiting longer and longer to get to court and so, overall, remanded prisoners increased as a proportion of the total prison population. This reduction in inmates is not, however, a downward trend. There are plans to build, and fill, more prisons in the future. I have used here the figures for 2019, to give a clearer picture of the typical prison population outside of the pandemic. The House of Commons Library produces reports on the demographics of the prison population, with the October 2021 edition available at https://researchbriefings.files.parliament.uk/documents/SN04334/SN04334.pdf [accessed: 13.12.21].

cling on to the idea that the police wouldn't arrest someone unless they were a danger to society. Prison is where we put criminals, and criminals belong in prison. Unless we come into contact with the system ourselves, we can keep believing that, fundamentally, it works.

But when you've heard the stories of the same life circumstances, over and over, that led someone inevitably back to prison again and again. When you've heard of the addiction and homelessness and abuse and trauma that impacted their direction in life. When you realise that for every whole-lifer, there are 10,000 more petty criminals with mental health issues and learning disabilities bouncing between the wings and the streets, you can't help but feel that there isn't a reassuring hard divide between the bad people on the inside and the well-behaved population on The Out.

To really get to grips with the failures of our prison system is to grapple with some of the biggest problems in our society. A society that accepts a care-to-custody pipeline and one in four of the prison population growing up in foster homes or residential care. A society that accepts one in three prisoners has a learning disability or difficulty, living on landings where eleven is the average reading age.[12] As if custody is the best place for people with these issues who require support.

A society that accepts institutional racism coursing through the criminal justice system. According to the 2017 Lammy Review, over a quarter of the prison population are from a 'Black, Asian or minority ethnic (BAME)' background.*

* When I've described people of colour and discussed the statistics around different ethnicities within the prison population, I've used the language used in the reports that I'm quoting. This is for purposes of clarity regarding the data and to ensure that I'm quoting the sources accurately.

A Black man is 228 per cent more likely to be arrested than a white man. Adjusting for all other data, Black people are 53 per cent more likely to be sentenced to prison in the Crown Court. Asian people are 55 per cent more likely. And if the stats could get even a little more eye-wateringly terrible, other ethnic groups are 81 per cent more likely to end up in prison than their white counterparts for the same offence.[13]

It's a society that thinks homelessness is normal and should be tolerated in one of the richest countries in the world, as we step over rough sleepers on our way to buy a £3 coffee. A society where fully 280,000 people are estimated to be homeless in England alone and then we go on to release one in six inmates to rough sleeping or other, more hidden forms of homelessness on top of that.[14] It's a society that has 4.3 million children living below the poverty line, relying on food banks to eat.[15]

It's a society that accepts drug abuse is the weakness of the individual, not a legitimate attempt to just survive a day behind the walls. It's a society that ultimately thinks prison is the best option for our most lost and damaged kids.

The people who make up the prison population are a symptom of these big, complicated societal diseases. The custodial system magnifies and concentrates the injustices and inequalities of The Out, but then hides them behind walls in the hope that if the problems are out of sight and out of mind, they'll simply vanish. And it's true that if we really want to solve the problems of the inside, we'll ultimately need to address the underlying problems that we allow to fester in society. But in the meantime, if our chosen medicine is doing more harm than good, then it's time to think about trying a new cure.

Why should you listen to me?

I began work in social care in the community eighteen years
ago. It started with youths at risk of becoming involved in the
criminal justice system before training as a social worker and
eventually going behind the walls full-time. Although I've
worked with women and visited women's prisons, the majority of stories I will share are from the male establishments I
experienced.

I was what the older generation of prison officers called a
'care bear' – and one of the few dozen civilian staff inside the
prison. I specialised in mental health and substance misuse,
running 'through the gate', 'dual diagnosis' and 'anger
management' services. Eventually, I travelled the world on
a research fellowship, visiting rehabilitation facilities and
prisons in the hope that I could learn how to really make a
difference from the inside.

I had a wide scope when it came to what my job actually
involved. There was already a housing team, although no one
had seen them on the wings in months and I wasn't sure if
they'd actually all quit. There was the drug and alcohol team,
all carrying caseloads of seventy crims each. A mental health
team, who were harangued and harassed by everyone, cons
and screws alike. There were already a couple of gangs workers and a few teachers, and three or four officers tasked with
keeping crims safe in custody. My role was to step in when
all that stuff wasn't really fitting together or if a con didn't
neatly fit into one team's strict criteria. Too mental for the
drugs team, too high for education, too gang-affiliated to stay
safe in custody. It was my job to work across all the teams
and, if not deliver him safely to the community upon release
fully rehabilitated, then at least stop him from killing himself
or anyone else while inside.

My caseload could run to seventy inmates if their needs were simple and their risk level low. However, I usually focused on twenty-five men who needed intensive support. They'd be referred to me through the weekly multidisciplinary meeting that was held to discuss the biggest causes for concern inside the establishment.

They all needed one-to-one support and I spent my days running up and down four flights of stairs across various landings, from the segregation unit to the detox wing, the vulnerable prisoners' unit (VP) for sexual offenders and ex-police to the foreign nationals wing, the hospital wing to the first night centre. If I'd been allowed to carry my phone behind the walls, I'd have reached my step count by lunchtime every day.

The issues with which they presented were as different as the wings they inhabited. Some were free to move about the prison during mass movement and come to the morning group therapy sessions I ran. I initially started the groups to save time. I thought that if I could cram twelve inmates into a one-hour session, I'd manage to get through all of my work and the associated admin quickly enough to leave on time each day. I didn't count on how important these groups would become over the years, but our classroom was not a cosy one. When this prison had been built over a century ago, it had not been designed for therapeutic interventions.

We had to make do with the space we had. Halfway through our morning sessions, the thrum of treadmills in the gym above would kick in and we had to raise our voices to compete. We once found a dead cockroach on the floor; even bugs that can survive a nuclear holocaust have a breaking point. The walls were bare and the paint chipped. The windows were cracked. When we closed the door, we had to jam a leaflet from the rack on the wall into the gap so it didn't swing back open with the draught. There was always a draught.

Of course, there were inmates who were too high-risk to receive an invite to our morning group therapy, although plenty who did attend were those prisoners from the wings of the notorious prisons you see on documentaries. I sat in rooms with some extremely dangerous men. But I don't simply want to talk about the high-profile prisoners or the murderers and rapists who make the headlines. This isn't yet another sensationalist tale of being banged up and working in England's most violent establishments. Those stories have already been told and, while they're gripping, they don't represent the day-to-day reality of life behind bars. What I've learned from my time on the landings, walking through the front gate upon release with these men and trying to help them make a go of it on The Out, is that prison is not full of notorious cons. It's full of men like the ones you'll come to meet in this book. Inmates without a history of violence, or inmates who spent most of their time in custody technically innocent and awaiting trial. Inmates who hadn't been diagnosed with mental health problems but quickly developed them.

Yes, I'll share the times I worked with paedophiles, murderers, the downright dangerous. But most of the men loitering on the landings aren't like this and imprisoning them in record numbers makes society no safer, the tax bill no smaller, the damage done no less. They're the majority who rot away behind these prison walls. Theirs are the stories that never make the news. Because if they did, they'd show in stark relief just how pointless, just how failing, our prisons are. Ultimately, I left the prison estate burned out by the sense that I couldn't make a difference from inside the crumbling walls.

Instead, I decided I wanted to give voice to the voiceless, share the stories of the men I met, show the humanity in the people we most fear or despise and hope that the world would be willing to listen. I could tell the world on The Out about the misery and poverty, the violence and mental health problems, the addiction issues, abuse and neglect, trauma and racism, that are the reality for the 82,000 men, women and children spending tonight locked in an 8ft x 12ft box with another inmate.

The men I'll introduce you to, the stories I'll share, are based on real people and events. While details have been changed or disguised and some descriptions and incidents are composites of different people and stories to protect anonymity, these are the human beings behind the headlines. The prison estate is vast, and I couldn't even hope to capture the entire breadth and depth of the experiences within the system. Instead, these diverse stories aim to each demonstrate in a different way the failure in our approach to incarceration.

Prison is a microcosm of society. An inner-city town. And of the half-dozen establishments where I've walked the wings, there were between 400 and 1200 souls crammed together from every culture, background and religion. Prison is young and old, gay, bi, straight. It's trans and queer. It's Black, white, brown and every ethnicity in between. It's a melting pot of every physical and mental health diagnosis under the sun. It's guilty, innocent and shades of grey. It's plea deals, remand, indeterminate and life sentences. It's segregation, detox units, VP units and hospital wings. It's shared showers, shared cells, shared toilets and shared meals. It's code blue emergency alarms, barking dogs, radio crackles. Mass movements and six-man unlocks. It's five storeys of landings, with mess nets draped over them to catch the furniture, TVs or bodies that fly over the edge. It's five-a-side football matches against the officers in the mornings then dirty protests in the afternoons. It's calls to prayer followed by an overdose on spice.

Prison has its own share of village idiots and town criers, but there are also the funny ones, the clever ones, the charming and charismatic ones. Then there are the psychopaths, the burglars, the rapists. The gangsters, the wrong-place-wrong-timers, the fraudsters and white-collar criminals. The nonces, the drug dealers, the addicts and the unwell.

Every day I came face to face with horrific life circumstances that led to incarceration. That's not to excuse the behaviour of those who commit crimes. Instead, though, it allows some understanding of why and how men and women and children end up inside. Understanding how they wind up in prison brings us one step closer to understanding how we can bring them back out into the community safely and with the ability to pursue a happy, meaningful, rehabilitated and fulfilled life.

The men I'll introduce you to aren't broken. Mental health issues, addiction, trauma, neglect, abuse or poverty might have pushed them to the edge, but the cracks in the system were there waiting for them. They are real people, with hopes and dreams and ambitions. They are sons, brothers, fathers. They could have had normal lives. They could have contributed to society. They still can, if we radically rethink our approach to incarceration, public protection and rehabilitation. It's the system that's broken. The prison estate is falling apart, bursting at the seams with its overcrowded landings, and cells infested with rats and cockroaches.

We're being conned out of every penny of the £21.5 billion that's being spent on prison and reoffending per year. Yet no one will admit that all of it, from the magistrates' courts to the supermax cat As, is The Emperor's New Clothes. And so instead, they quietly fund a handful of people like me to walk the landings, desperately trying to rehabilitate people in an environment designed to debilitate.

This book is my attempt to change the conversation in some small way. These people are part of our communities and we're failing them, and ourselves, if we are not willing to listen. They are no different from you and me. We must open our eyes to the reality of the broken system. If we truly care about the society we live in, if we want to be part of a safer and fairer world, then we must dare to look at the reality of our prison estate with compassion and humanity, with objectivity and rationality, and then demand change.

Because, as every crim I've ever worked with knows, the first step towards making things better is admitting there's a problem in the first place.

CHAPTER 2

Doing Time – The History of Prisons

Prison smelled of stale cigarette smoke and sweat, and sometimes incense and sometimes weed and crack pipes. It smelled of hundreds of years of sadness and desperation and anger and hurt and depression and anxiety. It smelled of defeat. It smelled of grown men who gave up caring about themselves long ago, if they ever did.

There was never silence. The soundtrack of prison life was full of banging metal gates, emergency alarms, assertive hollers of 'Back behind your doors, lads.' Pool balls were bounced around the table and sometimes put inside socks to wrap around people's heads. Speaker systems blared from the cells of enhanced inmates, while football matches were fought and lost. Every movement of a crim back onto a wing was completed by the shout of 'One on.' Dogs barked. The swearing became banal background noise, punctuating every sentence. It was the common language of that world and one the staff adopted to communicate effectively, too.

In my time, I saw people die of old age, die from drug overdoses, suicide and murder. Some of those deaths happened quietly, behind cell doors, or in an ambulance on the way out to hospital. Others happened in front of the wing, with arms of fellow inmates twisting from door hatches, holding mirrors to get a better look. I worked with officers who could talk a prisoner down from jumping over the railings and those who told men with profound mental health issues to 'Get it over with and hang yourself – just don't make a mess.'

I watched prisoners high-five and congratulate each other at the news of a child's birth on The Out and I saw them cry on each other's shoulders when a fellow inmate had killed himself. I watched them raise money for charity, fast for Ramadan and mop shit off the walls.

I had rape threats heckled from faceless windows on the wings, followed by kindness, compassion and generosity on the landing. I saw officers waiting for blood tests after an attack, desperately hoping they hadn't been infected with HIV or hepatitis C. I heard of an officer being covered in shit when a whole wing took a disliking to her. I watched the news and read the headlines as my colleagues were banged up themselves for sexual relationships or for smuggling phones and drugs in for inmates.

I watched lines lowered out of windows – a carefully constructed chain of bed sheets passing around the drugs and weapons that were flown over the walls by drones, or brought in during visits or by bent staff. Then I saw wings torn apart as cells were spun to hunt for the contraband.

I met devastated mothers in visits' halls, broken-hearted by their sons yet loving them unconditionally. I heard stories in the smoking shed of the mother arrested for spitting a wrap into a coffee cup and handing it over to her son, only for him to die of an overdose back on the wing.

I watched on the news as the police hunted for escaped cons. Then I tried to do my job through locked cell doors in the constant bang-up that followed.

To be stood in a prison during mass movement was to be reminded like nowhere else of my status as just a body among the hundreds of other bodies who also happened to occupy the space and time of that precise moment. But I was also part of a system that stretched back hundreds of years and has carried on as it always had after I left.

But to truly understand how and why prison is failing so badly, first we need to look at how we got here. 'Here' being England and Wales holding the title of the highest prison bill in Europe, spending £3.4 billion a year on incarceration alone,[1] with a further £18.1 billion on reoffending thrown in for good measure.[2]

'Here' is a prison estate where, in 2019, one in seven prisons in the country were given a performance rating of 'serious concern'.[3]

'Here' is Dutch judges refusing to extradite a British man back to HMP Liverpool because of the very real concern that the establishment wouldn't be able to protect his Article 3 Fundamental Human Right – the right to live free from torture and inhuman or degrading treatment.

A Brief History of Prison

The use of imprisonment as the primary form of punishment in England is only about as old as an average inner-city establishment, which being built in the nineteenth century may have seemed ancient on the days the roof leaked, but was actually just a brief moment in the long history of finding novel and inventive ways of punishing criminals. Before then, prisons existed but were used mainly to hold people awaiting trial or debtors who couldn't afford to pay what they owed.

Instead of imprisonment, when the very first societies began codifying laws, chiselled in stone, the phrase 'an eye for an eye' was literal. The Code of Hammurabi stands proudly in the Louvre Museum, Paris, demonstrating that since time began, there have been crimes and there have been punishments.

Back then, if Deano had gouged someone's eye out, he would indeed have lost his own eye. But he was found guilty of robbery and criminal damage – offences so serious back in 1750 BC that he'd have been sentenced to death, no questions asked. In China, punishments such as tattooing, castration or cutting off the nose were seen as fair trades for breaking the agreed-upon societal rules.[4]

It was the Romans who first used imprisonment as a punishment rather than simply for detention. When I learned about the Mamertine Prison built around 640 BC in the sewer systems below ancient Rome, I looked around my classroom, stinking toilets next door polluting the air, stale with the sweat of the tens of thousands of men who had previously served time, and felt a sense of recognition. I was being melodramatic, of course. My crims weren't forced into hard labour in a sewage pipe. But then in 2,500 years, maybe we could have expected a little more reform . . .

Throughout medieval times, Deano would have fared no better. He'd have still most likely been hung, his loss of life seen as a fair swap for his offence. Or maybe he'd have got lucky. In the 900s, King Athelstan raised the age at which a criminal could receive the death penalty from twelve to sixteen. He thought it was just 'too cruel'.[5] Maybe this Anglo-Saxon soft-touch king would have looked kindly on Deano and he'd have been put in the stocks or got a public whipping instead.

I thought about the rats sniffing around piles of rotten food in the exercise yard and wondered if, in a different time, a baying crowd would have thrown tomatoes at Deano in the town square. On the other hand, over in Japan, he could have been buried alive or chopped up with bamboo saws.[6]

The Vikings were keen on blood money payments, buying their way out of a murder or offence by paying compensation to the victim's family.[7] But then Deano had fuck all. That's why he'd set up his business in the first place. If he couldn't have afforded to pay or wanted to prove his innocence, he'd have faced trial by ordeal. Maybe he'd have been tied up and thrown into a lake, his guilt obvious if he floated. Innocence would only be determined if he was half-drowned before being pulled from the water. Or, he could've been forced to carry a hot iron bar. If his hands were still blistered and bloodied after three days, he'd have been deemed guilty.[8]

It was Henry VIII who popularised the concept of the worthy and unworthy poor. Those who were old or disabled were worthy and given a licence to beg. But to beg without a licence resulted in whipping, with punishments becoming more severe for repeat offenders.[9]

In the eighteenth century, Deano could have been sent overseas, transported to the Americas or Australia, sentenced to a life of hard labour in the colonies. I look at his pale, blotched face and wonder if he'd even have survived the crossing. Yet when America began its fight for independence in 1775, and before prison colonies in Australia had been established, shipping off the problem people of society out of sight and out of mind was no longer possible.

The boats, previously used for transportation, were instead moored around the country and filled with convicts. These hulks housed hundreds in squalid conditions, and inhabitants would be required to perform manual labour all day before returning to the crowded, disease-ridden ships at night.

What all these sentences had in common was that they were designed to punish the offender. There wasn't much thought of rehabilitation or reform, or whether or not chopping off the hand of a thief would actually help him to find his way back to the straight and narrow. Retribution was the order of the day and a punishment to teach the crim a lesson, whether with an eye, his life or his loss of liberty and with back-breaking toil. They also sought to deter any would-be

scoundrels from the notion of committing a crime. For surely
Deano would have thought twice about nicking that Boris
bike if he knew he'd hang for it?

These *lex talionis* – laws of retaliation – have long endured
throughout Europe and the rest of the world, and still leave
their mark on our confused system of criminal justice to this
day. These ideas remain a common part of the contemporary
conversation around crime and punishment. There's barely a
day that goes by without the comments section on the latest
clickbait article lighting up with the *capitalised* phrase 'AN
EYE FOR AN EYE'. But this rationale for imprisonment
doesn't quite stand up to closer scrutiny. Deano nicked a bike
and damaged a garden shed. He doesn't have a bike to give
back to the council or a shed to replace his neighbour's, but it's
been arbitrarily decided that this is worth two years of his life.

Our ludicrously complicated sentencing laws, developed
haphazardly over the centuries through statutes and court
cases, mean he'd have got the same sentence for a racially
aggravated assault.[10] Likewise, administering drugs to obtain
intercourse[11] would have had the same outcome. The total
haul of bagels and salmon, combined with the garden shed,
came to a value of less than £1000. But his crime was deemed
to be as serious as an assault against another person. His
incarceration would cost the state over £44,000 per year.[12]

Leaving aside the wonky maths and skipping back to the
eighteenth century for a moment, utilitarian philosopher
Jeremy Bentham was hunched over his desk, busily sketching
out the panopticon prison design. Hailed as a modern piece
of architectural brilliance, his idea was to create a prison
where all inmates could be viewed at all times, by just one
guard, housed in a central room. He postulated that human
beings are rational and pleasure-seeking, reducing and avoiding pain wherever possible. Therefore, if the potential pain
of punishment in prison could outweigh the pleasure derived

from committing crime, the general public would all choose to be law-abiding.[13]

More importantly, however, he thought prisons could be run privately and for profit. The key to the panopticon prison would be productive labour. Contracts would be awarded to private jailors. They'd then be motivated to look after the health of their inmates through a series of targets. The jailor would be financially rewarded or punished based on how many inmates he managed to keep alive. He believed a jailor could be encouraged to provide safer and healthier conditions if he was fined when crims died. Bentham would probably look on approvingly at the UK and US these days, where big profits are being made and prisoners are used as cheap labour, but more of that later. Because in Bentham's lifetime, these ideas of privatisation ran counter to most reformist thinking.

In the haphazard prisons that did exist in the eighteenth century, men, women and children mixed together in shackles and irons, paying their jailor for the privilege of a roof over their heads. Inmates had to pay for food, pay for straw to sleep on and even pay for their release. If they couldn't afford to pay, they stayed, even if their sentence had been completed.

Really, compared to all that, Deano should've thanked his lucky stars that the reformers came along. At the turn of the eighteenth century, perhaps because all of these convicts were now out hard-labouring in full view of Londoners, rather than over in America, the public attitude to punishment began to shift.

During the previous century, the Bloody Code had added more and more offences that warranted the death penalty to the statute book. Stealing from a rabbit warren, going out after dark with a blackened face and destroying a fish pond would all result in the hangman's noose.[14] But at the same time, the Industrial Revolution had brought tens of thousands into the poverty of inner-city living. Enlightenment thinking had spread and the public appetite for capital punishment was quickly deteriorating. Who now could honestly say that they wouldn't, if they found themselves in Deano's position, pilfer a bit of food to feed their family or steal a horse to be able to pay the rent? The juries of the day started to refuse to find people guilty or undervalued stolen goods to help a crim escape with his life.

Into this landscape of retribution and punishment stepped John Howard, High Sheriff of Bedfordshire, who visited the uncontrolled prisons and hulks of the eighteenth century and saw sex workers and beer being brought in for the inmates who could afford to pay. This wasn't reshaping the criminals into upstanding members of society. He was shocked by conditions that were breeding more criminality and debauched behaviour.

He campaigned for shackles and irons to be removed. It was normal for a con to be locked away until he could afford to pay a fine for his release. Howard demanded this practice be abolished. If a con was committing crimes from a position of desperation and poverty, he was unlikely to be able to stump up the payment for his release.

Elizabeth Fry, influenced by her Quaker beliefs, was dubbed the Angel of Prisons for her campaigning and social work for women and children who were imprisoned. Like Howard, she was unable to turn away from the horror after seeing it for herself and the two of them helped to promote the belief in a more humane system of punishment.

But as the reformist movement gained traction, so too did its critics. As if pulled from a Twitter rant today, anecdotes of comfortable and luxurious prisons began to spread. There was a much-reported tale of a 'poor ragged sweep' who was imprisoned 'for some trifling offence'. The story went that upon arriving in custody, instead of hell, he discovered paradise:

the warm bath into which he was put much delighted him, but nothing could exceed his astonishment on being told to put on shoes and stockings . . . His joy was complete when they took him to his cell . . . and, half-doubting his good fortune, hesitatingly asked if he was really to sleep in the bed! . . . the governor . . . asked him what he thought of his situation? "Think of it, master, why I'm damn'd if ever I do another stroke of work!"[15]

The public were concerned that the holiday camp conditions that Howard and Fry were advocating would lead to more crime, as ruffians and scoundrels decided to commit offences so they could enter the palatial establishments. This line of thinking was bolstered by the apparent failure of the reformist movement over in America's first prisons.

Newgate Prison, New York, was pioneering in its early approach. But by the 1800s, financial difficulties had set in. An ex-offender at the time spoke of the officers in the same way many inmates speak of them today: 'It was hard to expect a capable man to lead the life of a turnkey for $500 per year, especially when he had to stay inside the stockade almost constantly.'[16] Even 200 years ago, this ex-con knew staff would hardly be motivated to work under poor conditions for low pay. Even then, funding for rehabilitation wasn't a vote winner.

The world watched on, assuming Newgate failed because it was soft on criminals, rather than because its staff were poorly paid and ill-trained, and the inmates were living in overcrowded conditions. As it built more prisons, America went back to hard labour and completely silent regimes. The men who came to rule these prisons believed that 'the reformatory plan, or the system of attention, kindness, and forbearance, had failed, and will fail, wherever, or whenever it is put into operation'.[17]

And so, it was in this climate that England saw the great, state-run Victorian prison building project commence. A confusing mixture of *lex talionis*, religious reformist ideals, utilitarian philosophy, deterrence and economic drive all culminating in the building of Her Majesty's Prisons. 'Victorian' has become the byword for describing these crumbling buildings that still stand sentinel in most major cities.

Pentonville, in central London, was finished in 1842. In the six years following, fifty-four more prisons were built with 11,000 spaces. The buildings themselves have barely changed since the nineteenth century but, by the turn of the century, there was already growing concern about conditions. In an effort to improve the situation, the 1895 Gladstone Report emphasised that prisons should turn inmates into better people than before they went in, stating 'we start . . . [from] the principle that prison treatment should have as its primary and concurrent objects, deterrence and reformation.'[18]

The shift towards rehabilitation was also seen in the development of the prison categorisation system and prisons specialising in the type of offenders they housed. HMP Holloway, London, began operating as a female-only prison between 1902 and 1903 and borstals, which housed young offenders, opened at the same time. There was a growing acceptance that women and youths couldn't be adequately cared for, kept safe or rehabilitated in the mixed-gender systems of yesteryear. Progress was also made when it came to housing male prisoners, and the first 'open' prison was built in 1934. These prisons focused on rehabilitation and resettling the offender back into the community. Reform advocate Sir Alexander Paterson said at the time: 'You cannot train a man for freedom under conditions of captivity.'[19]

At the start of 1940, there were around thirty-three inmates for every 100,000 in the population. With the Second World War came an influx of prisoners. Staffing levels remained low while the criminal estate grew by 50 per cent.[20] But the horrors of forced labour camps, concentration camps and gulags saw a renewed emphasis on reforming the prison estate. The 1948 UN Universal Declaration of Human Rights introduced the right, for all, to live free from torture. At the same time, politicians voted in favour of a bill to suspend the death penalty for five years.[21]

A focus on post-release support developed, with the first pre-release hostel opening in Bristol in 1953, giving inmates support to find their way again on The Out. A halfway house, of sorts, to reintegrate ex-offenders into the community. Nowadays, while women and children remain under differing regimes, the majority of inmates are adult males and they're housed in four main types of prisons. Once sentenced, inmates are categorised from A to D. Cat A are those deemed to be at high risk of escape and at high risk to the public if they manage to break out. Cat Bs can be locals or training prisons. Locals take everyone directly from the court, so house any type of offender, including the murderers and sex offenders you might assume went straight to cat A. Locals are also the places that take almost all of the remand prisoners, the people who haven't yet been convicted, totalling 12,000 people on any particular day.

Training prisons hold longer-term sentenced cons and, along with cat Cs, are meant to prepare prisoners for resettlement and release. Finally, cat Ds are 'open' and the stepping stone between custody and community. In a cat D, an inmate can go out and work in the day and return in the evening. Around 1 per cent of the prison population is cat A, while the majority languish in B and C cats, desperately applying for cat D status.[22]

The training and resettlement prisons seemed like a development in the right direction. Yet these positive moves forwards were hampered at every step of the way by overcrowding and a lack of resources. The overcrowding was dealt with by sending more cons to prison and building more cells.

After decades of campaigning, the death penalty was abolished in 1965 in Great Britain. Public outcry had followed the execution of Timothy Evans, a man with learning disabilities, in the yard of Pentonville, London, in 1950. Overwhelming evidence had emerged in the following years that he was innocent.[23] His posthumous pardon galvanised public support for fairer treatment of those charged with crimes. Yet in every decade that followed, there was another report, inspection or act that stated clearly that prisons 'were now in overcrowded and unsuitable conditions'.[24] Successive governments seemed either incapable or uninterested in listening to the messages coming from inside the walls. Overcrowding prevailed, reform efforts failed.[25]

This, perhaps, you might not think is a problem. And in the last fifty years, there's been a strong and vocal opposition to humane and sanitary conditions in prison. With the media narrative as it is, it's political suicide to suggest better conditions and treatment. Make prison so horrible that everyone will be too scared to ever commit a crime. A tabloid frenzy based on Bentham's utilitarian philosophy. While evidence stacks up to show reoffending is reduced if family and community ties are strengthened, the data doesn't matter.[26] To this day, there are reports that allowing incarcerated children to Skype their loved ones and have in-cell phones to stay in touch with their family means that soft-touch prisons are better than hotels.[27] Or horror is proclaimed that cons in open prisons, the ones specifically designed to support offenders to resettle back into the community, allow the inmates to participate in Park Run.[28]

Regardless of the reformist ideals, conditions were getting worse anyway. When the clock struck midnight and the

1980s gave way to the 1990s, Strangeways prison was holding 1600 inmates, rather than the 900 it was designed for. In Manchester, they weren't just doubled up, they were three to a cell. There was no in-cell sanitation, just a pot in the corner. There were rats, there were cockroaches. There were reports of a small group of bullying and aggressive officers, who went to the staff pub at lunch and came back in the afternoon looking for a fight.[29] Strangeways had a reputation for being inhumane, dirty and violent. Troubled men, a mixture of remand and sentenced, were thrown together behind the crumbling walls. There were plenty of warnings that the place was a powder keg about to blow.

And then on April Fools' Day 1990, the biggest prison riot in British history began. A 25-day stand-off ensued in which 194 were injured and two died. The damning inquiry and subsequent Woolf Report that followed is still one of the biggest public rebukes to the 'it's a holiday camp' narrative. Reforming crims was the most successful way to reduce crime, but attempting to do so in buildings like Strangeways would never work. Remand inmates, non-violent offenders and those suffering with profound substance misuse and mental health issues would be better served in almost any environment other than prison. Woolf knew that treating these people like scum, subjecting them to conditions not fit for an animal before tossing them back out into the community, would never create *less* crime.

The Strangeways riot and Woolf Report succeeded in introducing a ban on the unsanitary and degrading practice of slopping out. Yet in 2010, the prison's Independent Monitoring Board reported there were still 2,000 cells in the estate without any in-cell sanitation. Up to 4,000 inmates were still shitting in a bucket at night.[30] Well into 2019 there were still prisons where eating and sleeping next to a bucket of your cellmate's faeces was acceptable.[31] After his years incarcerated, Nelson Mandela said that 'no one truly knows a nation until one has been inside its jails. A nation should not be judged by how it treats its highest citizens, but its lowest ones.'[32] We wouldn't allow our dogs to sleep and eat next to their own excrement.

But slopping out wasn't even the biggest criticism levelled at the prison system by Lord Woolf. The main observation of the report was that the overcrowded conditions decreased the chance of rehabilitation and possibly made criminal behaviour worse. As it had been for the past 150 years, complaints of the problems associated with overcrowding were ignored and, instead, the Tory government decided to go full force in the other direction.

Between then and now, the prison population has risen from 45,000 souls in 1993 to a high in 2012 of 86,000 individuals.[33] Yes, more prisons have been built, but those men in the old Victorians still remain doubled up, the prisons holding way beyond their originally intended capacity.

And since Strangeways, both government and opposition have tripped over themselves to convince the public that they're the party who are 'tough on crime'. They've increased the length of prison sentences year on year while feeding the baying media and public the narrative that prisons are soft.[34] If only they were tougher, society would be safer. These are lies. This is spin. The evidence clearly states the opposite to be true.[35]

This explosion of the prison population coincided with the move towards privatising the estate. In 1992, HMP Wolds, Yorkshire, became the first privately run prison in England and since then, there's been a free-market free-for-all. The private sector happily embraced the job of prison building for the government and megabucks contracts were awarded for their enthusiasm. The companies that were entrusted with the job of managing our criminals were businesses like G4S, who in 2021 were fined £44 million by the Serious Fraud Office for a scandal involving the electronic tags offenders are supposed to wear upon release into the community. Not only were they profiting from locking people up, but they were also lying, cheating and breaking the law to make even more money out of incarceration.[36] Serco got in on the action, too, and also received a £22.9 million fine for similar fraudulent activity involving the Home Detention Curfew electronic tags.[37] Millions of pounds of taxpayers' money spent, while Deano was behind bars for a pushbike.

By 2021, there were fourteen privately run prisons in England and Wales out of a total of 117. Owing to the super-size of many of their new buildings, the private sector holds around 18 per cent of all prisoners.[38] The employees of these private companies are offered lower wages and less training than their public sector counterparts.[39]

The boom in prison building has gifted England, Wales and Scotland with the highest rates of incarceration in Western Europe. There are thirty-eight countries in the Organisation for Economic Co-operation and Development (OECD), and they are predominantly economically wealthy and politically democratic. Of these countries, England, Scotland and Wales together are deemed to be a 'high crime society with a particular propensity for all violence, short of intentional homicide'.[40] In Holland, community treatment and specialised mental health services have been used to divert prisoners away from prison. As a result, there's been a 40 per cent reduction in registered crime and many prisons have now closed down.[41] In Norway, a concerted shift away from punishment towards rehabilitation in the 1990s has seen reoffending rates drop to 20 per cent up to two years after release.[42] Just a reminder that despite all these additional prison contracts being awarded, the UK's reoffending rate remains around 48 per cent after just one year of release from custody.

The businesses that lock up inmates have an active interest in ensuring that their buildings are constantly full. Reoffending prisoners mean big profits. We've entrusted our prison estate to a wealthy elite who financially benefit from more crime. Yet they have gone largely unpunished while breaking the law themselves and fraudulently taking taxpayers' money.

Of course, the prisons get fined when an inmate dies in custody (Bentham must finally feel vindicated) and there are certain tick boxes they must check: access to education and healthcare are requirements. And there are some amazing men and women working within these establishments whose personal ethics mean they labour tirelessly to help prisoners rehabilitate and walk away from a life of crime. Those individuals are the reason that there aren't more riots, more protests, more deaths. Those individuals are the reason criminals don't commit more crime upon release. But the fact remains that private companies want to make sure they have a steady supply of cons, ready to fill beds and turn a profit. It's counter-intuitive to their business model to want to rehabilitate.

Prisons also utilise inmates as cheap labour. In America, this has been compared to 'the new Jim Crow' and de facto modern-day slavery.[43] But this isn't just an American phenomenon. Contracts worth £30 million apiece have been negotiated between private companies and the government. While prisoners receive only a few pounds a week for their work, the *Guardian* uncovered companies like Virgin Atlantic and the Macmillan publishing group using inmates' labour to complete monotonous and mind-numbing tasks such as cleaning in-flight headsets and sorting returned books.[44] These tasks arguably do little to rehabilitate a prisoner or train them for employment on The Out. It's not such a far reach to think that the boredom and repetitive nature of the work may actually convince crims that going straight is just an arduous slog and crime is far more exciting.

Instead of opposing the swelling incarceration rates and privatisation, the Labour government that came next seized on the popularity and fervour of the 1990s 'tough on crime' stance, introducing IPP sentences in 2003, with disastrous consequences.

These sentences mean that an inmate can spend a whole lifetime behind bars for a non-violent offence if they have previous violent offending behaviour for which they've already served time. IPPs were doled out by the judiciary like Santa at Christmas, on the government's orders, and now hang over an inmate's head like the Sword of Damocles. Even when released, having served his time, the inmate isn't free. He could be recalled to prison at any moment, for almost anything. The majority of recalls to prison aren't for lawbreaking. They're for drug relapses, mental health breakdowns or behaviour deemed 'unacceptable' by the Probation Service.[45]

IPP was a bad idea that became a badly written law, which became a badly executed policy. It swelled the prison population and swells the pockets of those who have a vested interest. So overused and misused were these sentences that they were abolished in 2012. Even David Blunkett MP, the champion of the IPP sentences, now expresses 'regret' about them.[46] That 'regret' doesn't go very far for the inmates who are still locked up, sleeping tonight in a double cell at Her Majesty's pleasure. Almost two thirds of prisons in England and Wales are reported to be crowded and the top ten most overcrowded are stuffed to 147 per cent overcapacity.[47] IPP only exacerbates this problem.

Just to stick the boot in, Chris Grayling MP jumped on the 'tough on crime' bandwagon when he banned books from being sent into prison and then spent £72,000 of taxpayers' money in court trying to defend his decision, which finally, after months of chaos, was ruled to be illegal.[48]

And as if it couldn't get any worse, in 2010, the prison

estate saw its budget effectively slashed and burned. Front-line staffing levels were reduced by 30 per cent and suddenly, by 2013, 27,650 staff had become 19,325.[49] Already dealing with massive levels of overcrowding and collapsing buildings constructed centuries earlier, the decimation of staffing levels would have a horrific impact. The estimated loss of experi-ence on the landings owing to these cuts was 80,000 years.[50] The prison estate still hasn't recovered. The government has since realised how catastrophic these cuts were and are trying to tempt new staff into the roles. The recruitment drives see little impact as inexperienced new officers, left to clean up the mess, leave the service as quickly as they start. The staff who remain will most likely work in one of the seventy-eight out of 117 prisons that are operating above their approved capacity level.[51]

The violence and deaths that have subsequently occurred are in direct relation to these cuts to staffing – a government policy that dances perilously close to criminal. Throw spice, a high that was originally legal when it first appeared on Brit-ish streets, into the mix and what followed over the next few years was an inevitable catastrophe.

Prisons were failing on every metric as the Covid-19 crisis struck. The government finally realised the squalid, infested, overcrowded conditions were ripe for the rampant spread of the virus. We decided to follow the example of other countries and release some non-violent offenders near the end of their sentences. France swiftly released 10,000 inmates to reduce the risk of a deadly outbreak behind the walls and saw no uptick in crime or public outcry.[52] Even America kicked out tens of thousands of non-violent crims or those who were coming close to release anyway.[53] Our own government set up a programme to do the same. By mid-May 2020, just fifty-five prisoners had been released under the scheme that iden-tified 4,000 inmates who were eligible.[54] It seems even when money is increasingly tight, we're still intent on wasting it on incarcerating non-violent offenders who have been identified, by our own government departments, as a low risk to society.

The original theory and ideals behind the modern system of incarceration were that the loss of liberty was punishment enough, while imprisonment protected society through incapacitation. The UN Nelson Mandela Rules of 2015 extended and codified the minimum conditions and treatment a prisoner should receive. The prisoner may be locked up, but this doesn't negate his fundamental human rights and the right to be free from torture. Yet there's been a slide towards the belief that incarceration alone isn't punishment. The conditions should be horrendous – part of the punishment – and support grows for the misguided belief that bad conditions deter offenders. The data disputes this argument and the stories I share should demonstrate, sometimes viscerally, why this belief is wrong. It was into this, one of the most expensive, overcrowded and ill-conceived prison systems in the world, that I stepped over a decade ago and saw up close for the first time the human cost of the failures of this system.

CHAPTER 3

How to Build a Criminal – Institutionalisation

It wasn't long after his first conviction that Taylor dragged a snapped biro across his skinny arms. The cuts were jagged and messy, but not deep. He clenched the sleeves of his jumper tightly when he was on the wing, hiding the injuries, hiding his embarrassment. The small cuts became swollen and red as prison grime infected them. Finally, an officer noticed his withdrawn behaviour and a nurse was sent to clean him up with antiseptic and plasters.

He was eighteen years old, but everyone said he looked more like twelve. The officer tried to refer him to the mental health team, worrying about the youth. But he wasn't hearing voices, the wounds weren't deemed deep enough to demonstrate real suicidal ideation. He was offered an appointment with the GP in three weeks to prescribe antidepressants. What would have been seen as extremely worrying behaviour in any rational society didn't even get a mention at the shift handover.

When the cutting in private didn't relieve the tension inside, Taylor started to smoke spice. The legal highs that had swept through communities on The Out had found their way behind the walls. No longer legal, but still undetectable in piss tests, spice had become the drug of choice inside. The effects were on another level. It caused hallucinations, overdoses, fits and psychotic episodes. But it was an escape, and everyone seemed to be using something or other to kill the bird, kill time.

Bang-up gave Taylor too long behind his door to contemplate his future. And he didn't like what he could see. So instead, getting high seemed a sensible alternative to all those thoughts. He couldn't even afford to buy phone credit and tobacco, so it was inevitable drug debts would bring even more trouble to his cell door.

Taylor would serve a short sentence, then be released. Each time he came back to prison, he'd got a little taller, life being measured in the bigger kit he was issued on his return. When he finally stopped growing, he had size 15 feet and was given his own pair of prison trainers, his name etched on them in felt-tip pen. His return in a few months was seen as so likely, his kit was stored for next time.

When he first came in, he wasn't cut out to be a crim. He was vulnerable, soft. When he realised that keeping his head down and keeping quiet rarely got him what he wanted or needed, he began to act like a spoiled teenager. He started throwing tantrums, hoping that if he kicked up enough of a fuss, he'd be noticed over the crazier and scarier inmates.

I'd heard about Taylor months before his thick file was dropped onto my desk. During the weekly safer custody meetings, designed to create wrap-around support for only the most problematic prisoners, he'd be brought up repeatedly by exasperated staff from every department. His details repeated so often, I knew his prison number by heart before we met.

Taylor drained resources, constantly threatening suicide, making superficial cuts, telling staff he'd swallowed bleach or razor blades. He'd threaten to kill cellmates then he'd get into debt almost immediately on the landings and be moved around the prison until there was nowhere left to put him.

One minute he'd be in floods of tears, crying, begging for a phone call to his sister. The next he'd be threatening to cut his own ears off. Seconds later he'd be threatening to cut your ears off. A lot of it was just noise, but he said exactly the right things to make sure you couldn't walk away.

Taylor didn't meet the criteria for support from the mental health team. They were too busy desperately seeking outside hospital beds on psychiatric wards for the clinically ill. The drug and alcohol team didn't want to touch him. Their caseloads were full of men addicted to alcohol and heroin; the men most likely to die while they were being medically detoxed.

Yet each time he returned to the establishment, his behaviour deteriorated further. Where once he'd been a fragile child, now he was becoming increasingly difficult to manage. As his actions became more erratic and dangerous, patience began to wear thin. Where once there had been sympathy and compassion for this youth, frustration among staff and inmates grew. He was becoming the biggest nuisance on the landings.

I started working with him by accident, really. He'd already been in and out twice when our paths crossed, and I became entangled in witnessing his slow descent towards institutionalisation. It was the first week of December and the centrally controlled heating system had been cranked up to the limit.

It was pouring with rain and all outside exercise had been cancelled. No one wanted to walk loops of the yard when the weather was this bad. The whole establishment felt damp, steam rising from bodies and condensing on the windows. Restless energy vibrated and the volume of the place seemed to have been turned up a notch. With no one burning energy out on the yard, it was even more crowded and claustrophobic inside.

I was searching for a quiet space to write up my notes, but every office seemed to be taken. A large stack of bright orange cardboard folders threatened to topple from the desk as I entered the prison cell that was used for the officers' office on D wing. Officer Owen was sitting behind the desk, his thinning hair smoothed back to cover the bald patch that was visible as he hunched over his paperwork. He glanced up at me as I entered, smiling briefly before returning to his notes.

'Do you mind if I try to get a bit of my paperwork done in here? I won't cause you any trouble,' I said as he held out his mug to me.

'Brew up and you're always welcome,' he said, shuffling his papers to one end of the desk so I could squeeze in alongside him, 'but I've got these four reviews to do.' He pointed at the orange files as he turned to walk onto the wing.

I stirred three sugars into his tea with a cracked single-use spoon. Before settling into the corner and firing up the creaking desktop computer, I heard him bellow Taylor's surname down the landing.

'Dawkins.'

I was halfway through resetting my password on the prison database when Owen, trailed by Taylor, came back. The youth eyed me suspiciously but slumped into a chair as Owen started leafing through the file.

'I didn't do anything, guv. I swear,' he started, but Owen waved his hand for quiet.

'You're not in trouble, son,' he replied. 'You're here for your ACCT review.'

Taylor's eyebrows furrowed in confusion and his eyes shot back to me, searching for an answer.

'Because you hurt yourself. You're on an ACCT.' Owen waved the orange file in front of Taylor.

'Since when?' Taylor shot back.

Owen muttered under his breath; frustration at his colleague who had opened the document but not explained to the kid what it was crossed his face. I watched him physically shift, pulling himself together.

'It's what we do when you hurt yourself. You get one of these. Assessment, Care in Custody and Teamwork. It's so we can keep an extra eye on you. Try to help you with what's troubling you. Refer you to people like miss' – he pointed in my general direction – 'if we think you need any additional support.'

He held out the document to Taylor, showing him that he was currently on four-hourly observations. A member of staff would check on him every four hours day and night, to make sure he hadn't harmed himself again.

'And here' – Owen pointed – 'is where we do the referrals to help you stop self-harming. So, let's talk about what's troubling you.'

Over the next half an hour, I tried to tune out their conversation. But as Taylor erratically recounted every aspect of his troubled young life, I caught the headlines: three months left to serve. Theft. A breach of a community order. No, don't want education.

'Religion? Can the chaplain visit?'

'Fuck that.'

Smashed cell. Got put on basic regime. No TV. Cutting. Ligatures. Hate my cellmate. Going to kill him.

'Need help. Real help.'

'With what?'

'Dunno, guv.'

'What about groups? Talking it through? It sounds to me that you like talking.' Owen smiled wryly.

I looked up and he was staring at me, eyes pleading. I nodded imperceptibly. Yes, I'd give it a try. He could come to my group therapy.

There were plenty more ACCT reviews for Taylor after
that. Self-injury ebbed and flowed, sometimes weekly and
other times daily. Sometimes a noose, sometimes a blade.
There were never-ending drug debts that got him beaten
up and moved around the prison. Weekly security reviews
when he reported others for dealing and threatening him
over his debts. He'd get done in after getting caught trying
to nick someone's trainers or tobacco or shower gel. The
shit-smearing first started when he didn't have enough phone
credit to call his mum on her birthday. He learned all these
behaviours while inside the walls, watching how others survived the chaos and copying their example.

He wasn't just causing this madness to get what he wanted.
Taylor had some deep emotional wounds, but he lacked the
tools to excavate and fix them. He hadn't yet realised that
prison wasn't designed to care about his feelings or his needs.
He hadn't considered that a shrinking staff team had to try to
give equal attention to 1,200 men. Hadn't thought that he'd
be banged up in an adult prison, living 120 to one wing, with
no one to ask him how he was coping.

In here, Taylor and his emotions were nothing special –
one in four of the men on the landing had been in care during
their childhood.[1] It seemed like all of their fathers had either
been absent or beating the shit out of their mums if they
were around. So what if his mum had been on crack? Hadn't
everyone's in here? It's just the way it was.

And who cared if he was worried about his upcoming
release? Some 15 per cent of those on the landing would be
going through the gate homeless. Couldn't read the forms
to claim benefits? Tough shit. The average reading age was
eleven. No one in here could. He was expected just to deal
with that. And if he couldn't, he was told his acting out had
nothing to do with mental health and was a behavioural
issue for which he should be punished. He'd get a nicking, a

negative entry on his file and then his TV would be removed, he'd be put down in segregation or he'd lose time out of his cell. All these methods were tried to get Taylor to behave.

I liked Taylor. He was sensitive at times, able to listen and understand when I explained to him how difficult his behaviour could be. At first, I could slice through the bluster to uncover the lost kid inside. He was funny and could be incredibly generous with no ulterior motive. But he hated to think the staff had seen any of these acts of kindness. He was scared in prison and wanted to give off the impression that he was a gangster. He hid his softness as deep as he could until one day, all the bluster of acting like a bad man turned him into one.

In our one-to-one sessions, as if to prove to himself that he wasn't a nice person, he'd push against me, shouting, crying, pleading, begging, threatening. There was never any real aggression, never any hatred towards me in the beginning. But in time, as prison became his real life and the real world became a distant memory, he adapted and adopted the attitude and behaviour of an inmate.

Taylor was a lost kid who I watched become a criminal in custody. I could suggest alternatives to smoking spice, but then I didn't have to sit in a cell each night contemplating what a shitshow of a life I had. Whatever coping strategies I tried to teach, I wasn't sure how practical their application could have been when he was left to count the cockroaches running across the floor.

His arms became criss-crossed in the self-inflicted injuries that gave him some release or reprieve from his self-hatred. It was just what people did inside to cope. It became normal. So, too, did the headbanging, the screaming, the brawling. Even a dirty protest wasn't that unusual.

So Taylor's smeared himself in shit today?

'Oh, OK,' I'd reply calmly. 'I'd been hoping to drag him along to group.'

But his stench mingled with that prison aroma you can't scrub away.

Instead of group therapy, he got a nicking for the shit-smearing: a negative entry on his record that meant he'd have fewer privileges in the coming weeks. He'd covered his cell walls in it and an officer had written him up for damaging prison property. It had taken half a day to find the cons trained in biohazard cleaning to come and sort it out.

He asked me to go to the hearing with him, to answer the charge in front of a governor and try to mount a defence. I escorted him from the wing, grateful that he'd had a shower that morning.

'Easy questions first,' the governor said.

The governor tried to smile, but it didn't reach his eyes. He appeared numb to the cutting and the faeces and the threats and the violence. He shuffled the stack of paperwork, the dozens of nickings for bad behaviour that he was tasked with dealing with that morning.

'Who are you?' he asked.

'Prison Number A7015446,' Taylor said, unthinkingly.

'And what's your name?' the governor said.

'Dawkins,' he replied.

Was it at that moment I knew he was lost? When he called himself a number instead of a name? When the holler of a surname was all he had left of who he was before he was an inmate? In truth, I barely noticed. The exchange between criminal and governor so normal that it took me a moment to register that prison was seeping into him, becoming part of him, defining him. It happened often when I was completing assessments or referrals. An inmate would rattle off his prison number when I asked who he was, then look puzzled when I'd repeat, 'No, but *who are you?*'

There had been a directive that all staff should refer to the inmates by their first names or at least add a 'mister' before the surname was shouted down the landing. The rumour was that some crims in another establishment had mobilised and sued the prison, fed up with the lack of respect that a sneered surname implied. But old habits die hard. Besides, there were plenty of crims who felt that they didn't want to be on first-name terms with other murderers, thieves and gangsters, let alone screws. I always told the men they could call me by my first name instead of 'miss', in an effort to humanise myself to them. I'd hoped that it would not only break down barriers and allow some trust, but that they'd also be less likely to try to kill me if they saw me as a person.

It didn't catch on. They were numbers and I was 'miss', and it felt completely normal to speak to each other like this. It cemented that they were crims and I was staff, and the divide between us was so big it could never be breached. Prison Number A7015446 became indivisible from his crimes.

But maybe I should have seen the creation of 'Taylor the Criminal' the moment he put on his prison tracksuit and became just another unidentifiable inmate, blending into the hundreds of other nameless men. A uniform designed to stretch and fit with however much weight was lost or gained in prison. An economical costume that was deemed suitable for work, exercise and downtime. An outfit that you wouldn't be seen dead in on The Out, but in there could be jazzed up with sports logos drawn on in biro and headbands made from torn sleeves, in an effort to maintain some sliver of individuality.

Or perhaps it was the day I arrived at his cell to find him in tears, begging me to try to get him a toilet roll as the whole wing kicked and screamed from behind their doors at the deg-radation of not being able to wipe their arses because there was none left in the building. When an officer laughed in his face and said that if he liked to dirty-protest so much, what was his problem? The shame of begging for toilet roll slowly chipping away along with a thousand other humiliations.

Was the final step towards institutionalisation the warped reality and coping strategy of cutting himself? Taylor had never hurt himself before he came to prison. He'd never considered it as a possible response to difficult emotions. There isn't enough information to compare self-injury in the community and self-injury in prison. On The Out, it's usually secretive, hidden. There simply isn't data on the prevalence of adult men harming themselves in the community. But it isn't endemic. Inside, though, it never seemed to end. Over 11,000 inmates were reported to have self-injured 52,339 times from March 2020 to March 2021.[2] These are only the cases that were recorded. It's only from a distance, years after Taylor's first conviction, that I see how prison normalises these actions, tolerates this behaviour as attention-seeking rather than an act of desperation. The trauma of incarceration visibly scarring his body.

What happened to Taylor? I couldn't make his biological family give a shit about him. I couldn't just magic out of thin air a supportive social network who would help him out, practically and emotionally. I couldn't erase the memories of abuse that woke him, sweating, in the night. He had to deal with life alone.

I couldn't provide him with a secure house upon release or find a job for an illiterate 22-year-old spice addict with no work experience and a criminal record. Every time he went out, he was leaving to the same nothing he left to the time before. And all these things are proven to increase the likelihood of him returning again and again and again. And as he received more convictions, the chance of him going back inside kept on growing exponentially.

I didn't need to read the dozens of studies to know that substance misuse problems, learning difficulties and no one looking out for you made life extra difficult after release.[3]

I saw it over and over again with hundreds of men. Taylor became just another crim, bouncing from street to landing and back again because there didn't seem to be any possible way to exit the merry-go-round. I didn't need to check the endless governmental data that proves that short sentences and time spent in prison makes them more likely to reoffend, makes them more criminal in their behaviour. I saw it every day, as prison and criminality became the defining feature of those men. As it stripped away their humanity and reduced them to their charge sheet and prison number.

And I understood why Taylor, ultimately, decided that the only way to avoid disappointment and pain was to care even less about himself than anyone else did. Trying to find self-determination in a place designed to create hopelessness was a challenge for the most resilient men. Taylor didn't have that skill.

Instead, he watched other crims and learned different ways of coping. Drugs, fighting, cutting, tying nooses around his neck. A 'Fuck You' to the system. You can't break me if I break myself first. We cared about him, yes. But not enough that it gave us sleepless nights. No one in the whole world cared that much about Taylor.

He's inside now. Friends who still work in prison mention him from time to time, tell me that he's back, that some things never change. Except he's older, tougher. He'll be nearing thirty, half his adult life has been spent behind the walls. Too old for anyone to care about his troubled start in life. No one supported him when he watched his mum getting beaten up, no one supported him when he was abused in care. And when the culmination of all this was prison and self-injury and drug abuse, we just blamed Taylor.

Old enough to know better, he's now just another number, another tracksuit. He's been reduced to his crimes, dehumanised and institutionalised to such a degree that there's no longer the possibility of a place for him in society. He's accepted that this is who he is, that his horizons finish at the end of the wing. And it should be so horribly shocking. But it isn't. It's the everyday, the banal reality for tens of thousands of people. Taylor is no exception. His behaviour may have been more disruptive than others, but the descent into institutionalisation is happening on every landing, every day. It breeds hatred and a distrust of society, it divides us from them. It increases criminality and creates criminals. If this is prison working, I'd hate to see what failure looks like.

CHAPTER 4

But What about 'The Paedos'? – Sex Offenders

Scar tissue ran down the side of Jeff's neck, crept under his sweater and onto his chest, a reminder of the day the other inmates had found out his offences and served up some prison justice. Jeff had tried to see his sentence out on the main wings, with the general population. He'd lasted a week.

The other cons had become suspicious of the old boy on the landing. They waited until association, the hour a day when most of the wing is unlocked at the same time to take showers, make phone calls or get some exercise. Then a group of them entered his cell and rifled through his paperwork. There's no privacy in prison, so although all legal mail between con and solicitor should be confidential, Jeff had had to store his forms in a shared cell that was left open whenever he was unlocked.

In the time it took Jeff to finish his shower, the whole wing had found out that he was a nonce. He returned to his cell just as the water had finished boiling. Sugar was added to cause maximum damage. It was launched towards him in a violent kettling that missed his face but put him on the hospital wing for two weeks. His scalded skin would scar deeply.

Whenever you talk to people about prison, about its failings, its brokenness, about how we need to radically rethink the system, the average person will nod along. Then there will be a pause, a beat, and I prepare myself for the question. But what about the paedos?

There's usually some degree of understanding and empathy for youths like Taylor – a recognition that maybe our current system of incarceration isn't the best option. Those feelings rarely extend to the paedophiles. Years before, while still working out in the community full-time, I came to understand why.

As I sat down to meet Jeff, I felt the sweat pooling in my armpits. I shifted uncomfortably on the plastic chair. The air was stifling, yet my skin was uncomfortably cold. I'd never been inside prison before. I'd never sat down to have a conversation with a convicted paedophile. I had the sinking feeling in my gut that for all my bravado, I was completely out of my depth.

The man in front of me was swallowed by his prison tracksuit. The elastic at the ankles had come away or been torn out and the material flapped loosely to display gnarled ankles. I felt a pitying ache as he crossed and uncrossed his legs, folding in on himself, appearing feminine and delicate. Wrinkles etched his face, creasing into jowls at his neck. Wiry, unbrushed hair sprang from his head in receding patches. I knew Jeff was only in his fifties because I'd spent days poring over his case file, preparing myself for the meeting. But he looked old enough to be my grandad.

I was in my early twenties, working on The Out with 'complex and chaotic' clients. It was my job to make sure he managed to maintain his tenancy, didn't drink and didn't reoffend in the community. Jeff wasn't due out for another four weeks, but he was deemed so high-risk that I'd started working with him in advance of his release date. His file was full of acronyms, denoting his specific risk factors. High risk of offending. High-risk because he threatened staff. High-risk because he'd turned up drunk to the office wielding a knife before. High-risk because he'd constantly use racial slurs. High-risk because he frequently attempted to groom his community support workers. I'd read through the handover notes. It started innocently with a handshake, maybe accidentally brushing against you. Sitting too closely on the sofa on home visits. Testing boundaries. High-risk because he was manipulative and sly.

It wasn't hard to convince my manager to add Jeff to my caseload. I was desperate to prove I could work with the most feared service users. My manager had probably run out of the more experienced staff willing to work with Jeff. It had been win-win.

And so, I found myself loitering outside the prison walls. Nerves had made me set off extra early, so I smoked anxiously, waiting for the allotted appointment time to roll around. The prison was surrounded by shops, cafés, homes and schools. It cast a shadow over the neighbourhood that was gentrifying all around it – a neighbourhood that Jeff would soon be returned to. The air was warm with the promise of summer and I was uncomfortable in the long sleeves and high-necked jumper I'd chosen to put on that morning. Because what else can you wear when your day involves a trip to the VP unit of the local cat B?

In less than a month's time, I'd be meeting Jeff on his day of release, supporting him to attend probation and escorting him home. Hopefully without any mishaps. Our appointment that day would be our first meeting, where I'd hoped to develop a working relationship and plan his release in finer detail.

A giant of an officer met me at the gatehouse, helped me to cram my belongings into a locker and signed me in. It was as intimidating and overbearing as all those prison dramas would have you believe. The conversations and shouts and arguments of hundreds of men behind the walls echoed, accentuated by the emptiness of the yard we crossed to reach the VP unit. I felt eyes on me from every barred window and pretended I didn't hear when the catcalling began.

I had to wait while the officer opened and closed every gate – a natural and swift movement he'd perfected over his years in the service. I startled every time it slammed, metal on metal. To hide my fear, I made inane small talk. He humoured me and played along with the charade that this was all absolutely normal.

He swung open the final door and we stepped onto the unit. It was silent. A world away from the main prison. Every inmate was behind his door. But it wasn't peaceful. That smell that infiltrates every prison filled my lungs. Bleach and vomit, and shit and sweat and cooking food and rotting souls. Mess nets draped across the landings, adding to the feeling of claustrophobia.

Jeff was already waiting for me in a classroom, tapping out a disjointed rhythm on the sticky lino floor with his flip-flops. He smiled as I entered. The officer reassured me he'd remain stationed outside the door. Told me just to call to him if I needed anything.

Over the next hour, Jeff continually turned our conversation onto the subject of abuse. His face became animated as he talked about the traumas he'd suffered as a child. I naively thought that I needed to nod empathetically and listen to this. But somehow, it felt wrong. His teeth exposed as he maintained unblinking eye contact. It felt like he was enjoying telling me these stories. I felt I was being manipulated and didn't know how to make it stop.

I steered the conversation back to his housing, his plans for release, shuffling uselessly at the assessment paperwork I needed to complete. But he was slippery and managed to worm back towards talking about his offences. He'd drop in the names of his victims, suggest they were friends who were fond of him, who would be waiting for him when he got out.

I lost control of the conversation, of the situation, and I could viscerally feel his revelling in my discomfort. I was never at physical risk. The huge officer at the door was more than enough security. I could have fought Jeff off by myself if I'd have needed to. There was no risk of violence, yet I still felt like I'd been assaulted as I left the session. He'd got into my head and I felt powerless and scared.

I wasn't trained and I wasn't capable of working with Jeff. I was too young, too full of false confidence. I'd been so desperate to prove I could work with him, yet in reality I was a deer in the headlights. In time, I learned that working with men who have committed sex offences against children required special skills, but back then I didn't have a clue what those specific skills were, so instead I vowed to have firmer boundaries. Laser focus. Not even for a second would I let my guard down. It shook me up and for a while I questioned whether I was up to the job at all.

After that meeting with Jeff, I understood clearly why no one likes the nonces. Not the officers, not the public, not the tabloids or the politicians. Definitely not the other crims. On the hierarchy of crime, the paedophiles are usually considered the lowest of the low.

Once I went behind the walls full-time, any conversation about my job would eventually turn to this specific type of offender. More than almost any other crime, theirs strike at the very core of our fears. Because if ever there was a justification for prison, then surely keeping innocent children safe from paedophiles would be it. No reformer ever wants to be seen to be even remotely sympathetic towards these crims. While in prison, we lock them away on the vulnerable wing, trying to make the problem disappear. But just like all of the other cons, the overwhelming majority of them will one day be released, and we can't ignore them if we really want to make society safer.

It would be easier to leave them on that VP unit and pretend they don't exist – save the reforms and rationality for the more 'deserving' cons. But unless we address this, the most controversial topic, then any argument for systemic overhaul will always be marred by the question 'What about the paedos?'

Appealing to humanity and compassion when discussing the correct punishments or treatments for offenders doesn't work so well when it comes to nonces. But although an emotional reaction and tendency towards retaliation may feel good, make us feel superior and justified and contented, it doesn't mean it's the correct response.

The tabloids love reporting on those with sexual convictions involving children. They go into lurid, triggering detail with almost as much glee as Jeff did that day I sat across from him. Articles describing them as 'monsters' and 'beasts' build a picture of these offenders as a completely separate species to you and me.[1] These animalistic portrayals of those with sexual convictions then shape public opinion and create an atmosphere where the very treatments that are proven to reduce offending are impossible to carry out in the community.[2]

Inside, the crims love heckling abuse and attacking them whenever it's possible to reach them. The tabloids then report on this violence and, if not lauding the behaviour of the attacker, then definitely not condemning it, either.[3] The officers ignore them as best as possible. A silent, begrudging locking and unlocking of the scum of the establishment.

After Jeff, I continued to work with men with sexual convictions from time to time. And sometimes it was difficult and horrific, and triggering. And other times it was fine. It was work that usually centred around specific tasks: securing housing or managing substance misuse detoxification. I didn't work with these crims around their offending behaviour. I didn't know how to do that work safely for both me, them and their victims. Some of them were on waiting lists to be transferred to specialist establishments, where they'd spend months on another waiting list before starting a course to manage their offending behaviour.

They weren't allowed to attend my group sessions, because it would have been too risky to mix them with general population. They'd be attacked. Sometimes, a convicted paedophile would think he could survive on the wings. He'd hide his crime from other cons, pretend he was in for fraud or had caught a robbery charge.

The officers would know. All of the staff would know. One perfunctory check of the new con's electronic file and soon the whole staff team would circle him with more caution. And he'd always get found out by the crims.

After the kettling, Jeff was shipped up to the VP unit, spending the rest of his time inside with limited access to employment, training, therapy, education and the gym. For those with sexual convictions against children, access to services in prison is even more limited than for the average cons.

He could have tried to get a move to one of the special prisons that provided treatment programmes to offenders like him. But to be accepted, he had to admit what he'd done and admit that it was wrong. Jeff did neither and so he wasn't eligible for the courses that would attempt to stop him from offending in the future.

Even if he had displayed guilt or remorse for what he'd done, the places in these prisons and on the sex offender treatment programmes were limited. Even if he'd wanted to go to a specialist establishment, there probably wouldn't have been space for him anyway. Most cons like Jeff waste away their whole sentence, never having to consider the impact of their actions and how to stop them in the future.

As of March 2019, there were 13,359 prisoners convicted
of sexual offences in our establishments.[4] There are different
types of sex offenders. Flashers, child abusers, men who rape
their wives, the friend who gets drunk with you and believes
a slurred 'no' means 'yes', gang members using rape against
rivals, those who watch child pornography. There are men
who urinate in public and those who 'upskirt' women on
public transport. There are the Hollywood moguls and New
York socialites. While we tend to lump them all together in
prison, literally and figuratively, the treatment required to
make sure society is safer varies wildly.

So when I talk about men like Jeff, I'm not talking
about your run-of-the-mill sex offenders. The tabloids seem
strangely silent when it comes to the 773,000 adults aged sixteen to seventy-four who experienced a sexual assault from
March 2019 to March 2020.[5] Or the 87 per cent of female
victims who know their perpetrator. No one seems too concerned that by March 2020 4.3 million women and 989,000
men living in England and Wales had experienced sexual
assault since the age of sixteen.[6] Or that only approximately
16 per cent report the offence to the police. These journalists
only seem to notice when a woman is found to have made
a false accusation, rather than the woeful conviction rate of
5.6 per cent of reported rapes.[7] That's a whole lot of sexual
assault happening and very few convictions. This kind of sex
offender, on the whole, remains free.

And while these figures show us that there are even more
dangerous men out in the community, that doesn't take away
from the truth that there are around 1,500 extremely dangerous – again, mainly – men who prey on children, behind the
walls. And while they're in prison, there's no doubt that on
The Out, we're safer. But after their release, what then?

I could argue that every man, woman and child inside our
prisons should be treated with a basic level of dignity and

respect, regardless of their crime. Because to do so makes us better people and a better society.

But instead of thinking about the human rights of the offender, maybe it's easier to consider the victims and the potential future victims of these men. How do we protect them? Because what we do now doesn't work.

I never did end up meeting Jeff out in the community. He set fire to his cell a week before his release and caught an arson charge. But I've no doubt he'd have hurt many more boys when he was finally released. He was dangerous and cunning and clever. There are plenty of sex offenders like Jeff, and worse, filling VP units up and down the country. But we're barely treating them. When the MOJ conducted research to see if its own sex offender treatment programme worked, it easily found 13,219 untreated sex offenders to compare with only 2,462 offenders who had started treatment between 2000 and 2012.[8]

The MOJ's core treatment programme is a voluntary one that automatically excludes the participation of certain categories of offenders, including those with mental illnesses, those with an IQ of less than 80, those deemed a suicide risk, those diagnosed with severe personality disorder and those who don't speak English.[9] If I read that list out to a room of officers, they'd laugh in my face. The MOJ's exclusion list is a pretty good description of the prison population. So instead of treating and rehabilitating, instead of making society safer, we're locking them up for a set period of time and then we're simply releasing them. And that thought is terrifying.

The obvious answer proposed to me by many people is to bring back the death penalty. Kill them. Then they're no longer a risk. The truth is, though, the death penalty doesn't work. Handing power to the state to kill 'with premeditation and ceremony' is not only barbaric in theory, but it's also 'inequitable in practice'. Data from the USA suggests that the death penalty is applied unjustly against people, 'largely dependent on . . . how much money they have, the skill of their attorneys, [and] race of the victim . . . People of color [*sic*] are far more likely to be executed than white people, especially if the victim is white.'[10]

Even the police in the USA agree that it doesn't prevent crime. 'A survey of police chiefs nationwide found they rank the death penalty lowest among ways to reduce violent crime . . . reducing drug abuse, and creating a better economy with more jobs [ranked] higher than the death penalty as the best ways to reduce violence . . . states with the death penalty have the highest murder rates'. And this says nothing of the scores of innocent men and women released from death row. 'Nationally, at least one person is exonerated for every 10 that are executed.'[11]

The death penalty is a disgusting and vicious form of punishment. And it doesn't even work. But if the death penalty doesn't work, there's only sparse and patchy evidence of what does.

About one in six prisons in England and Wales has the ability to run a sex offender treatment programme, yet nearly every establishment has a VP unit that houses sex offenders. If the government believes this programme works to reduce the harm committed by crims with sexual convictions involving children, why then do we not immediately ship every paedophile off to one of these specialist establishments and sign them up for a treatment programme?

If we really want to keep children safer, why doesn't every sex offender immediately begin an evidence-based, data-driven programme of therapeutic interventions, group work and appropriate courses to support him to stop being so dangerous?

The difficult, honest answer is that the majority of these treatment programmes don't work. And no one can quite agree on what does. Certainly not psychotherapy.[12] Possibly chemical castration.[13] Globally, relapse prevention continues to be used as a treatment method even though there's no evidence of its effectiveness.[14]

While it's common that sex offender treatment courses address areas including 'self-esteem, personal distress, victim empathy, and denial', there's no supporting data to suggest doing so reduces reoffending.[15]

The MOJ's own research on the sex offender treatment programme used inside prisons showed that not only did it *not* reduce offending, but participants actually *increased* their offending upon release.[16]

Maybe it's for the best, then, that the MOJ could only find 2,562 convicted sex offenders who started the prison-based sex offender treatment programme between 2000 and 2012 in England and Wales.[17] Based on their data, we were actually doing a better job of rehabilitating when we just left them to rot on the VP units.

There's also little detailed research into what works, because it's impossible to collect data on what paedophiles who *don't* offend do to stop themselves from doing so. No one wants to admit to these tendencies, but if we can't find out what successfully stops them from offending, evidence-based interventions will always be lacking.

Research shows that some interventions, involving therapy and supportive networks, work better than others. They're just not the treatments we're widely using in our prisons. These treatments need to be tailored to the specific needs of the offender, delivered by highly qualified, competent, confident and compassionate professionals.[18]

I might have had a bucketload of false confidence when I first met Jeff, but I was definitely not highly qualified or competent. I was a kid, hoping I could save the world with a bit of empathetic social care. Even as a social worker, my training included only one two-hour lecture on sex offenders. And that made me the most qualified person on the wing to deal with Jeff. Officers receive no specialised training to work every day alongside paedophiles. When you don't feel confident working with an inmate who has sexual convictions involving children, it's difficult to believe it's possible to be competent and professional.

Research also shows that treatment should be delivered 'in a manner that is responsive to various characteristics of the individual, such as language, culture, personality style, intelligence, anxiety levels, learning styles, and cognitive abilities, in order to increase their engagement and participation in treatment to ensure maximal effectiveness'.[19]

I once tried to access a translator to help me assess a foreign national inmate. He was only in for shoplifting but had cut his wrists seven times in the previous forty-eight hours. He'd bitten the stitches each time, hoping to bleed out before the nurses could get to him. He couldn't understand a word of English and I had no idea what language he was speaking. The prisoners we usually relied on to translate in desperate circumstances couldn't figure it out either. They argued between themselves for half an hour before they finally settled on a Moldovan dialect as the likely language.

I spent the whole lunch break on hold to the translation services, waiting to see if they could find someone who could speak anything remotely similar to this language. I was still listening to the hold music when a nurse called me out of my office, back to the hospital wing. Over the lunch break, these cons had spread the message around the foreign nationals in the building and found another inmate they thought might be able to help figure out what the disturbed and suicidal man was saying. I thanked them but explained that owing to confidentiality, I'd have to use an official translator.

Three hours later and a translator still hadn't been located.

The inmate had now started smashing his head against the cell wall in between tearing his jumper into small pieces and swallowing them one at a time. He was the first inmate I'd seen who had to have all of his clothes removed and was given only an un-tearable blanket for his own safety. Shortly afterwards, security brought down the Moldovan con from general population and we used him as the official translator.

If I couldn't even locate a translator for a man intent on killing himself, it seems unlikely that anyone would give a shit enough about the paedophiles to make sure their therapy was delivered in a culturally appropriate style. Add to that the fact that we treat learning difficulties, mental health issues and addiction issues completely separately owing to the way they're funded, you'll understand why our current treatment programmes just don't work.

So when I'm asked, 'What about the paedos?' I want to make it crystal clear. The current system we have doesn't protect you or your children. In fact, just like with the average general population criminal, your taxes are being spent on things that may actually make society less safe.

When I first stepped foot inside prison thirteen years ago, I didn't know how to work with sex offenders. I suppose I can take comfort from the data that shows apparently no one knows how to work with them. Or, if we do, we're not doing much of it.

But for all those depressing statistics, there are some small pockets of work going on that seem to be achieving real results when it comes to stopping cons from reoffending. Up in the Midlands, they've got a team running workshops and providing support on the inside and out in the community. They call these 'Circles of Support and Accountability' and their data shows impressive reductions in reoffending compared to the rest of the general prison population.[20] This inside-out approach not only allows the foundations to be laid while in prison, but it also supports the offender to resettle into the community upon release. This is vital, as research has shown that some sex offenders are so fearful of their return to the community and the response they will be met with that they find prison preferable to release. This creates a situation where some offenders may be motivated to reoffend, in part, because they find prison a safer environment than the outside world.[21]

The circles of support offer an offender positive working relationships prior to release and allow him to know in advance who will be there to help him navigate his reintegration. Instead of solely focusing on the offending behaviour, they model positive behaviour, support the man to reintegrate into society in an appropriate way and create a safe space for him to ask for help if he feels the urge to offend again in the future. They show him how to have normal, functioning and healthy relationships with other adults. Like all other programmes that address reoffending in the general prison population, this one works because it highlights the importance of compassion and support, of showing the offender that there is an alternative possible life beyond one of crime.

The more socially isolated the offender, the more likely he is to reoffend. This is true for any type of criminal. But the increased likelihood of isolation that men with sexual offences against children face just makes this fact worse. These truly supportive working relationships are cited over and over again in research as a huge protective factor against reoffending.[22] So while monitoring and sex offenders' registers are often seen as the only solution to protecting society from people with sexual convictions, in reality the approach of compassion, community and non-judgemental support is what actually works. It might not be a popular opinion to treat these men with humanity and offer them support, but it works to stop them reoffending. And that should matter more than anything else.

There's also a higher incidence of recidivism if an ex-con can't secure stable work or housing after release. Even the companies that agree to take a look at a crim's CV will go nowhere near sex offenders. Housing providers routinely refuse to consider the applications of arsonists and sex offenders equally. Even the most well-meaning residential rehabilitation facility will refuse a con if he's on the register. Without access and support to navigate the housing, benefits and employment systems in an effort to put in place the foundations for a life beyond offending, the possibility of reoffending increases. The circles of support work with the offender to help him access the tools necessary to live a life beyond his crimes.

There's also a centre out in the community offering additional support to sex offenders in an effort to stop them from reoffending. It offers vital services to those with 'atypical sexual preferences' as well, which means people who are concerned about themselves and their thoughts but haven't offended can access support. These services actively try to work with people before they get so far as offending, which is surely a good thing for the safety of society.

The location of the support service is secret, because it would probably get burned to the ground if the general public ever found out where it was. This leads to the confusing situation where there's a service that's reducing offending, making society safer and could, arguably, make us even more safe if it could reach more potential offenders before they commit any crimes. Yet they can't advertise their work, they can't publicise the support they offer. They can't reach those thousands of potential offenders who are out in the community before they commit crimes.

Usually, they just have to wait until the man has been convicted, worked his way through the prison system and then been referred to take part in their interventions long after the crime has been committed. Although the circles are showing positive outcomes in the community, there are still only limited services that go 'through the gate' and provide support from custody before re-entry into the community.

There is also a helpline that exists for those who are worried they might commit an offence. It actively supports people to ask for help and stops them from progressing their thoughts into further actions, yet it is not widely publicised. That helpline's impact is unmeasurable. How can you report on how many crimes you've stopped from taking place? How do you prove a negative? But the data they *can* collect on the groups aimed at men concerned they might offend or teen-agers displaying inappropriate behaviour suggests this is one of the only interventions that's doing more good than harm.

Collecting data on convicted offenders is easier, though. And what these circles of support in the community appear to do is reduce reoffending.[23] They work. Research suggests that there's some degree of public acceptance for treatment rather than just punishment. But this acceptance reduces rapidly when people are surveyed on whether or not they'd accept treatment facilities within their own communities. This is a difficult and emotive issue. No one wants a sex offender community service on their doorstep. However, this community treatment and support is necessary, because those prison treatment programmes sure as shit aren't working. They must take place in someone's neighbourhood.

The media plays a part in fanning the flames of this hugely controversial topic. There's a disparity in attitude towards community treatment between those who regularly read the tabloids, with their dehumanising stories of 'beasts' and 'monsters', and the rest of the population.[24] Seeing sexual offenders as 'other', and actively attempting to stop them from reintegrating into society, is one of the quickest ways to increase recidivism.[25] Almost all sexual offenders will be released one day. They require treatment and support that works. So not only is reporting in this way distasteful, but it's also dangerous. Research shows that tabloid readers were the least likely to support the very community services that actively reduce the risk posed by sexual offenders.[26] These services are necessary if we are to mitigate the risks posed by those with child sexual convictions.

Laws, punishments and treatments should be used to make society a better and safer place for all. Even if our primal instinct is to look the other way, or chase sexual offenders out of our communities, or pretend they're subhuman, we must fight our basest instincts and understand that tailored, professional and compassionate support services protect us all. We have a duty to fully research and look objectively at what works to reduce offending. And then we must start doing it.

I wasn't trained or qualified or capable of working with Jeff when I first met him. My intervention did nothing to reduce his risk. I only hope that one of these rare community services did eventually reach him. Because he was released. Because he did return to that community outside the prison walls.

Research and reform are needed – the data we have proves that to be true. But the controversy around sentencing and punishment doesn't end with people with sexual convictions. There are also the crims who kill other people. The murderers.

CHAPTER 5
Looking at Life – Murderers

Mo came to my attention because the other prisoners referred him to me. They'd seen him struggling. They were good like that. I knew they supported each other in the group, but I hadn't realised that their support extended to others on the wing who didn't attend.

It had been a rough weekend for everyone. Having fewer staff had meant near constant bang-up. Outdoor exercise had been cancelled. Visits had been shortened. The classroom smelled acrid, the result of a cell fire started in protest at the regime. My eyes stung from soot still hanging in the air, but it masked the odour of the men who hadn't had access to the showers for three days. Everyone was trying to keep their cool through gritted teeth, talking quietly to one another, sipping coffee from Pot Noodle cups.

I lifted the radio to my mouth. 'Permission to join the net?' I asked and then told the central communications team my location.

The radio crackled back, filling the room with noise. A moment of anticipation before the battery promptly gave up.

As usual, there were twelve of them that morning and just one of me. All I had as protection was an emergency bell on the wall behind me. I wasn't even sure it worked. I'd never had to press it. In that classroom, I had what the textbooks called 'dynamic security', which basically meant interpersonal skills and peripheral vision.

Titch started chewing his lips. I saw him look over at Jimmy and raise an eyebrow. A message passed between them. He was looking for reassurance before he started talking.

'What is it?' I asked.

'I dunno if I should talk about it, miss. Confidentiality in our groups and all that.'

'If you tell me you're doing drugs in prison, I'm going to report you. If you tell me you're going to hurt someone, I'll report you . . .' I started up with my usual warning, the one that reminded the crims that I expected emotional honesty in the groups, but honesty about committing crime? That was a different story.

'Nah,' Titch cut me off, 'what d'you think of me? It's not about me. There's a guy on the wing.'

Slouched men sat up to attention. The cons were communicating with body language and eye contact. They were visibly twitchy, wondering if Titch was about to start grassing someone up. However tight the group was, however much we supported each other emotionally, a snitch was still a fucking snitch in prison. No one was about to sit back and listen as Titch stitched someone up.

He read the room. His eyes flickered around and landed on Jimmy again. Jimmy frowned – there was an almost invisible wink: *Do you know what the fuck you're doing here?* he silently asked.

I scanned the room too, grasped the feeling of the group. I looked at him, square in the eyes, hoping that my stare could convey my thoughts: *Don't grass anyone up in here, Titch. It's not worth it, man.*

He read me.

'No,' he repeated. 'Nothing like that, you dickheads. I was just gonna say I'm worried about that new guy.'

The room exhaled, bodies sat back and relaxed in their seats.

Mickey turned to Titch. 'That new guy on the threes?'

'Yeah, yeah, I've seen him. The guy who won't stop crying?' Jimmy said.

'He's not in a good way, miss. He asked for a listener last night. I heard them talking,' he added.

Listeners were the inmates specially trained by the Samaritans to provide emotional support to other cons who were struggling. If he was requesting a listener, it meant he needed help.

Titch caught my eye. 'For real, miss, you need to go and take a look at this guy. He needs your help.'

'He's on the threes?' I directed the question to Mickey. 'Which cell is he in? Anyone know him, what's his name?'

'He won't talk to any of us, miss, didn't hear from him all weekend. Fuck knows who he is – never seen him before,' Mickey replied.

Titch confirmed the same story. 'Never seen him, but if anyone needs your help, miss, it's him.'

'No one knows him?' I asked incredulously.

Everyone who came and went from the detox wings always knew someone inside. Their criminal activity was so consistent, their stomping grounds so similar, that they always crossed paths with one another.

'For real, miss,' Jimmy stated.

'Who's he sharing with?' I asked.

Suicidal inmates, inmates who cried non-stop, inmates who refused to leave their cells and inmates who asked to speak to listeners were never single cell. It was unfortunate to be the poor guy doubled up with an emotional cellmate, but at least it meant that there was someone there to keep an eye out. We relied heavily on the prison population to keep each other alive. The crims doubled up with suicidal inmates were probably far better at therapy than any of the staff paid and employed to work inside.

'He's high-risk, miss, he's in there on his own.'

Mickey let the sentence hang in the air. We all knew this wasn't an ideal scenario.

'Fucksake,' I muttered under my breath. Out loud I said, 'All right, all right, I'll sort it out. No worries.'

For the remainder of the session, I used this as an opportunity to discuss and reflect on how far the crims had come in their own recovery.

'Do you lot remember what you were like when you first came in?'

We laughed, almost in relief, at the progress they'd made. Some of them had been at death's door when they'd first landed on the detox unit. Some of them had cried uncontrollably, like this new guy. But were now functioning, focused and positive; alive and hopeful. They congratulated each other and afterwards filed back onto the landing smiling. It felt good to look back sometimes, to see how far they'd come.

I tidied up the classroom, stacked away the chairs and followed them back out onto the wing, hollering 'Twelve on' as I went. I headed straight to the officer's room to see if I could find out more about this inmate no one knew.

Officer Wendy had her feet up on the desk. Big black boots resting on top of a stack of ACCT documents, a pastry in one hand, newspaper in the other, crumbs flaking down her shirt. Some officers genuinely cared and worked hard to help crying, suicidal new inmates. Wendy wasn't one of them. Officers like this wound me up, so I knew I had to keep myself in check and approach her with caution.

Asking an officer like Wendy to do anything that might look like work was always a gamble. It was as though I had a finite number of favours I could ask for. I had to weigh up

whether or not asking her to open up the cell door of this specific inmate right now was more important than asking her
to unlock that specific inmate tomorrow. Officers like Wendy
gave the good ones a bad name. I normally flattered, praised,
begged, cajoled Wendy just to do her fucking job. I decided,
for that moment at least, to leave her in peace with her pastry
and paper, and investigate this new con myself.

'Do you mind if I grab the ACCTs, Wendy?' I said, pointing to the pile of files under her feet.

She mumbled through her mouthful of croissant, lifting
her legs. She plonked her boots immediately back on the
desk, giving me nowhere to spread out the documents.

I pulled up a chair, balanced the seven folders on my knee
and started leafing through them. Four of the names I knew
– they were crims I worked with. Mickey had attended my
group this morning and his ACCT document should have
been brought to me by an officer at the start of the session,
but that didn't always happen. I pulled out a pen and wrote
an observation for him:

Client attended group 09.30–11.00. Appeared well kempt
and no obvious signs of distress. Discussed with the group
his visit with mother over the weekend and client stated that
it had left him feeling more positive. Engaged well throughout, good eye contact. States his mood is currently '7 out
of 10', whereas last week felt it was at a '5'. No immediate
concerns: agreed to attend the session again tomorrow and
verbalised clear future planning. Expressed an interest in
beginning education, which should be discussed during
next ACCT review.

It would have been a useful handover note if anyone read it,
but it also served the dual purpose of clearly showing that
he wasn't feeling suicidal at my latest contact with him. As

deaths in custody had increased, so too had my arse-covering tendencies.

The next document was huge, with a stack of extra observation forms stuffed into it. This clearly wasn't my man. The man I was looking for wasn't known to anyone in my group and they had said that he was brand new in. I got to the final ACCT and saw Mo's name written on the front. He was in his forties and on remand. Flicking past the contents page, I went straight for the section that explained why the inmate was suicidal. It made for interesting reading. This was his first time in prison. It wasn't impossible, but it was pretty rare for someone to start offending in their forties.

I continued to read. 'Pregnant girlfriend' came next. OK, so first time in custody with a kid on the way. This was starting to make sense. Finally, the officer had noted down 'murder charge'. Oh. So, he'd never been in prison before, had a kid on the way and was looking at life. That'd do it, I supposed.

I waved the file in front of Wendy. 'You heard anything about this guy, Mo?' I asked her casually, hoping her love of gossip rather than commitment to the job would get her talking.

'Yeah,' she said gleefully. 'He's all over the news, just flipped out and killed his cousin. He's climbing the walls coming off the drink, crying he never meant it. Stayed at the scene, waited for the police – owned up to it and everything. Don't know what he's crying about, mind you. Fucking scum, if you ask me.'

'He's single cell because of the murder? Has he threatened anyone since he got here?' I asked, again trying to disguise my work talk for light-hearted gossip between friends.

'No, nothing since he got here. They're always like that though, aren't they? The ones who act the worst out there coming in here and start crying for their mum. Realise they're not so big and bad, after all.'

'Do you mind if I take a look at him? He's got an observation due anyway, so I'll do it for you if you like?'

Hiding my request for an unlock like I was offering to help her out worked and Wendy hauled herself up from the chair and headed up to his cell to crack the lock for me. She opened the door without knocking, swinging it wide open, not bothering to check if he was sleeping, or having a shit.

'Knock, knock. Someone here to see you,' she shouted as she threw the lock so he wouldn't be able to shut the door fully.

At least she did that, making it less likely I'd be taken hostage if he decided to drag me into his cell.

As a civilian working behind the walls, I wasn't allowed to enter cells without an officer. It was partly for my own protection, to minimise hostage situations where do-gooders who aren't fully trained in personal protection get locked in with a con. I also suspected it was because far more civvies than you'd like to believe smuggled in drugs, phones and other contraband. And I knew of at least two nurses who were caught shagging prisoners in their cells during my time.

Whatever the reason, I had to stand in the doorway, slightly sideways on as a tactic to reduce the risk of being pulled in by this violent murderer. But this killer didn't look capable of taking anyone hostage. He was at his desk, with his head in his hands.

'All right, Mo? I run these groups every day where we sit and talk about our feelings. Some of the other guys said they were a bit worried about you. Do you mind if we talk for a minute?' I asked.

He swivelled his face towards me but remained bent over. He was tear-stained. Snot leaked from his nose and he wiped it away on the already filthy sleeve of his prison-issued sweater. I noted the laces had been removed from his trainers.

From the corner of my eye, I saw Titch and Mickey

hovering at the end of the landing. They kept enough distance to give us privacy and couldn't hear what Mo and I were talking about, but I knew they were watching.

'Sorry,' he replied. 'I'm not usually like this. I don't know what's happening to me. I never cry.'

'It's all right, man. I'm not judging you for crying. Do you want to tell me what's going on for you?'

'My girlfriend's pregnant. She'll leave me. I don't know what to do.'

'Will this be your first?' I asked.

'Yeah. We've been trying for years. She's due in four months.'

'Congratulations,' I said, and he breathed out a desperate laugh.

'Yeah, cheers. I can't wait to be a dad.' He smiled, although it didn't reach his bloodshot eyes.

'Have you spoken to her since you got here?' I already knew what the answer would be.

He'd never been in prison before, so he didn't know the process for getting phone numbers added to his PIN. He didn't have a cellmate to help him through the intricacies of the system, getting the necessary apps in and his phone numbers authorised. By the time an officer clocked on to this during his first ACCT review, it was the weekend and the backlog from Friday night meant the phone numbers wouldn't be cleared for a few days. He had no way of contacting the outside world.

Mo needed to learn quickly how to navigate prison to make life in here slightly more bearable. It was clear he had no idea how to add money to his account, no idea how to order tobacco from the canteen and no idea whether or not he could trust either the cons or the screws, or me.

'I could ask one of the guys to come up and help you to put all the apps in?' I suggested gently.

He snivelled again, swiped at his nose and pulled his head up.

'Would you? I haven't a fucking clue what I'm doing here.' He gave a forlorn chuckle.

'Sure, you want me to get someone? We can get those things sorted for you now.' I beckoned Mickey over.

'This is Mickey. He might look like a scary fucker but he's all right really.' I pointed and smiled.

'Mickey, this is Mo. He needs to sort his apps. Do us a favour and help him out? I'll go and get an update on your PIN and phone numbers, see if there's anything I can do to get them approved today, OK?'

Mickey offered an outstretched arm into the cell, not stepping inside without an invite. Mo stood, rubbing his hand on his trackies, and shook Mickey's.

'Come in, man.' He offered Mickey the plastic chair and sat down on the bed.

'Am I OK to leave you to it for a bit, then? I'll come back later and let you know how I get on with the phone.'

I briefed Wendy back at the office on the conversation as I scribbled, knowing that she was barely listening. Then I headed for the chapel to see if they could help me to get the numbers approved quickly.

The chaplaincy team worked their magic and by the afternoon the phone numbers were approved, an emergency tobacco pack provided (which he'd have to pay for as soon as he had money in his account) and a canteen order for some chocolate completed (again, to be paid for the following week). Mo was no longer hysterical and felt better for making a plan.

Mo hadn't been a 100 per cent legit member of the public before the night his cousin had died. He'd done his share of brawling as a teen and dealt a bit on the side. He'd driven a car without insurance a few times and bought stolen goods down the pub once in a while. But nothing like this. What led a man to live a fairly normal life, reach his forties and then go out, get drunk and kill someone?

Mo said he'd suffered with depression his whole life but in the six months before the crime, a dark cloud had loomed over him. He'd been drinking more and mixing it with cocaine and cannabis. His depression had spiralled, he'd started having panic attacks and he'd felt constantly anxious.

Before the crime, he'd gone to the doctor, worried about himself. The insomnia and mood swings had been happening for weeks. He'd been on a waiting list for basic primary care support in the community when it happened.

His memory of the night was blank. Blackout drunkenness. Even watching CCTV footage of the incident couldn't trigger recollection. But he could identify himself on the video. He knew he'd done it. Lunged at his cousin outside a takeaway, thrown him through the window. Glass had embedded into his neck. He'd bled out in minutes.

Mo's solicitor had told him he was looking at a minimum tariff of fifteen years before he'd be considered eligible to apply for release. The solicitor thought he should change his plea to guilty. He started fanatically reading, in a desperate effort to educate himself on the law around murder.

Despite knowing the difficulties he would face, he entered a plea of not guilty. Although he'd handed himself in, admitting his cousin had died because of his actions, Mo couldn't accept that he'd meant to do it. He'd get a manslaughter conviction, that was never in doubt. But for murder, the main sticking point in Mo's case was whether or not he had the intention to seriously wound or kill. The prosecution needed to prove 'beyond reasonable doubt' that he had the *mens rea* – the mental element, the intention – to kill. Mo's trial would focus solely on this point. He'd be held for the full six months on remand while the prosecution built its case. His first child would be born while he awaited trial.

It had taken me a while after working with Jeff to figure out if I was capable of doing the job without judgement. I'd spent a long time reflecting and ultimately decided that I'd signed up for the job to help the people no one else gave a shit about. The invisible people who moved around the same city as us but who we never acknowledged. So I treated Mo with the same degree of humanity I did all of the crims, although I was acutely aware that some people would deplore my showing sympathy to someone who had taken an innocent man's life. I understood the gut reaction to hate a man like Mo. But I believed that there's humanity in everyone. Because I didn't believe anyone was a hopeless case. When I signed up for this job, I didn't add a clause to my contract saying: 'I'll only work with the deserving criminals.' I'd agreed to work with whoever needed my help. It wasn't my job to judge. The jury would do that. And so would the whole family, who'd been torn apart that night too.

Mo started coming to group, but he remained on the open ACCT for a long time. Circumstances triggered him to suicidal thoughts regularly. His girlfriend couldn't make a visit because she had a hospital appointment. Or he'd be hauled out to court for a pre-trial hearing and get the feeling that it wasn't going to go his way. Each time, we'd increase his observations and hope to hell that he wouldn't join the fast-growing list of deaths in custody by suicide that was averaging around two a week across the estate.

The group was supportive, giving Mo the space to speak, to vent, and offering positive affirmations. They reassured him with their own stories, validating his feelings. Titch, on a life licence himself, offered emotional and practical help. The two of them would talk through the mental gymnastics of accepting a life behind bars.

Mo was gentle and often so honestly emotionally vulnerable that it made the classroom quiet with contemplation. He cried regularly and I believed his anguish at having killed someone was genuine. He asked his solicitor if he could write to his auntie and uncle to apologise, but he was advised against it. Only his mother was still speaking to him. If remorse was a living thing, I think it would've been Mo.

Working with him was easy, in a way. His openness, his acceptance that he'd done wrong and his searching for a solution to make things right demonstrated to me his willingness to change. But my role wasn't focused on showing him how to put this learning into practice on The Out. I was supporting him to prepare for a long stretch. We were working together to develop the tools to survive getting ready for trial and the subsequent prison sentence, without losing his mind.

I felt morally torn. I could never understand what the family was going through. I didn't know if they wanted him lifed off or were open to forgiving him. Emotionally, I understood the need for him to be punished. But rationally, I couldn't comprehend what society was hoping to achieve by incarcerating him for decades in a failed system. He didn't need rehabilitation in the usual sense. He wasn't a hardened criminal. But those issues with alcohol and cocaine, his depression that had led him to use in the first place – they were problems that a long prison sentence wouldn't solve. If anything, staying banged up would exacerbate them.

While Mo was panicked about how long he'd get, I was left thinking that whether he got a manslaughter or a murder charge, in the end, he'd eventually be released. He'd be on licence for the rest of his life, but he'd be returned to the community. And it was hard to believe that after serving decades, he'd be a better person for it.

People who commit violent crimes like Mo should be

punished. It's right and proper that for serious and violent crimes, there should be consequences. Loss of liberty is our go-to method of punishment and in these cases can also work to protect society for a period while the offender is incarcerated. But while the punishment is occurring, the best thing for the community, the taxpayer and the offender is to implement a robust series of interventions, like our Norwegian counterparts, that prepare a crim to return to society and repay his debts practically. It benefits no one to leave him inside to harden and criminalise further, to become institutionalised and bitter, only to be released when he's unable to be employed, unable to give anything back to society.

Since 2006, on the diktats of government, the length of sentences handed out for serious crimes has increased exponentially – two and a half times as many people are serving sentences of over ten years now. For serious offences, the ones heard in the Crown Court, the average sentence is 58.3 months. This is over twenty-four months longer than in 2006.[1] And I know that some people are so dangerous that they need a longer time away from the community to be able to come back safely. I understand that. But what I don't understand is how a system that's failing on every metric is meant to suddenly rehabilitate a man because his sentence length has doubled.

We're no safer on The Out now than we were back then. Lengthening prison sentences hasn't made for less crime. Data shows us that length of sentence and increased incarceration doesn't reduce the violence and crime in a society. I think I'd be able to swallow the idea of longer sentences if I was convinced that daily intensive rehabilitation was taking place behind the walls. Or if these men were asked to work on day release in a capacity that served the community. Or they were at least housed in a building that the inspectorate deemed 'fit for purpose'. No length of sentence can make a man into a better member of society if he has to serve his time inside the prison estate as it is now. It's like knocking down his house then asking him to rebuild it without any tools. And surely, what we want is for him to repent, rehabilitate and be given the opportunity to spend the rest of his life making amends for his crime.

I sat quietly in group as Titch led the session. This criminal class, this criminal classroom. I was trying to teach them the skills to live a fulfilled, meaningful and offending-free life. But out on the wings, he'd be schooled in criminality. If he wanted to make amends, if he wanted to give back to society, he'd have to wait until the end of his sentence.

My mind kept taking me back to the Norwegian prison system I'd been researching. I'd watched a documentary and remembered hearing one of the officers say that our countries aren't different. Like the UK, in Norway too, everyone will be released one day. The Norwegian officer had said that the most important question was 'Who do you want for your neighbour?'

Life doesn't mean life behind bars, because with the right interventions, most people are capable of rehabilitation, reform and change. The Norwegian reoffending statistics prove it. But in an English prison? I'd take Mo now over Mo at the end of a fifteen-year stint any day. I understood the instinct for retribution, but I wasn't sure what his incarceration would ultimately achieve.

The afternoon before he went out to court, I saw him pacing the landing. He was trembling as I reached out to shake his hand. I looked him up and down.

'Roll the shirt sleeves down and cover the tattoos. Look the part. And take off those prison rosary beads. Get them off. Remember to tuck your shirt in.'

He was too anxious to say anything but he nodded that he understood.

'Take care of yourself. Seriously, take care. I'll be here waiting. You got this.'

I didn't see him during the two-week trial. He was taken to court early and brought back late. I was always far beyond the walls when he returned to his cell each night. The group gave me updates on how he seemed from shouted conversations under cell doors and out of windows after bang-up. But none of us knew which way it would go. Didn't know whether he deserved those fifteen years his solicitor had warned him of or not.

The jury didn't either. They were locked in debate for days and couldn't come to a unanimous decision. The judge had to intervene. He directed them to return with only a majority verdict. He was eventually found guilty. He got twenty-one years.

In 2003, the average minimum a crim spent in prison before being eligible to apply for release for murder was twelve and a half years. By 2016, it was over twenty-one years.[2] The prison staff team was decimated over this period. Overcrowding problems persisted, more buildings deemed unsuitable for habitation, more violence, more deaths. Of those released, one in two continue to reoffend within the year. It can't make sense in any rational world to think that just doubling down and doing more of the same thing, for longer, will improve outcomes.

Mickey loved telling us in group that insanity was doing the same thing over and over again and expecting a different result each time. Sentencing people to serve longer stretches is like a crack addict thinking that if he just takes more, it'll all get better. More of the same failing system can't be the answer.

In such a brutalising system, it's no wonder that so many prisoners want to block it all out and just get high . . .

CHAPTER 6

Tried to Fund a Place in Rehab – Substance Misuse

My head snapped up from the education referral form I'd been hurriedly scrawling. I heard a voice I recognised, but I had to do a double take before I realised it was Shaun. He'd lost a lot of weight since I last waved goodbye to him at the gates two months earlier. It meant he'd been back hard on the drugs. All the weight he'd put on in prison had melted off him and his cheeks looked sunken. His eyes were bloodshot and his matted hair puffed out in sweaty, greasy tufts.

His prison-issue jumper had stains down the front and his white socks were greying. He was, however, wearing a brand-new pair of sliders and he'd already put his rosary beads back on. Physically, he looked like total shit. But he was smiling, sauntering as if he hadn't a care in the world. In his head, Shaun was still the good-looking badass he used to be. I knew he'd seen me, because his swagger slowed – he'd hesitated to look for a nearby cell he could dive into and avoid me altogether.

He was hoping I wouldn't remember him, hoping he could just ride his comedown in peace without having to think about bettering himself again. He looked beyond me down the landing, pretending to get the attention of someone behind me. I waved back at him, not letting him get away that easily. Shaun was visibly embarrassed that I was seeing him in such a state. He approached me, standing as close as people get to one another in prison. Never closer than a fist's reach away.

He still carried himself with that larger-than-life presence, but the minute our eyes met, he deflated. He slumped and seemed to shrink to half his size. He was defeated and devastated, and I could see he just wanted to burst into tears.

'Miss,' he started, almost pleadingly.

There was a layer of grease covering his skin and he had that smell that told me he was struggling with the detox. It was Monday morning, so I guessed he was picked up on the streets on Thursday, overnight in a police cell, court on Friday morning, into the van Friday afternoon before finally landing back on the detox wing by midnight. That meant he'd have gone four days without crack or heroin. He'd be on the lowest dose of methadone because the nurses wouldn't have been able to confirm his script over the weekend. Although doctors on The Out keep normal working hours, unfortunately the prison estate doesn't, which means crims like Shaun have to wait until Monday afternoon to get the methadone dose their bodies rely on.

However much he might start using and abusing drugs later on in his prison sentence, right then, my first priority was to make sure he wasn't about to die on me and that he was being detoxed properly. Only once we had got him stabilised could we start back down the long road to recovery. I smiled gently.

'Let's get you sorted. Have they got you scripted properly? What do I need to get for you right now?'

'I feel like shit, miss.'

'We'll sort it, OK? I got you.'

For two hours I chased community doctors to send faxes for prescriptions. Shaun signed four different consent forms to allow me to speak to various medical professionals. I begged the healthcare team for an emergency appointment with the prescribing nurse to get his script sorted before the end of the day.

Judging by the state of him, he'd been on full-throttle self-destruct for the past eight weeks without respite. I didn't know how soon after his release he'd managed to score. Sometimes it's minutes. Sometimes it's months. He'd tell me the whole story later, once he'd stopped clucking and climbing the walls during withdrawal. Once he'd stopped being sick and choked some food down.

The volume of the wing went from just about tolerable to deafening as soon as Shaun Armstrong got over his first days of detox. He was constantly in motion, ducking and diving. Morning unlock was punctuated by screams from Wendy.

'Armstrong, get away from the meds queue.'

'Armstrong, why are you unlocked? Back behind your door.'

'Armstrong, stop running!'

Boundaries in prison between staff and crims are taken seriously, and rightly so. I worked with criminals who were at times manipulative, selfish, self-centred, dangerous, head-fucking, out of control and downright crazy. In prison, you're not allowed to have favourites, though everyone knows that everyone has favourites.

Fuck it, Shaun was up there in my top ten. Physically, he stood shoulder to shoulder with me in height, but his presence always made me think of him as much taller. His tenacity, his determination to play the system. The effort he put into grafting on the landing was exhausting to watch but strangely admirable. He was a hard worker, I'd give him that. If only he could have channelled that energy positively, he'd have been a billionaire.

But his ambitions ran no further than managing his drug

dependence while in prison. He was a master of distraction, running rings around staff during medication time. Like *One Flew Over the Cuckoo's Nest*, the detox wing would dutifully queue up every morning to be handed their daily dose of methadone, Subutex, uppers and downers, vitamin pills and weight gain shakes. Shaun had already put in an order with the other crims the night before and would create some mayhem or other, buying them a moment to hide his drug of choice before flashing their tongue and open mouth to the nurse. Back in Shaun's cell, they'd remove the meds from wherever they'd manage to secrete them and by 11 a.m., he'd be rolling around the landing like the last man at a rave. High as a kite and loving life.

In Shaun I saw a spark that was rare in a place designed to sap the life out of everyone who had the misfortune to step inside. The way he carried himself, the way he fixed his hair in a carefully gelled sweep. The way he so dramatically played at being crazy when the nurses were around, in the hope they'd give him a couple of sleeping pills, all demonstrated to me a lust for life that could power him a million miles away from this shithole. Shaun was better than this place. He was too alive to be spending his time only half living in prison.

But while it was amusing to watch, I was always on high alert when I saw him circling any one of my clients. Nothing good could come from talking to him. He was probably trying to recruit Deano or Taylor into his latest cunning plan, convincing them to get their girlfriends to bring in drugs or embark on some complicated scheme to rewire the TVs to get Sky. I warned them not to get involved with him, but Shaun was still managing to get his drugs from somewhere.

Shaun thought he was subtle. He'd been getting away with his petty criminality inside for so long that he congratulated himself for always getting one over on the system. He didn't know that day in, day out I was completing security information reports, grassing on his suspicious behaviour. In fact, I put in so many reports about Shaun, I got an email direct from the head of security thanking me for my contribution and saying I was one of the top five snitches in the establishment.

When Shaun managed to get a referral to work with me, he approached our first session with the gleeful assumption that if he played it right, he'd be walking away with a doctor's referral and a note on his file saying he really did need an increase in those lovely opiate-based painkillers. He was quick to remind me that he'd initially been prescribed them for the injury he received last time he was in custody. The fall from the top bunk that he'd sued the prison for and got a six-grand payout.

'Now, I'm not saying you'll be in trouble. I don't want to get you in trouble. But if I can't get an increase, I'll be forced to inform my legal team. And what's your full name, miss? Just so I can make sure I get the details right when I speak to my solicitor.'

It was a risk, inviting him to group. But he so clearly had the potential to stop wasting his ingenuity and charisma on criminality. Shaun was absorbed in maintaining his little kingdom on the wing. That got under my skin. If we could shift his focus and show him there was a different way, I had no doubt that he had the wits and persistence to change his path.

There wasn't widespread support for Shaun's gatecrashing of our classroom. Mickey had pulled me to one side beforehand and raised serious concerns that his presence would upset the group dynamic with all his bullshit and noise. Mickey had seen people like Shaun come and go from the group for years and knew his sort. He was probably stealing meds from half of the attendees and if they didn't feel safe talking with him in the room, it would never work. I warned

Shaun it would be a trial session, no promises he could keep coming.

As group began, Shaun was poised to perform, sat on the edge of his seat, wondering what was in it for him. Always looking for what he could get from the situation, he started to sway slightly, rolling his eyes around crazily, in a weak performance of someone hearing voices. He tapped his feet and twitched his legs. Everyone pointedly ignored him and his obvious attempts to attract attention.

Mickey had asked if he could do the group rules that morning. He stood up, unfolding his massive body as we all sat staring up at him. He cleared his throat and I nodded for him to begin.

'Just for you lot who are new to group, I want to make clear that in this room, for an hour a day, there's no shit talk. We're all here for a reason. If you've got an agenda, leave it at the door, lads. You won't just be wasting your own time, but you'll be wasting my time, too. I just wanted to let you know, you're all welcome to the room, to the group, but make sure you're able to look at yourself in the mirror afterwards and know that you've been honest with yourself this morning.' Mickey smiled and winked before he sat back down.

Shaun spent his first session with us in stunned silence, staring open-mouthed at the other crims. They were getting real, talking deep, being honest about their hopes and fears and feelings. He'd stopped fidgeting, his frenetic energy subdued.

'Do you want to say anything, Shaun, just before we finish up? How did you find your first group?' I asked.

Wide-eyed, he muttered his thanks to the room for putting some things into words for him.

'Keep coming, mate,' said Mickey. 'This thing that we're doing right here works, but you have to put into it, you have to get real with yourself, too.'

He slapped him on the back and Shaun nodded that he'd think about carrying on attending.

Shaun did come back, but he was reticent and untrusting at first. He'd channelled that admirable drive into the wasted causes of his criminal lifestyle and his prison persona for so long that he seemed unable to grasp that I had no ulterior motive, aside from making sure he became a better version of himself. He seemed to regard the level of honesty that came from the other cons and myself as suspicious. As if I'd use his emotions against him or as if I were storing up all the stories and ideas shared to use one day as evidence in court to prove something about himself that he didn't want the world to know.

It seemed that Shaun couldn't quite comprehend that our group therapy just 'was'. He kept searching for the catch, not understanding why the other cons were coming and talking and getting real. He always looked baffled during those early groups, as if he were missing out on the swindle; as if the other crims were playing the system in a way he couldn't quite understand. He was perplexed.

When the serious offenders started crying in group, they weren't rewarded by me in any way for their tears. No one in the group ever took the piss. And then Shaun started noticing that no one took the piss after the group, either. The vulnerability the crims displayed in the classroom didn't seem to follow them back onto the wings. In fact, the ones who did cry seemed lighter, calmer and freer when they returned to the landings. Shaun noticed that rather than seeming paranoid and anxious when they left group, having allowed others to see their weaknesses, they seemed even more self-assured.

I'd print off articles about cons who had changed their lives. I'd print off motivational slogans from Instagram. I'd print off cell workouts he could do and the inspirational stories of Iron Man triathletes who used to be criminals. I'd print off job adverts from companies that would employ ex-offenders. I'd slide them all under his cell door, day after day, leaving breadcrumbs for him to follow. Over the coming weeks, I watched Shaun while I was on the wing. Instead of running up and down the landings causing a nonsense, he was spending more time in the gym, more time in the library, more time in my groups. There had been a shift, some slow changes germinating. It was a good start, we'd laid the foundations, but then he was released before he'd been ready to open himself up to the group.

As he left the landing for release, he called out to Wendy, 'Don't give away my cell – I'll be back in a couple of weeks,' still thinking that if he was pissing off the staff, he was winning.

Shaun was one of those petty and persistent offenders who came and went so often, I sometimes didn't have time to archive his paperwork before I had to restart it all again. In 2018, over 25,000 people were sentenced to serve less than six months.[1] Of them, 60 per cent reported a drug or alcohol issue and, just like Shaun, committed crimes that were linked to addiction.[2]

Although community sentences are more effective at reducing reoffending than custodials, especially when it comes to people like Shaun with a large number of previous offences, I agreed that he'd be back soon. The use of community punishments has more than halved since 2008.[3]

The government's own data shows that these short prison sentences for theft and drugs actually increase the likelihood of reoffending when compared to other sorts of treatment or community sentences.[4] Yet these are the mass of offenders, churning in and out of the gates each year. I'd witnessed that revolving door in full swing over the years and was just waiting for the morning Shaun dropped back onto the wing. Desistance theory states that moving away from a life of crime is a process requiring long-term support to get to the bottom of the offending behaviour. Just as I felt I was getting somewhere with Shaun, he'd been released. I hoped that when he did return, we could pick up from where we left off. Meanwhile, reoffending costs £18.1 billion per year.[5]

And now there he was again. He'd made it two whole months on The Out before he was brought back into custody for shoplifting. I had eighteen weeks to work with him this time before release. There was no judgement from me. I knew not to expect miracles. I knew that a few tentative therapy sessions wouldn't change the world. I understood that a lifetime of learned behaviour and addiction couldn't be forgotten overnight. But most of all, I knew that what we naturally framed as failure wasn't necessarily failure. Stumbling blocks and trips and falls on the way didn't mean the journey was over. It wasn't over until it was fucking over. I'd promised to turn up every single day and try my hardest to make a positive difference to the lives of those men. Those short-stay sentences might have got in the way, they might not have worked, but when a man with Shaun's spark came along, I knew I'd do everything I could to get him to channel it right.

Addicts relapsed, again and again, but that didn't stop me from returning to work each day with unlimited hope and shoulders wide enough to carry their burdens until they were capable of carrying them themselves. Shaun was making progress last time around and he'd make progress again. Failure wasn't failure. What happened would be a lesson learned. If he was willing to move forwards and try again, I'd work with him every single time he returned until we could break the cycle. I refused to give up on him, because he never was, and never will be, a hopeless case.

Two weeks later and the meds queue was taking an age. The nurse's computer kept crashing and if they didn't get a move on, there'd be no time for group. There was a tension, pinched voices as the inmates tried not to show they were struggling after only a slight delay in their methadone.

Of course, Shaun had managed to push his way to the front of the queue, charming nurses and irritating crims, got his script and was returned to his energetic glory. But strangely, instead of harassing the rest of the line, instead of ducking in and out of cells, that morning, he grabbed the mop and bucket from Mickey and skipped towards me.

'Do you want me to mop your classroom while you wait, miss?' he asked.

'Yeah, sure, why not.'

I left the door wide open and let him in. I stayed on the threshold, keeping one eye on the meds queue, one eye on him, making sure there was no ulterior motive for the offer of help. I watched him as he diligently mopped from the back corners towards the door.

'Do you think this is my rock-bottom, miss?' he asked.

I looked at Shaun, assessing him.

'Do you want to talk today?'

He sighed, rolled his neck to crack it.

'Suppose it's about time I did,' he said finally.

Once we were all finally seated and group had started, Shaun told us he loved the thrill of shoplifting. As a kid, his first memory was pocketing pick 'n' mix on a day out to Woolworths. Told us he got good at it, too. Started nicking things for other people, selling them on, turning tidy profits every day. He was always chasing new highs. It started with alcohol, spending his earnings on vodka. Cocaine next. When he first got banged up, he couldn't deal with the boredom, the monotony. With a racing mind and nothing to do, he'd started smoking weed to kill the bird.

'None of this super skunk shit they smoke now, just a

mellow buzz, pass away the layover listening to music and zoning out.'

He'd never served more than a year in one stretch, bouncing between The Out and the in, building a community, friendships, a life, in both places.

'Real life looked so fucking dull,' he said. 'I thought it was a mug's game, working a nine-to-five.'

He looked at me, hands dancing as he talked.

'You get paid peanuts, miss, to spend half your life in here.'

I laughed.

'It's true. I get paid to be here. And then I get paid when I walk out the gate every night. You're still here for free. And being king of the wing doesn't look all that exciting to me.'

'For real, miss.' He laughed and sighed, stretching his legs in front of him and his arms behind his head. 'It's not fun anymore. Not like it was. I'm getting too old for this. It's hard work grafting all the time.'

He told us he'd started using heroin in prison. When mandatory drug testing was rolled out across the prison estate in England and Wales in 1996, crims who had previously blazed away their bird knew that cannabis would stay in the system for thirty days. His cellmate had offered him heroin. It only showed up for a couple of days and the high was nothing like he'd ever felt.[6]

Of course, I'd smelled the weed and spice and crack and heroin burning from behind cell doors. The acrid taste of bad-quality drugs hanging in the air, mingling with the incense bought on canteen to cover the odour. I'd dealt with men rolling into group off their nuts, or swaying on the landings, zombified. I'd heard stories like Shaun's before, prison rumours of addiction starting inside, but Shaun was the first to talk about it openly in group. By 2018, almost 15 per cent of inmates surveyed reported they'd developed a drug problem once inside prison – a doubling from the figures reported in 2014.[7] As of September 2021, 16 per cent of the prison population were in custody on drug-related charges, with another 10 per cent of the prison population serving short sentences for theft offences – the offence of the addict.[8] The maths seems blindingly obvious.

One in seven inmates developed a problem while in custody and then when they commit crime to fund that addiction, we bang them up again, always on these short sentences that only break their ties with the community, uproot their lives and make them more likely to reoffend on release.

Shaun told us he didn't mind prison. 'I was just in and out. I could score in here just like I could on the streets. It didn't make a difference.'

I winced, knowing the statistic that a third of inmates thought it was easier to find drugs in prison than on The Out.[9] They were meant to come in here to sort their shit out. We were meant to keep them safe, patch them up and send them back out clean and functioning. We were meant to get them off the drugs and drink and break that constant cycle of reoffending. While one in two of the released inmates reoffend within twelve months, if he's on a short sentence, like Shaun had been the twenty-two previous times he'd been inside, there was a 67 per cent chance he'd be back before the year was done.[10]

'So, what's different now? Why are you coming to groups?' I asked.

Shaun had watched others display vulnerability, speak honestly in this classroom. But he hadn't tried it for himself and I thought maybe that was as much as he'd say for the time being. He was silently weighing up the moment. He rocked back on his chair, looked up to the heavens and then he told us.

He'd starting injecting this time round. Promised himself he'd never do that. Hated those fucking junkies, never thought he'd end up like them.

'Watch your language,' Mickey interrupted, bristling at the word 'junkie', which was one of the only banned words in the classroom.

'Well, I'm one of those fucking junkies now, so I can use that word if I want,' Shaun shot back.

Shaun told us how he'd never, ever considered injecting. He hated the people who did that. Thought they had a problem. Thought he was in control if he was just smoking.

'It's stupid, I know, because I've been in and out of here more times than you've had hot dinners, miss. But I honestly thought I had this thing under control. I didn't mind prison. Now, I know that was never true. I'm fucked. I'm an addict.'

He dropped his head, creased forwards and let out a sob that vibrated around the classroom.

The group members who went to Alcoholics Anonymous and Narcotics Anonymous applauded him, but then we sat silently.

Mickey put an arm on his shoulder, but we remained quiet to see if Shaun wanted to say any more.

Finally, he straightened, shaking Mickey's arm free. He blinked tightly.

'I haven't used since I got back in. I'm on a script, but I've been clean for seventeen days.'

The group turned to look at me, waiting for a response. I stood up and crossed the room to shake his hand.

'Well done. Seventeen days drug-free, you should be mad proud. Thank you for opening up today, it must have taken a lot of courage to decide to do that.'

The whole group applauded then, standing one by one to shake his hand, too.

We celebrated the success, we learned from the trips and falls, and we kept moving forwards. Why did we stand up knowing we'd be knocked down again? Because we were not born to lie with our faces in the dirt. Get knocked down. Get back up, brush yourself off. Keep trying.

After that day, Shaun was flying. Being a drug addict and a criminal had taken up a hell of a lot of time and energy. Surviving in prison had taken intelligence and determination. Unfortunately, the failings of the system made it easier to excel at criminality than to channel that energy towards going straight. Rehabilitation was the exception, not the rule. Finding role models who had left the gates and never looked back was almost impossible. The expectation was that they'd always be back. Yet the men behind bars had bucketloads of wasted potential. We overlooked their skills because they'd been directed for too long towards the next scam or swindle or hustle. But we'd be better off recognising them, understanding them and nurturing them towards change.

Shaun was never a lost cause, he just needed to learn that there could be another way. To see that another world existed beyond the landings – a world where he could thrive if given the chance. And when Shaun grasped this, he realised how much more he could achieve in his life. When he started channelling that energy right, Shaun never looked back.

The change in him was undeniable. We booked a one-to-one session so we could start planning his future beyond these walls.

'Can I see the paperwork before we do it tomorrow?' he asked.

I handed over a blank support plan. There was a grid on the page – columns at the top with titles like 'What I want to achieve'; 'How will I achieve this?'; 'What help I need to achieve this'; 'When do I want to achieve this by?'; 'What could stop me from achieving this goal?'

'Cool,' he said. 'I'll get it done tonight.'

Never before, or since, had an inmate offered to complete their own support plan. Shaun was different. That spark in him had become a fire and, finally, he was charging head first in the right direction. He was ready for it.

The next day, he presented me with his completed support plan. Goal one was detox off his script; within six weeks. Goal two: give up smoking; six weeks again. Goal three: get fit. Goal four: get a personal training qualification, with a three-month deadline.

When we met to go through the support plan, I didn't need to do much talking at all. Shaun had it all figured out – he just needed me for the practicalities. To come off his script, we first had to arrange a medication review, then look at dropping 40ml down to 30ml, 30ml down to 20ml. After 20ml, he could drop straight down to zero, with a week of sleepers and vitamins to get him through the physical withdrawal.

I'd given up smoking a year before and told Shaun that I'd done it without any patches or gum. 'It's mind over matter,' I told him, but I also warned that giving up methadone and cigarettes at once was bold. But now he had an idea, a goal to work towards, he was dogged.

'I can get you a meds review in three days' time. How's that sound? You ready to drop to 30ml, then?'

'Yeah, that'll feel good, miss.'

'And what about the smoking? Is that going to stop in six weeks' time?' I questioned.

'I'll stop smoking the day I reduce my script down, so in four days. Do it all at once, nice and neat.'

During his meds review, the prescribing nurse looked at him dubiously as he declared he'd be fully detoxed in six weeks. She worried that it was too much, too soon. But he was determined and the nurse finally agreed.

He never complained, even when the flulike symptoms took over and you could see him going hot and cold, shivering with a running nose. In group, everyone would ask him how he was feeling and he'd resolutely reply, 'I'm holding it down.' His energy had settled to calm. He knew what he wanted and he held it together with grace.

By week three, he was putting in applications to increase his time in the gym. He was in no fit state to be throwing weights around, but he took himself up there as often as he could. When he wasn't in the gym, he was reading everything he could find on fitness and nutrition, and managed to build himself a twelve-week workout plan, starting the day he finished on the meds. He brought a copy of the food available on canteen and meal options to one of our sessions and we cobbled together the healthiest dishes we could come up with from the hideous choices. I tried to hold back my disgust at the limited meal options, but we figured out the best of a bad lot, carefully calculating the protein, fat and carb ratios of each possible combination.

When I gently asked him if he thought he was pushing it all a bit too fast, he barked at me.

'Don't be like that, miss. I need this. I need you on my side.'

I never questioned his plan of action again.

Shaun came into his own in our group sessions. His demeanour relaxed and he developed a gentle way of challenging others. He arrived on time, he rounded up other prisoners to attend and he checked on others afterwards if they'd had a tough group. He completed every piece of homework I could think of setting him and updated his support plan week on week.

As he progressed and grew stronger, a few on the wing started to wonder when he'd fail. Some other cons were going out of their way to pick arguments with him. He tried to keep his head down, but there was always someone in the background making a sarcastic comment. I saw how other cons started treating him differently, giving him a wide berth, avoiding conversation with him. During one session, as we sat out on the landing with all of his personal training workbooks spread out in front of us, another crim wandered past and muttered, 'Fucking teacher's pet.'

It was a natural reflex when I worked in prison to constantly question the crim's motives, to not take what they said at face value and to wonder if I was a pawn in their game. I had all these thoughts while working with Shaun. Maybe this was just one big, elaborate effort towards some master plan madness. He wasn't suddenly a model prisoner. He still constantly gave Wendy shit and would happily steal any pens I happened to leave lying around.

However, he was so focused on success that nothing was going to stop him. He stopped the script and smoking. He followed his workout plan to the letter and secured his first personal trainer qualification within the three months. He met his targets.

And with these successes came inevitable change. As Shaun challenged and fought his addictions, he moved closer to the real world and further from the relative shelter of the detox wing. The detox wing, although mental at times, was a close-knit unit. The officers were experienced at handling the mental health issues specific to addicts. The addicts came and went through the metaphorical revolving door on short sentences. They were in and out and knew each other well. With the methadone finished, it wouldn't be long before he'd be moved out onto general population.

I worried about how it would affect his progress. The main wings were rougher and meaner. His access to the group would be limited. I didn't want to see all of his effort swallowed up, his attention distracted back towards scoring and grafting. He had six weeks left to serve and I had to find a way to maintain his focus through those final weeks, prepare him properly for The Out.

I asked him if he'd think about going to rehab. The words hadn't finished coming out of my mouth before he screeched 'Yes.'

Even though all of Shaun's offending had been related to drugs and alcohol, even though he'd started using heroin when he was in prison, he'd have to wait until the end of his sentence before he could be sent to a facility to address those issues. And even though it was obvious that this was the kind of support he desperately needed, he was going to have to do his time first.

For the one in seven crims in on drugs-related charges and the one in eight in for theft, getting a place in rehab would be like winning the lottery and the odds of receiving the funding to go seemed just as unlikely.

Even after all the work Shaun had done, even though he was the kind of criminal who was constantly out stealing and getting high and would continue to do so for the rest of his life if he didn't stop using, there was still no guarantee of getting into rehab. His community drug and alcohol team would have to support the application, agree to foot the bill. Which borough he resided in would be the deciding factor between whether he got released to rehab or released back out to nothing. Some areas had more funds to spare than others, some had already used up their budgets for the year. The local authorities didn't work together, so even if one had some cash left over and another was running short, they couldn't share. In reality, though, with demand as high as it was, I never found a local authority that ever had enough money to spend on everyone who needed it.

I'd been keeping Shaun's community substance misuse worker updated of his progress while he was inside. She was amazed, elated.

'I bloody knew he had it in him!' she sang down the phone when I told her he'd finished his script.

She fought tooth and nail to get his application for funding in front of the community panel and then battled even harder when the powers that be said they wanted to see 'more commitment from him in the community first'.

The funding panel didn't believe rehab would work for a con who hadn't actually ever managed any clean time on his own on The Out. They were under the misapprehension that it was easier inside to stay free from drugs. His community worker pulled out his offending record and a calculated cost to the community of all the crimes for which he'd ever been convicted.

'And these are only the ones we know about.' She pointed emphatically at the wedge of paper that made up his record, holding it up for the funding panel to see.

They relented, but only agreed to ninety days in rehab instead of 180. Shaun hadn't proved to them he could engage in treatment outside of prison and they didn't want to blow too much money on him.

We then had to find a rehab willing to take him, within the budget they'd given us. Somewhere that had a free bed on his exact day of release, so he could be whisked from the gate directly to the facility, escorted to make sure he didn't have just one last use on the way.

I took Shaun off the wing and into a private office for the two-hour phone assessment with the rehab. I fetched him a cup of water and sat doodling on my notepad as he repeated to the centre manager all the details of his life I now knew so well. He put on a phone voice, desperate to impress, desperate to convince them he was willing and worthy of help. His legs bounced throughout, nerves coursing through him. He absent-mindedly stole my pen and starting fiddling with it, holding it like a cigarette. Every so often, I gave him a thumbs up, nodding along to his convincing responses. Eventually, he held the phone out to me. It was damp with his sweat.

'It all sounds good to me, but obviously I'll have to take it to our weekly meeting. It's not me who gets to decide, but I will be recommending we accept Shaun.'

I thanked the man on the phone, trying to keep the grin from spreading. I couldn't get Shaun's hopes up yet. We could always fall at the final hurdle. It still wasn't certain that Shaun would get the help he needed.

I took him back to the wing. 'One on!' I hollered, waving at Officer Owen as I turned to leave for the night.

Of course, Shaun got into rehab. Of course, he did the full ninety days. Of course, he managed to convince them to let him train as a peer mentor and stayed on, working to support others. Shaun had that spirit. He was a grafter. He could achieve anything if he put his mind to it.

I called once a week for the first six weeks then closed his case, finally sliding it into archive, wondering if it would ever need to be retrieved again.

He'd been in prison twenty-two times when we got him into rehab. Each time he'd served less than twelve months. The majority of sentences, he was in for less than six. A full 25 per cent of the prison population is in for theft and drugs charges, with 20,000 people each costing £44,500 per year for their incarceration alone. Even at a conservative estimate, the tax bill for Shaun's prison time ran to over £500,000. That price tag doesn't include the cost of the police and courts or the costs the victims incurred when he was out stealing every day. Even those rehabs that celebrities go to don't cost that much. Some of the best rehabs in the country are less than £10,000 a month.[11] If Shaun had secured the funding for a six-month rehab stay, the real holy grail, it would have cost one tenth of what was spent on his incarceration.

But maybe Shaun wasn't ready for rehab after his first or second or tenth offence and all that taxpayers' money would have been wasted. Maybe he still needed sentencing by the courts to learn from his mistakes. But short sentences don't work, they increase the likelihood of reoffending compared to community orders.[12] One in five people on a six-month sentence are released homeless and 67 per cent will reoffend again within the year.[13]

If the government advised the courts to work on the presumption of a community order for any sentence less than six months for theft and non-violent drug offences, economists have calculated it would save us at least £83 million each year.[14] Maybe then we wouldn't desperately have to beg for that rehab funding, maybe then the prisons would be a little less overcrowded, maybe then we'd be able to focus on doing meaningful work inside.

But it isn't just these short sentences that are problematic. Incarceration for drug-related offences just doesn't work. Portugal has now decriminalised drugs and has seen positive outcomes for the individual, the community and the tax bill. Drugs and drug dealing aren't legal there, but possession can be dealt with through fines. Alternatively, if caught with a personal supply, the drug user can be summoned to a panel comprising a social worker, mental health professional and lawyer. The drug user is assessed and, if an addiction issue is found, treatment is offered. Drug overdoses and deaths have decreased, HIV rates have gone down and drug-related crime is no longer the massive issue it once was.[15]

Reduced incarceration rates have saved the money necessary to provide the treatment. If we followed Portugal's lead and treated addiction as the public health issue it is, we could reduce the prison population by a third immediately. Rehabs support their attendees to become drug- and alcohol-free. Prisons just create more addiction. If we can actually reduce problematic drug use, there are long-term savings as crime is reduced, and addicts require less NHS treatment and are able to re-enter society with employment and as a productive member of their community.

The money is available for rehabilitation, the money is already being spent on things that don't work. The government would rather look tough on crime instead of actually fixing the problem. Unless we learn to channel that money to where it's needed and into what works, we'll be all the poorer for it.

Before he went to rehab, we held a goodbye group for Shaun and everyone had a little glow of pride, knowing that somehow their peer support had helped to make a difference. The group had developed momentum. Shaun's successful exit from prison powered the confidence and hope of everyone else. The crims were getting it and an excitement about future possibilities was palpable.

During those months I loved working on the detox unit. It was a welcome break from the days I was spending in segregation trying to work with prisoners whose violence made it a challenge even to get in the same room as them. If supporting a crim to manage a substance misuse issue was difficult, managing an anger issue could be even harder. Prison exacerbates substance misuse, but the violence it breeds and perpetuates is on another level.

CHAPTER 7

Containment and Confinement – Violence

I heard Kai before I met him, screaming from the twos. For once, I wasn't the intended victim of the abuse coming from the segregation windows. He was exchanging horrific insults with another prisoner housed below him. I stopped outside the windows, listening as they screamed back and forth. It didn't sound like prison bluster. It sounded like if their doors were to be cracked, one would be dead within minutes. I recognised the voice calling back to him. It was Daryll, down the seg for fourteen days for having a phone in his cell. Just another day in paradise as two inmates on my caseload were threatening to murder one another.

It was my job to defuse this rather than walk on by. I joined in the hollering, calmly, strongly, loudly.

'All right, enough. Both of you now. Quit the cursing and I'm coming in to speak to you.'

Daryll had been working with me for a few weeks already. He recognised my voice immediately and fell silent. Without someone to spar against, Kai stopped, too.

'Is that you, miss? You coming to see me?' shouted Daryll.

'If you two stop shouting long enough.'

I looked up to the two windows and squinted against the sun. I felt Kai's eyes on me but couldn't see him through the reflective glass.

'You all right up there? Is it OK to come chat to you, too?'

I heard a gruff grunt and narrowed it down to two different cells.

'All right, give me a minute. Sit tight, keep it cool.'

I was wary. Segregation was where the really violent ones went. So dangerous to staff and other prisoners, they were effectively placed in solitary confinement. This was deemed a more sensible tactic than looking at the problems in the system and society that caused assaults in prison to reach record highs in 2016 of 26,022, up 27 per cent from the year before. Attacks on staff had increased by 38 per cent, with 6,844 in twelve months, and showed no sign of abating.[1] Instead of meaningful research into this violence and real reform to keep prisoners and staff safer behind the walls, segregation was just rebranded and became the Care and Separation Unit (CSU). Everyone still called it 'seg' or 'the block'.

Segregation could be a barbaric affair. No natural light, bare cells. Some staff felt their role was to punish the criminals who broke the rules and broke the law. If a crim had assaulted an officer, then he didn't deserve the time or attention I offered. He was bad and that was that. In one prison, the staff never handed me referrals to see if I could make any progress with a con. Even if one of my regular clients was hauled down to seg, it felt pretty obvious that I wasn't wanted or needed in there and so I could only start working with him again once he was returned to general population. It was an environment I dreaded visiting and did so rarely, secretly glad that the officers didn't expect me to spend any time in there.

Thankfully, Kai had rolled through the gate of a different establishment, where segregation was a purpose-built block. It didn't need mess nets. The crims in seg didn't have TVs or stereos to throw over the railings, to bludgeon staff with. There were no tables and chairs out on the wing like in the main block, so for a prison it actually felt quite spacious.

There was a small exercise yard for the legally mandated minimum of half an hour outside every day.

Each cell had its own toilet and shower, which had the double benefit of being more comfortable for the prisoner and also saved costs. Fewer staff were needed to escort prisoners to the once-weekly wash they were entitled to under prison rules and the whole wing smelled much more pleasant for it.[2] Although it probably sounds idyllic compared to most other establishments, it was still solitary confinement in an empty cell, no larger than a service lift, for 23.5 hours every day, and when it popped off in there, with twenty of the most violent inmates, it could be louder than the biggest five-storey wing in any prison.

Kai's details had been slid over the desk to me during the weekly multidisciplinary meeting. He'd been in for less than twenty-four hours and was on a three-man unlock, a procedure where three officers donned riot gear and were on hand any time his cell door needed to be cracked open. He'd turned up the day before, ghosted from another prison. We'd been given no warning of his arrival, but it seemed that his previous establishment had stitched us up. Sometimes, when a prison got fed up of dealing with a particularly difficult con, they'd try to arrange exchanges. Give us one of yours and we'll give you one of ours. Once we opened the gates and he crossed the threshold, the troublesome inmate became our problem. And there was no return or refund if we weren't satisfied with who we'd received, if he wasn't as promised in the description. It was a shady tactic, shifting the problem along, but everyone did it.

Funding depended on achieving targets and targets included reducing assaults, violence and days spent in seg. Particularly as more prisons were privatised, turning a profit was key. Although shipping inmates around the country only moved the problem on and created a level of churn that increased instability and volatility in the estate, profits trumped constancy.

But we hadn't even traded Kai, hadn't even managed to move on one of our own problem cons in exchange. His old establishment was full, running beyond maximum capacity, and claimed Kai was the only crim who could possibly be shipped out. Kai had been dumped at our gates and since then the place had been going wild. No one had got so far as to ask for his prison number before he was throwing punches and threatening to kill people.

The CSU governor told us how Kai had launched himself off the van, immediately assaulted an officer and pulled a blade out of his mouth ready to cut someone else. He'd kettled another youth in his last place and had been ghosted out of every other establishment that ever had the misfortune of accepting him, after having spent notoriously long stints in seg. He was deemed unmanageable, violent without provocation and a lost cause we'd been dumped with.

He'd spat, he'd kicked, he'd threatened life. He'd been brought to seg by six of our biggest officers, and he hadn't calmed down even when they'd finally bolted the door behind him.

Once they'd safely wrestled him behind his door, the healthcare team had peeped through the window and swiftly put him in the 'behavioural' not 'mental' category, which meant he was fine to stay down the block. But the guv knew we couldn't just leave him there. The prison estate was getting slammed in inspections and we knew it wouldn't be long before they came knocking at our door. There were regulations and policies around keeping a prisoner in seg, especially one as young as Kai. We'd have to demonstrate clear evidence that we'd done everything possible to stabilise his behaviour and get him into the main prison.

'So. . .' The guv clapped his hands together, looking around the table at the mental health nurses, the chaplain, the safer custody team. 'What's the plan, then?' He looked at me. 'Can you do your thing through a locked door?'

It was a request more than a question.

Officer Rav came out to greet me and sign me onto the wing.

'Thank fuck for that,' he said as his voice echoed in the new silence.

'I suppose that's Kai, then? How long has it been going on for?'

'They've been going at each other for over an hour,' he said. 'You're not here to work with him, are you?'

Rav was right to be concerned for my safety. Kai was an unknown quantity. No one really knew if he'd try to stab me because we hadn't yet got hold of his youth records, and the case notes from the shared online database were sparse. It was risky, but it was also my job. To work intensively with the men who drained resources and assaulted others or injured themselves.

Although I'd be meeting Kai through a locked door, there was still a gap at the bottom and a few millimetres at the hinges. If he wanted to, he could throw piss out at me, spit at me or, if I leaned in close enough to the gap to hear him speak, he could shank me with a blade jammed into a biro.

I knocked lightly and stood back. Nothing.

'All right, is it OK if I open the flap so we can talk?'

A grunt.

I took this as a yes and gently swung the metal away from the narrow strip of plastic that was meant to give visibility into the cell. Kai was staring out of the window, turned away from me. I thought he was going to start his screaming again and ignore me entirely, but his head tilted when I introduced myself.

'And you're Kai, right?'

Again, another grunt. He was listening, but he wasn't ready to talk.

'Give me ten minutes of your time,' I said. 'I'm not a screw. It's my job to work on keeping everyone in here chill, calm and in control. What's going on for you to be making a noise like that?'

He pushed himself off the window ledge and, filled with threat and menace, he came towards the door. When he brought his face close enough to the panel so I could see him, it was like he was looking through me and, although the anger surrounding him was palpable, I didn't feel like its target. Still, the aggression pulsed from him.

I could see that this kid was rage. Wound tight, coiled like a snake, always ready to pounce, to attack. He was only twenty-one but had the eyes of someone who had lived life, *seen* things. He hadn't yet grown into a man, but he wasn't a boy any more, either.

He was pale, the scars on his arms and face showed the signs of knife fights. His skin was lighter in places where the tissue had scarred and darker in others where the wounds had been deeper. From a distance, they were barely noticeable. But in my job, these were clear tells. Kai's rage wasn't just bravado: he'd been stabbed, shanked, scarred multiple times. He wasn't the kind of kid to avoid a fight.

It was a stilted conversation and he didn't want to talk much at first, but he stayed stood on his side of the door and listened as I spoke and I took that for a good sign.

'All right,' I said as I gently thumped goodbye on his cell door in the way I often did instead of a handshake, 'I'm going to catch you tomorrow. It's my job to help you keep cool in here. We're going to be all right, Kai.'

Rav raised his eyebrows at me as I slumped down at the desk and started hunting through the paperwork to write up his notes.

'You're going to work with him?' he asked again.

'They've asked me to,' I replied, 'and he said he'll talk to me if I come back tomorrow.'

It didn't sound like a very big win, but then with Kai, I didn't know what the goal really was. I needed to build his trust, but that would take time. It was going to be a tough job to make any positive progress through a cell door – or worse, with a herd of officers standing over us. And in this case, what did positive progress even look like? All I knew was that after twenty-one days in segregation, the senior management would be getting very twitchy. I also knew that the Secretary of State needed to approve any stay longer than forty-two days. Our prison didn't want that kind of attention, so I did what I could to support the team effort and get him into general population, even as I worried about his violence towards the other inmates I was supposed to be looking out for.

He responded well to bluntness, direct questions and no-bullshit statements. I asked him to list exactly what made him angry. He thought for a while, kissing his teeth and pacing his cell as if just asking him to think about what made him angry should've been on that list. I realised that he found it hard to talk. Not because he was shy or holding back, but because he didn't have the vocabulary. Every other sentence he'd stop, not knowing the words, and would suck in air quickly, spitting out curses instead. He didn't have the language skills to express himself and I had to speak plainly so he could understand me.

'We're going to make a contract. What pisses you off and what pisses me off. Then I'll promise not to do those things and you'll promise not to do my things, OK?'

His demands were all easy to fulfil. I had to tell him what time and day I was coming and not be late. He warned if I didn't come when I said I would, he'd never trust me. And then he said that I shouldn't bad-mouth his mum. When it came to my list, he seemed suspicious and wouldn't agree until he'd heard what I had to say.

My list for him was a little stronger:

- No matter how well we get on and how well you work with me, any threat you make to anyone during our sessions, I'll report.
- If you're ever feeling so angry that you might be a risk to me or anyone else, you need to warn me. I won't hold it against you, but I expect a warning so I can leave you to it, to calm down.
- You will never be violent on the landings. If you're feeling angry, you'll ask to go back behind your door.
- Don't bad-mouth my mum.
- Don't ever lie to me but, more importantly, don't ever lie to yourself.

He agreed, laughing that I'd included the rule about my mum in there, too, but then I'd heard what he'd been saying to Daryll that first day and I never wanted to hear that shit about my own mum.

Later, I typed up the notes and slid a copy of our contract through the gap, asking him to stick it up on his side of the door so he could be reminded of it each time we leaned our heads in for a chat.

For men like Shaun, I'll always argue that custodial sentences aren't the solution. But for cons like Kai, the answers aren't so clear-cut. It was obvious he needed to be in a secure setting – there was no way I could even consider starting to prepare him for release. He wasn't even able to leave his cell without an escort of officers in full kit. Violence hung thick in the air around him. I was in no doubt that without a long-term intervention of epic proportions, he'd end up seriously injuring or killing someone.

Working with Kai felt like the highest-stakes game I'd ever played. And I was holding a fucking terrible hand. He needed to be securely held, but that couldn't be done indefinitely. His behaviour could be contained for a period in the establishment. But what then? The prison estate didn't have the resources to lessen his risk. It was clear from even a brief meeting that Kai required intensive, consistent support. He needed specific referrals to specialists. Even with the right interventions, it would take years to make tangible progress.

He was put on three-man unlock for the first three days, but the prison couldn't keep that up forever. We were running on a skeleton staff most of the time. Finding officers well-trained in this type of control and restraint and then dragging them away from their normal duties every time Kai needed to be brought out of his cell was costing money. Following the staffing cuts, there just wasn't the manpower to manage crims like Kai at this intensive level.[3]

His hearing for the nickings was a perfect time to reassess his risk, see if fewer officers would be needed to open him up in future. I was asked to attend, to help support him to stay calm while he answered the charges against him. Arriving early to the seg, I found the governor flicking through his paperwork, preparing for the meeting. He wanted to know how our work together had been going.

'He's agreed to work with me. We've made a contract and he's told me what makes him particularly angry.'

'I'm not on that list, am I?' he said, lips curling into a smile.

The officers were sweating before we'd even cracked the door. It was a sweltering summer and they were in full riot gear. I continued to talk to Kai, reassuring him as they got into position.

Even before the head of seg had drawn his keys, Kai had

moved to the back of his cell and kneeled down, his back to us. I withdrew.

As he began to crack the door, the governor beckoned me forwards.

'If you're happy to, me and you can walk him in,' he said.

And so I looked back at the biggest men our prison could muster, riot shields at the ready, and stood in front of them as the door opened.

Kai turned while still on his knees, stood up with his arms outstretched so he didn't alarm anyone, and walked forwards. He moved towards us slowly. I braced myself for my first prison assault.

'I'm right here and you're going to keep your eyes on me. Ignore these guys behind me, OK?' I said.

'I'm good, miss. I'm good. I'll walk with you. I'm cool. I'm calm.'

I made the hand gesture at him that meant 'look into my eyes', pointing two fingers at my face and then back at him, and he did. I held his focus the whole time he walked towards me, even as I felt the crowd of officers start to move and a wave of adrenaline build.

'You got me, miss?' he asked. 'Stay with me, miss. Stay next to me.'

I muttered to him the whole way. 'You're doing good. I'm here. We're cool.' Soothing words, the tone more important than what I actually said.

As we set off to leave the wing and headed into the office for his adjudication, he flinched. He'd felt the movement of the officers behind him.

'It's cool, it's cool. They're behind us but I'm here. Eyes on me, we're doing this together.'

He took a seat opposite the governor. The officers crowded into the cramped room and lined the walls around him. I hovered back now, by the door, but still in Kai's peripheral vision. I breathed and it felt like the first time I'd inhaled in ten minutes. The guv could see some small progress: he hadn't tried to kill me at least. I'd been used as bait, but it had worked and he'd shown that he had some level of control over his behaviour.

The guv read out his nickings and then asked him if there was anything he wanted to say. Kai glanced at me and I made another hand gesture. A flat palm, horizontal to the ground, gentle movement up and down. The universal sign for 'keep it cool, keep it calm'. He looked back at the guv and shook his head.

The governor didn't have the power to give out a very serious punishment, all he could really do was remove his privileges, like his TV or his time in the gym. But Kai didn't have any privileges to begin with. The governor looked down at his paperwork, chewed on his cheek and then finally said the case was going to be referred to an independent adjudicator. An independent adjudicator was an external judge who would look at the facts and could then add up to forty-two days on his sentence, without Kai ever having to go to court.[4] Only the most serious and violent assaults ever got referred to an external adjudicator – but in the same breath, the governor said the unlock could be reduced to two officers.

Kai smiled at the guv, thanked him. They reached across the desk and shook hands. He was unbothered by the possibility of a few more weeks inside.

I shouldn't have been relieved, but I was. I couldn't imagine in what circumstances it would be safe to release Kai back into the community. At least additional days would push that reality back just a little further. Yet this reaction in me just highlighted the futility of Kai's imprisonment. I knew that with the resources we had, all this sentence would ever be was containment. Kai would still be dangerous at the end of this stretch. Even with a governor who actively supported me and my job and officers like Rav who were compassionate to their charges, I still wouldn't be able to mitigate Kai's risks enough.

Instead of thinking about that future release date, which seemed far too close for comfort, I decided to focus on the goal of mellowing him enough to get him over to the main prison.

Twelve days into his stay in seg, Kai had settled so much that he was trusted to go onto the yard with me and only one officer. He didn't talk much, so we walked laps.

'Does this help?' I asked. 'Being outdoors?'

'It helps,' he mumbled. 'But I prefer it when I can exercise properly. That helps the most.'

They'd never let him in the gym, so it would have to be cell workouts to begin with. I started to slide printouts under his door. To keep up his motivation, I'd challenge him to do more than me and I completed the workouts myself each morning in the gym before work. I knew Kai's pride wouldn't allow me to beat him. Every morning I'd walk past CSU and shout up to him.

'I'm on three sets of twelve pull-ups now.'

And he'd reply, laughing. 'Fuck off, miss I only stop my press-ups for food.'

His behaviour improved rapidly over the next two weeks and the violent outbursts dropped. He'd gone from three-man unlock, fighting on the floor with officers, to me and him unaccompanied on the exercise yard, killing ourselves in the summer heat with press-ups, sit-ups and dips off the metal bench.

Talking seemed easier after a workout. I had some misgivings that I was helping him to get physically stronger to fight, but on the whole, it appeared to be working. Kai was now able to walk into the adjudication room with just me, no shields surrounding him. It wouldn't be long before he was able to move back into general population, but I wasn't sure it was the best thing for him. However bad seg could be, however much it messed people up, I just didn't think he was ready for the landings.

After one particularly brutal workout when the temperature was heading into the high twenties, we both sat back on the floor and started talking, for real. In his stilted, staccato rhythm, he told me about his family. Deep, brutal truths delivered pop, pop, pop, like gunfire. A mother who he'd seen raped and then beaten up with the blunt end of a gun before he was ten years old. He told me he'd wandered the streets and a kind auntie had taken him in before he inevitably ended up in the care of the state. He was in youth custody by his thirteenth birthday. He told me about his dad, and the eight siblings that he knew of.

'He's a wasteman, always hanging around by the Tube station. He's a crackhead,' he said.

A brother was doing life for murder up in Yorkshire. He couldn't see his mum, because of a court order that wouldn't allow him at the address. When he was sixteen, he'd taken a knife to her boyfriend and stabbed him. Kai said it was her pimp and he'd been protecting his mum from being attacked. But none of that really mattered, because his mum backed up this guy's story and even if Kai had been legally allowed back at the property, he wasn't welcome.

I asked him what he wanted from life, if he saw a future where he could escape all this and be the best version of himself: the version I got along with when we sat on the yard floor after an intense workout. He looked bemused, as if the thought had never crossed his mind that it could be any different. He gazed upwards, watching the clouds pass, unable to explain out loud what he was thinking about. He didn't talk much. We sat in peaceful silence until an officer told us our time outside was up.

It was meaningful work, but it wasn't enough. I wasn't a psychologist. We didn't have the privacy or space or time to do structured sessions. His needs had never really been assessed. He couldn't spend his whole stretch in prison being managed down the block. None of it was enough. I thought of the stories he'd told me and knew that this prison would never be able to unpick everything that needed taking apart with him. We weren't designed to do that work. We only had the resources to hold him until he'd eventually become somebody else's problem. Containment. That's all my work with Kai was. Holding him together enough so that the gaping chasms in funding and resources and staffing levels wouldn't blow wide open.

And although I should have been happy that his behaviour was improving, I had to face the reality that he'd be moved into general population, where all of the other inmates I was trying to keep alive and safe lived. When it was time to move on, the only space available was C wing. There's never a *great* wing in general pop, but the Cs stank of weed and were filled with youths. The atmosphere was bouncing with nervous energy and too much testosterone. Although the isolation of segregation could exacerbate mental health issues, for Kai, in the short term, it provided the stability and calmness he needed. There were fewer drugs available and the officers were more experienced at managing difficult and demanding behaviour. Moving him out and onto an unsuitable wing looked good for our targets and it would please the inspectors, but it wasn't right for Kai at that point. Still, CSU was hardly the cure, either.

From the start, it was clear the officers on C wing didn't have a united approach to managing him. I walked onto the landing one morning and saw him with his top off, smoking by the pool table. Both were clear breaches of prison rules.

'Put down the burn and put a shirt on. I don't expect this shit from you, Kai. Come on, man, you're better than that.'

The other youths raised their eyebrows, half expecting him to swing at me right then and there. But he did as he was asked and sulked back to his cell to put a shirt on. Kai was testing boundaries and had found they were lacking. Everything I'd learned about him showed he did far better if, when he pushed up against those limits, they stayed strong and firm. He did well with structure, routine, knowing where he stood.

Unsurprisingly, after a week, his violence flashed. He bounced Taylor's head off the pool table and now they were both down the block, screaming murder at one another from morning until evening. Taylor had no chance of holding his own against Kai, but he couldn't lose face. He'd have to continue the shouting until he got his head kicked in again. Meanwhile, the reality of solitary confinement was taking its toll on both of them. And there lay the conundrum.

'He can't stay down here, it'll make him worse in the long run – I've seen it before,' said the guv.

The UN's Nelson Mandela Rules prohibit the use of solitary confinement for twenty-two hours a day or more. Prolonged solitary confinement of more than fifteen consecutive days is defined as torture. The rules take into particular account the age of the person incarcerated.[5] Kai was young, and he'd already spent so much of his life down the block.

The guv had seen first-hand over the years what the data and research showed: that the people we confine exhibit maladjustment disorders and problems with aggression, both during confinement and afterwards. That inmates often have difficulty adjusting to social contact post-isolation and may engage in increased madness on the landings and hostility towards staff afterwards.[6] Seg might have been containing him for now, but we were just kicking the problem forwards into the future.

The guv hadn't read Lord Woolf's latest report on the use of segregation, but he'd have agreed with the sentiment.

> The complexity of segregation brings many challenges to already beleaguered prison staff and prisoners who for whatever reason, cannot manage or be managed in, the main body of an establishment. Segregation, though it may sometimes be necessary, must not be prolonged or indefinite ... Care must be taken to avoid, as far as is possible, the damage to mental health that exclusion will bring.[7]

My work with Kai was our attempt to take care to avoid that mental damage. I'd built some trust with him, I could usually keep him calm enough to have a conversation and throughout our time working together, he'd kept his side of the contract we made. But to expect a change in his behaviour overnight was like expecting a miracle.

The final time I saw him face to face, we'd just finished a session on the yard. There were three officers on that day. All good officers, who treated Kai with respect. They collected him from me and started walking him back to his cell. Rav opened the door and just as Kai took a step over the threshold, Rav lightly touched his shoulder, chaperoning him in.

Recoiling at the physical contact, Kai turned and swung in one movement. The other two officers jumped forwards. The alarm sounded and I stepped back, holding the gate for the flood of officers responding to the alert, allowing them in one by one to pile on Kai. I watched as my client and my colleagues fought on the floor, with no one left uninjured. It took half a dozen of them to wrestle control of him and in the end, everyone was covered in blood.

They got him back behind his door and he continued

banging, screaming, cursing, like that first day when I heard him before I met him. I didn't have the energy to attempt to calm him down this time. I felt defeated and was unable to approach him calmly.

'You broke his nose.' I rapped hard on his cell. 'You promised me you wouldn't fight and you did. He was good to you and you broke his nose.'

He muttered quietly to himself, backed away from the door, then lunged back around to face me, eyes narrowed and the words tumbling out.

'I didn't break my promise. They moved my cell. I don't have my contract – it's not on this door.' He was panting jagged, angry breaths. 'I wasn't on the wing and he fucking touched me,' he roared.

After that day, Kai was never allowed out with me again. He kept doing his press-ups and dips, but the days of us doing our workouts together on the yard were long gone.

I spent hot, tiring shifts stood by his door, staring at the chipping paint and bloodstains and shit-smears from all of the men who had left their mark. We talked, trying to map out and change the course of his life, with a locked door between us. I referred him for an assessment with the special education staff, wondering if the literalness with which he saw the world had led to the assault. Was Kai one of those prisoners with mental health issues or learning difficulties disguised by violence? There were so many men who were undiagnosed that it was likely.

And as summer rapidly turned to autumn, Kai was quietly ghosted out one night and I never saw him again. By the time his appointment with the specialist rolled round, he was long gone.

For a couple of weeks, we were given a little breathing space. Rav was still off work two weeks later when the inspectors arrived. The prison shone in its assessment that year. The shareholders got their payout. But the violence continued. Taylor was learning that he'd have to fight harder if he wanted to survive and another inmate just like Kai would arrive the following week, and the week after that, and the week after that.

There's no easy answer to managing the violence displayed by very damaged men like Kai. He was a risk to all the other prisoners when he was on the wings and he was a constant danger to staff, too. Putting a very violent man on a wing where the majority of prisoners are on remand or in for non-violent offences doesn't help anyone. Instead, it perpetuates and exacerbates an environment where everyone has to fight, to show strength, to be violent, just to survive.

But resorting to solitary confinement, a system that did more harm in the long run, a system that amounted to torture, wasn't the answer. Kai could neither be contained nor rehabilitated in the system as it was. And I didn't know what the answer was, but I did know that it involved specialist interventions, and decisions made in the best interests of the inmate. And it involved providing adequate staffing levels and then adequate support to those staff, who were living their lives in a state of hypervigilance.

Unless this happened, my colleagues would continue to get bloody noses and broken bones. They'd be bitten, scratched and spat at. Then they'd go off sick and they'd stay off sick, as the violence they experienced took a toll on their mental health.

There wasn't any consideration of Kai's mental health or any other possible issues he may have had. He was so violent that there was a consensus across all departments that his issues were solely behavioural. There was rarely such agreement between healthcare and prison staff. I, too, missed important clues that he needed specialist support because, like my colleagues, I fixated on his aggression. I forgot that, very often, behaviour is a symptom of something else below the surface.

It's important to remember that there isn't a clear divide between mental health issues and behavioural problems. The majority languished in this grey area. And while very violent inmates like Kai were kept segregated, on general population the behaviours displayed by inmates with mental health problems dominated daily life. Their actions could be even more traumatising and disruptive than those who displayed their issues through violence.

CHAPTER 8

There's Not Always a Mess Net to Catch You – Mental Health

A man stood directly in front of me, pointing a blade towards me. It was inches from my outstretched arm. I looked down the landing and couldn't see a single officer. He smiled politely and said, 'Would you like me to cut you a slice of bread?' before pushing the jam and butter towards me.

I was in Oslo Prison in Norway on the rehabilitation unit. It was lunchtime and I was sat at a long table stretching halfway down the wing. There were crims and screws seated together, but I couldn't tell who was who. Everyone was dressed casually in jeans and shirts and waffle-knit jumpers. The whole table switched to speaking in English to accommodate me, calling me by my first name. However many times I told the crims back home my name, they always forgot, always slipped back into the institutionalised 'miss'.

I'd been searching for charities to support Deano's business venture, when I stumbled across the application form for a Winston Churchill Memorial Trust Fellowship. They were offering free funding, and all you had to do was go off abroad and research whatever field of expertise you wanted, then bring your learning back to the UK and try to transform lives on home soil.

I'll have a bit of that, I thought, as I bashed out an email. Working with Kai had been exhausting and dispiriting. It had made me realise that it didn't matter how good I was at my job, without structural changes I'd be doomed to failure. I knew our system wasn't working, but if I could go around the world and find out what was, I might be able to implement some of their practices in our establishment. With the inspection over, I jetted off to find out just how good those Norwegian prisons really were.

On the table was a typical European spread of breads and cheeses, meats and jams, fruit juice and pots of tea. The plates were ceramic, the cutlery was metal. And that was a big, fuck-off bread knife. I nodded at the Scandinavian giant opposite, hoping he'd just put the blade down. All the men in there were massive, well fed. I looked at the smorgasbord in front of me. These inmates wouldn't last the night on the rations our crims were forced to survive on.

The only reason I knew the man sat next to me was staff was because he collected me from the front gate earlier that morning and the keys jangled at the pouch on his belt. Christian was going to be my guide as I explored one of the most successful prison systems in the world, where rehabilitation was expected and staff didn't routinely face assaults and attacks. He'd been in the service for twenty-five years and, in his bright blue jeans and tan boots, he carried himself with a reassuring confidence. Christian seemed proud to show me around – he knew the stats on reoffending and prison populations. He knew that what they did in Norway really worked. That wing was a world away from our detox unit. It felt more like a rehab, like the therapeutic community we fought to send Shaun to. There were framed pictures on the walls of skiers and outward-bound adventures.

'Are these the officers?' I asked, pointing to the photographs.

'They're the inmates,' Christian replied. 'Every so often,

we go on trips out in nature. It's good for rehabilitation, good for improving mental health.'

'Inmates from here?' I asked. 'But what if they escape?'

Christian laughed at me, crow's feet crinkling around his pale eyes.

'Where would they escape to, in the middle of the mountains? No, they come back and then we complete their rehabilitation and they're released in a better position.'

I felt like I was on another planet. Oslo Prison had a bad reputation in Norway and some wings were earmarked for closure.

'It's too old, it doesn't get enough light. It's harder to rehabilitate if the building isn't good enough,' Christian said, pointing around at the cleanest, brightest prison wing I'd ever seen.

The place was immaculate. No torn bed sheets tangled in the mess nets. No graffiti on the walls or half-ripped posters advertising the latest reducing reoffending initiative. It smelled clean. Fresh air and baked bread and washed linen.

When Christian had led me onto the wings, I felt immediately on edge. It was too quiet. Quiet before a storm kind of quiet. I'd become so used to the constant banging, screaming, fire alarms, personal alarms, radio crackle and slamming metal gates that I found the gentle silence of Oslo disconcerting.

My footsteps reverberated, but if the cons heard us move down the landing, they didn't bang or kick doors or shout out to get our attention. My heavy prison boots squeaked against the pristine floors.

Christian had done this sightseeing tour with dozens of foreign prison staff who, like me, had been desperate to see how Norway made such a success of reducing reoffending.

'Just wait until you see Halden Prison. That's one of the

most successful maximum security prisons in the world.' He smiled at my awestruck wonder.

The following week, I found myself in a fully kitted out studio listening to the vocals being recorded in the booth. The sound engineer leaned into the microphone.

'That's enough for today – great work.'

The musician took off his earphones and joined us in the studio. I watched as the men fiddled with dials and buttons and sliders, putting the finishing touches to the track.

'Would you like a copy of the CD?' Christian asked me. 'A memento from your time in our prisons.' Christian explained that the inmates using the studio would gain qualifications and real work experience while serving time in Halden. They'd be able to get work on release.

I followed Christian like an excitable puppy through the garage workshop where the officers and public could bring their cars to be repaired, allowing inmates to hone their skills in the trade. The equipment and tools sparkled, unscratched and unscathed from five years of use. I thought of Kai's cell door, peeling and covered in shit and graffiti and blood.

A metal detector framed the exit of the garage and as we passed through, Christian's keys set off the alarm. It pierced the silence.

'Is that because they steal the tools?' I asked.

He looked confused for a moment, as if he'd never considered the idea.

'I suppose that's why they installed it, but I don't think we've had any incidents like that.'

There was a different atmosphere there. The inmates back home would nick anything that wasn't nailed down. In Halden, the inmates were trusted. Trusted to do the right thing, behave well. Everyone spoke to each other so respectfully it was almost infuriating. I'd to take extra care to drop the expletives that peppered my language. That would have been considered rude or aggressive in Norway. But it wasn't that the Norwegian inmates were inherently better people. So what was it? Why was everyone nicking and grafting and fighting in my prison? Why were staff being assaulted and men overdosing on the landings? Why was it just so loud in my place?

'We had two stabbings on the wings last week,' I blurted out, unsure why I shared this information.

'That's terrible,' Christian replied, sounding genuinely concerned.

He led me out into the grounds and we strolled through the forest. It was almost winter and drizzle hung in the air, but the landscape was beautiful. A trail wound circles through the prison grounds. I could hear birds, the wind in the leaves.

'Sometimes when an inmate is really struggling, I ask him to take a walk with me. I find it can be the most amazing therapy.' His voice was gentle and I could imagine how soothing a stroll through the trees would be, talking through the problems of the wing with Christian.

'I don't think anyone is struggling in here,' I said light-heartedly.

But he took on a serious tone.

'The men in here have many problems. This is a high-security prison. Rapists, murderers, but also a lot of drug problems. Some of these men have huge addictions, anger issues. They have trauma. We must work hard with them to help them become better. It's not enough to take him out of prison – we must take the prisoner out of him.'

We reached a house within the grounds and he let me inside.

'Let's have a cup of tea and I can explain.'

Christian had arranged for me to visit the staff training academy, where all officers received three years' mandatory training, equivalent to a degree in the UK. Those officers who went on to work on the specialist wings, like the mental health or drug treatment unit, must've undergone further training. The first two years combined theory and practice, with a final year of supervised work on the wings.

Our own officers got between eight and ten weeks' training with a heavy emphasis on control and restraint, and security. Training in suicide awareness and mental health was minimal in the UK, but the best officers developed skills through years of hard-won experience on the landings. They may not have known the theory behind their methods, but there were many officers who learned through common sense and trial and error.

This doesn't necessarily need to be a disaster. Learning on the job is hugely important for staff: you can't truly understand how you'll react to a stab victim until he's bleeding out in front of you. Unfortunately, the officers who'd taught themselves to assess suicide risk or were able to pick up on the clues that an inmate was hearing voices ended up working on the highly pressurised units, where they witnessed horrors daily, where they quickly burned out. Like Rav, the most competent officers ended up dealing with the Kais of the estate. Then, like Rav, they went off sick or left the service.

There was meant to be supervision within our system too, through the first year on the job. But I'd never known a single officer to receive clinical supervision or debriefing after any of the several traumatising incidents they witnessed daily.

Christian explained that Norway had ten applicants for every one place on the training programme. The applicant needed to pass rigorous interviews, written tests and fitness tests, and be fluent in both Norwegian and English. While our prisons had a similar assessment format, I'd been in the gym when these prospective recruits were trying to hobble through the bleep test. I'm forever grateful that I never had to press the emergency alarm, because I'm in no doubt that I'd be halfway to heaven before most of those new officers had made it up the three flights of stairs to my rescue.

The selection process was robust in Norway and, although expensive, staff turnover in the country was minimal. As I swanned about the Norwegian establishments, back home the prison estate was haemorrhaging staff. Swingeing government cuts meant the most experienced officers were being given early retirement and the wings were losing their expertise by the day. Between 2010 and 2019, over 80,000 years of experience was lost from the landings.[1] The newly trained screws left to pick up the pieces were walking the wings without support, supervision or adequate skills to deal with the crisis. A third of new recruits were quitting within the first year.[2] Then prisons had to be even more lax in who they'd accept into the role, knowing that having any staff was better than no staff at all.

In Norway, recruits needed to wear their full uniform every day of training.

'They must learn how to wear the uniform,' Christian said. 'It's a privilege to do so. We all learn that a great responsibility comes with wearing it.'

I wondered out loud what they taught at the academy and how it worked so well.

'There's an independent research department.' He handed me a mug and sat at the kitchen table, indicating I should join him. 'When I was there, the research team was always battling the government. It needed to maintain its independence, to find out what worked, not just do what politicians wanted.'

I nodded emphatically, as if my prayer of a prison system using evidence-based research to drive policy had been answered. I told Christian that it was overwhelming to hear.

'How do you know what to do with your prisons if there's no research or data or evidence?' he said.

I wanted to haul Christian into my suitcase and onto the plane, drag him back to the UK and drop him off at Downing Street. It didn't seem like a faraway dream when he spoke, it didn't sound like some longed-for utopia. It sounded like it could be possible, that it was normal, that it should be expected. And I nearly yelped with joy when he told me that Norway hadn't always been like that.

'We used to just lock everyone up. Our reoffending rate was worse than yours. There was reform, huge reform, in the 1990s. We used to just care about revenge. It took a lot to change. A lot of hard work from government. A huge culture shift from the top down. But now we only focus on rehabilitation.'

He gazed at my hopeful expression.

'Don't lose the faith. We prove it works this way. Change can happen.'

Christian studied modules in mental health, criminology, psychology, law and the legal system during training – subjects that got maybe an hour during our officers' eight-week induction course. He repeated that phrase I'd heard so many times before in my research about the Norwegian system – he told me the focus should be on who would you want as your neighbour. It was such a vitally refreshing way to look at what exactly prison is for.

Halden is the most expensive prison in Norway and it costs around £98,000 to keep a crim there for a year – more than double what we spend in the UK. Yet Norway's recidivism rate stays stubbornly low at 20 per cent, even after two years of release, so they don't have to keep spending money on the crim. Once they've made the initial investment, he goes out and stays out. Costs are saved in the long-term. In the UK, it might be cheaper to keep them in one of our shitholes, but 48 per cent of them will reoffend within a year of release.[3]

On average, following his release, a Norwegian inmate

commits ten fewer crimes than if he'd not served a custodial sentence. This data adjusts for the time he was incapacitated from offending due to the prison sentence, so the figure is actually even higher than that. Each one of those future offences that has been averted is a cost saving, but beyond that, it's one less crime, one less victim, one less frightened community.[4]

And reports show that there are other economic benefits to the Norwegian model, including the increased likelihood of released prisoners entering the workforce. Typically, these men didn't have a history involving secure and sustained employment before incarceration. Prison didn't support them to get back into work: for many, it brought them into the workforce for the first time.[5] The reduction in social security payments and the increase in tax collected all feeds back into the economy.

Another way Norway saves so much money is by simply locking up fewer people than Britain. For every 100,000 people in the population, they lock up 58, compared to 146 in Scotland and 136 in England and Wales. If we followed suit, halving the number of inmates, we could double the spending and reduce crime in the process.[6]

'Come,' Christian said, taking my cup and washing it before leading me out of the house.

'Whose home is this? Do you live in the prison grounds?' I asked as we walked back to the wings.

'It's for family visits. Partners and children come to stay for the weekend with an inmate. It's a privilege for excellent progress. It's extremely important to maintain family ties in the rehabilitation process,' he said solemnly.

We entered one of the most secure units in the prison and Christian handed me over to Erik, the substance misuse unit manager. There were staff everywhere. He pointed out psychiatrists, psychologists and social workers. There were personal officers who had daily contact with inmates.

He showed me to the cells and I was introduced to another blond giant with ruddy cheeks, who explained he had a raging heroin problem before his arrest. His arms were scarred from years of injecting and I realised that for all Norway's robust social care system, there would always be people who fell through the cracks. But when they did, a whole community of support staff surrounded them to pull them back up.

The crim proudly showed me around his home. His cell was double the size of ours in England and he got to live in there alone. I was amazed by the light, pouring in from the unbarred window. His shower and toilet area had an actual door, so he could take a shit in private. Initially, I was shocked by the opulence of it all, then I recoiled at myself. Why was this basic standard of human dignity so strange to me?

I told the inmate that in England, we locked two grown men together for twenty-three hours in an 8ft x 12ft box, expecting them to eat, sleep and shit in the same room. If they were lucky, they'd get a curtain for privacy around the toilet. They'd have to shower in communal blocks on the wings. They were only entitled to one shower per week.

'How do they live like that?' he pondered. 'I wouldn't feel safe being locked in with someone. I couldn't cope. That would affect me deeply.'

I didn't want to tell him that most of his English peers weren't really coping, either.

He wanted to play down the prison itself – he knew that Halden's facilities were what made the headlines.

'It's not just the building, though. It's different here. The staff are respectful. They're calm. They don't judge you. I feel safe because of that, too. I'm calmer here,' the inmate said. 'The space is nice, yes. But don't forget, I'm locked in. In the news, they report that this place is a hotel. Remember: you can leave a hotel. Once I'm released, I don't ever want to return,' he told me as I turned to continue my tour.

Erik pointed out the group therapy room, where the local healthcare providers ran interventions, with staff often employed both in the prison and at local doctors' practices, too. This meant that if therapy was started in custody, it could continue, with the same therapist, into the community upon release.

Erik told me that self-injury was rare and there'd only been one self-inflicted death since Halden opened five years earlier. By the time 2016 was through, there would have been half a dozen deaths by suicide in one prison alone in London. In England and Wales, the prison suicide rate remains about ten times higher than the rate among the general public.[7]

'This isn't possible here,' Erik said uncomprehendingly. 'If he's harming himself, there's a problem mentally. He can't be in prison; he must be in hospital.'

'But what if it's not a psychiatric condition, just a psychological or behavioural issue?' I asked.

Erik was too polite to speak slowly to me like the idiot I was. He was too respectful for that. Still, I felt stupid when he answered me.

'We take psychology and psycho-social interventions seriously here.'

I'd forgotten that there was a rainbow of mental health in between the 'behavioural' and 'mental' categories we used to decide who has access to help in England. I'd forgotten that cutting wasn't fucking normal. I'd forgotten that death-in-custody notices should have been the exception, not the rule.

As Christian began to walk me out, he said, 'Not just the inmates. The staff, too. We must all protect our mental health. We have guidance sessions and supervision every three weeks.' He gestured to an office, where I saw an officer in the middle of one such session.

'We have access to therapists. It's a stressful job and we must protect our own psychology. Don't forget to always protect your own health too, when you go back home.' He tapped his head to emphasise the point.

'Your prisons are difficult, for the staff, too. Remember to care for the staff as well as the inmates when you return.'

As if the universe wanted to highlight how different our attitudes to mental health in prison were, Smithy was added to my caseload as soon as my feet touched British soil. He'd been discharged from the care of the mental health team because he wasn't psychiatrically unwell. But the wing staff still knew he had problems, even if he didn't reach the threshold for support.

In 2016 there was a total of 37,784 recorded incidents of self-injury, up 23 per cent from the previous year.[8] By 2020, the rate was over 55,000.[9] Smithy made up a good portion of those. He might not have been hallucinating, but there were profound psychological issues that became a source of constant frustration between prison and medical staff. Smithy bounced between never-ending mental health referrals and knock-backs until he inevitably ended up back on general population with an emphatic 'he isn't psychiatrically unwell' note on his file from the mental health team.

Like the Norwegian officers I'd met, on the wing the view was that if he kept threatening to kill himself and hurt himself, there was something mentally wrong. The psychiatrist's view was that these threats weren't symptomatic of a 'severe and enduring mental health issue', so he could be managed by prison staff. I understood and empathised with both sides. With no mental health training, officers found it incredibly difficult to manage prisoners who most definitely had issues, albeit not defined, diagnosable ones. They didn't get those three years of training or the clinical supervision necessary to process the trauma and tragedy they witnessed every day.

But I also understood the role of the psychiatrist and

the parameters of the healthcare team's tight budget. In the prison population, 71 per cent of males and 79 per cent of women report having mental health issues.[10] The healthcare team isn't designed to deal with psychological problems. They're designed to be the final safety net for the psychiatrically unwell. The psychiatrist's view was that no medication or psychiatric intervention would improve Smithy's situation. He didn't need a stay on a psychiatric ward, but he definitely needed something.

Smithy was an inmate the officers couldn't manage and the mental health team couldn't work with. He frequently made scratches on his arms, mixing the small amount of blood with water to make it appear worse, then holding his wrists up to his cell window and demanding officers fetch him a nurse.

Every evening Smithy would request a listener. The listeners received more mental health training than the officers and more supervision when they were struggling with the trauma they faced through their work. But their job was relentless and heaped incredible pressure on the employed con. Listeners could be called at any time of the day or the night for a suicidal prisoner. They then sat with the man and listened to his problems in much the same way the Samaritans phoneline did in the community.

The scheme single-handedly saves more lives in prison than we could ever quantify and Smithy's harming would have been much worse without them. But there were nights when no listeners were available, or a night officer didn't have the time to unlock and fetch the trained inmate, or an officer disliked Smithy and his demands so much that he refused to find a listener for him. Even the listeners found Smithy draining and difficult, and struggled with being woken every night to hear his problems repeated over and over again.

He'd torn up his prison-issue tracksuit and made a bandana, which he used to tie his hair back tightly. His fingernails were always just a little bit too long and his skin too dry. His hands looked to me as if he'd worked in kitchens plunging his arms in and out of hot water. Smithy had no family and you could tell. Other inmates were sent money so they could buy moisturiser or extra shower gel or wear decent flip-flops. Smithy wore everything prison issue. He had to ration his shower gel sachets so he could have his weekly shower as well as handwash his clothes in his cell sink. He could never afford to trade anything for a haircut. He wasn't unkempt, but he didn't live as comfortably as most other inmates, who still had at least one person on The Out who cared enough to send them a tenner here and there. No one cared enough to help Smithy out. The truth was, he just wasn't very likeable.

No one wanted to double up with him either, but if the doctor said he wasn't mentally unwell, he was fit to share. There wasn't the space for single cells. I thought back to the inmate in Norway. He'd been so relaxed, focused on his rehabilitation. He told me that he'd have been unable to cope if he'd had to share his space. I wondered if Smithy would have been more willing to engage with us, work with the staff, if he didn't have a cellmate.

There were tips and tricks to avoid doubling up with Smithy. Almost everyone on the wing had managed to get 'extreme violence' or their own mental health diagnosis added to their file, in the hope that the prison would care enough about Smithy not to bang him up with someone likely to kill him. Every week, the latest new arrival on B wing would be stuck in with him, only to realise within a matter of days why there had been space in the cell in the first place. It meant that an endless procession of crims moved through his cell. Some of them really were violent, and he was having a shit time of it behind the door as staff numbers dwindled and bang-up stretched for longer every week.

He was desperate to be sectioned. He steadfastly remained

focused on securing a transfer out of prison and into a hospital. He told us regularly that he wanted to kill himself, that he would do it. When the healthcare team relented to wing staff's demands, they'd come and take a look at him, deem his cutting to be superficial and tell the officers that he needed to be managed on an ACCT document.

If he'd run out of tobacco and didn't have any money to buy more, or if he'd been doubled up with someone he didn't like, the threats got worse. This was referred to as 'manipulative behaviour' – a rational choice to get what he wanted. I imagined Christian's shock that crims had to resort to such tactics. In Norway, if the inmates had an issue, they just talked to an officer or a therapist or a psychologist. In England, cutting to get tobacco was an everyday occurrence.

And it was normal for an inmate to stop me on the wing, insisting, 'Miss, miss, I'm hearing voices, I need mental health.'

Smithy was no exception. He'd often recount to me what the voices said to him, although most staff appeared to share the view that he was 'malingering' – a polite way of saying it was bullshit, that he was pretending. I agreed. But none of us stopped to reflect on why so many inmates were telling us they were hearing voices. What drove these men to want help or medication or something they couldn't verbalise so badly that they faked hearing voices? Smithy's malingering voices told him to cut himself, to kill himself, and that he shouldn't be in prison.

Every time Smithy seemed to be making progress, we'd call an ACCT review and discuss dropping his observations down, maybe to once every four hours instead of once an hour. Every time there was a chance we could close the ACCT document because he no longer appeared suicidal, Smithy would make it clear that he'd go right back to his cell and kill himself. He had our focus and he wasn't going to let it go.

He craved love and attention so badly that he'd mistaken the hourly checks on him for care and affection. He feared the staff forgetting about him and the feeling of abandonment that would bring. I thought of those wings in Halden, swarming with staff, all responsible for building and maintaining relationships with inmates. I wondered if Smithy had been banged up in Norway, would he have been behaving like this?

In my prison, there weren't the staff and there wasn't the time to pander to him. He was uniformly disliked for his underhand tactics. Staff had hundreds of other men to deal with. In the grand scheme of the chaos, Smithy was a time-waster. If we'd had the resources of Norway, if the staff had been given semesters full of lectures on ethics and psychology and effective communication, then maybe there would have been more sympathy and concern for him. If the officers had felt able to speak about their own mental health and had a space to discuss their frustrations openly every three weeks, then dealing with Smithy might have felt easier. But we didn't and so we were stuck reacting to his acting out. And everyone was fucking fed up of him.

Our sessions were on a never-ending loop, we were stuck in a stalemate.

'Get me out on a fucking section or I'll show you, miss,' he'd say.

'You can't threaten to harm yourself in the hope I'll be so scared I'll get you out of prison and onto a section. It doesn't work like that,' I replied.

I knew the way Smithy was trying to cope with prison was completely maladaptive, but that didn't mean he needed to be on a psych ward. He didn't need that, but then, prison wasn't helping him one bit, either. I tried to be clear with Smithy. I knew prison was making his behaviour worse, but he was stuck there and no amount of cutting would change that.

'You're not "showing me" anything by hurting yourself.

By hurting yourself, you're just hurting yourself. You get me?'
I said.

I thought back to Erik and remembered that psychiatric
illness wasn't the only kind of mental problem. My words
sounded bullshit even to me. Cutting should've never been
seen as rational behaviour to get needs met. It should've been
seen as the desperate efforts of a desperate man in a desperate situation. But my hands were tied. He didn't need to be
on a psych ward, but he sure as shit needed some sort of
support.

I clenched my jaw tightly as he screamed at me. 'Acting
out', we called it. I thought back to how quiet Oslo had been,
how calm, and wished that I could dump him on a landing
there. He wasn't a bad person. He wasn't any different to the
Norwegian inmates. But in a place like this, you had to shout
louder, cut more often, threaten life to be taken seriously.

'One on,' I hollered out to the wing as I brought Smithy
through.

I walked with him back to his cell on the twos, not wanting the conversation to end on this note.

'I'll come back on Friday. I won't make a referral to the
mental health team, but we can look at getting you into education so you can start getting off the wing more. There's also
a new hearing voices group. We can get your name down for
that and go from there?'

Our once-weekly education sessions were a poor imitation
of the garage and recording studio at Halden. Basic maths
was hardly the meaningful activity that would prepare him
for release, but it was all I could offer. I hoped it would be
enough to keep him distracted from acting out for a while.

He got to his cell and walked in.

'I want to show you something, miss.'

I hovered at the door as the temperature of the wing
dropped to ice-cold. I didn't know what exactly he was about

to do, but I felt the atmosphere change and had the sense one of us was going to get hurt.

He bent down, picked up his bed sheet and, in one swift movement, wrapped it around his neck and started coming towards me with purpose. I was on the twos on my own. All the other prisoners were down on the ones at the tables or playing pool. I could see them all clearly from my vantage point. It was only one storey, so no mess net blocked the view.

He was either going to attack me or dive over the railing, I wasn't sure which. As the seconds stretched, I felt like I had more than enough time to process what was happening. In reality, it could only have been a couple of moments and three strides before he was out of his cell and on the landing. As he came forwards, I stepped backwards, keeping out of reach of him in case he went to swing for me. At the very last moment, I realised he was aiming to jump the railings, not hurt me. He hesitated for a moment, looked back at me, wondering if I was going to stop him.

I wasn't allowed to place my hands on a prisoner. A fight kicked off, an inmate burst into tears or tried to touch me on the shoulder as they shook my hand upon release – in any and all of these situations, I wasn't authorised to touch him and he wasn't allowed to touch me. I didn't have the full training in control and restraint.

For fuck's sake, Smithy, don't do this, I thought as he started clambering over the railings.

The battery on my radio had died hours before, so I just had to holler at the top of my lungs 'Officer!' as I dived towards him and wrestled him back from jumping over the edge.

The crims down on the ones suddenly looked up and saw what was going on. They mockingly shouted, 'Run, officer, run,' as two screws bounded up the stairs to my aid.

He'd only been on the twos. Most crims had probably

jumped from higher buildings while being chased by the police, and he'd hesitated to be sure I'd stop him before he went over. As the officers got him off the floor and started walking him back to his cell, he turned to me.

'I told you I'd show you.'

I wanted to strangle him myself.

The nurse arrived to check on us.

'Unfortunately, you're choosing to hurt yourself. We can't stop you from doing that and nor can the mental health team,' she said as the officer started to pull his door shut.

Smithy smiled. 'But she did stop me, didn't she? She pulled me back from jumping.'

He'd gambled on the fact that I'd stop him. And he was right this time. But if the circumstances had been even slightly different, I may not have prevented him from going over the railing.

Norway highlighted the insanity of our own prisons. The way Smithy presented was not exceptional. It is estimated that over two-thirds of men in prison have a personality disorder and roughly half are suffering from depression and anxiety.[11] These issues can't be treated on overcrowded landings by untrained staff. They need therapeutic interventions, and these require a safe and stable environment to take place. There are one or two qualified psychologists in establishments housing over 1000 inmates. Under these conditions, it's obvious that issues will worsen, behaviour will deteriorate and prisoners like Smithy will continue to escalate risky behaviour in the hope of receiving interventions and help.

And as their behaviours escalate, the pressure on staff increases. They witness more horror, more trauma. Their own mental health starts to suffer. Some 48 per cent of officers reported their on-the-job training as poor or very poor.[12] They simply don't feel supported or trained to deal with men like Smithy.

I felt shaken and worn down. Rationally, I knew his actions were horrific examples of a man in need of some serious psychological support, but I couldn't help resenting Smithy. Why couldn't he just accept that he wouldn't be getting any help? How many times did I have to tell him it wouldn't work?

I requested a full debrief with my boss before going home that day. She provided me with the kind of clinical supervision that all the staff on the specialist Norwegian units receive. It was easier for me to ask for this kind of support: I was the woman who walked around the prison all day telling everyone else to talk about their feelings, after all.

But what about officers like Rav? He still wasn't back in work, even though the bones had healed. And Wendy, who had to deal with this shit every day and responded by behaving just as badly as the cons. Wasn't her behaviour an attempt to survive the day inside here, too?

I thought of the supervision that officers in Norway received, and they rarely had to deal with any incidents like this. Stuff like this happened every day for Rav and Wendy, sometimes more than once. If I believed the cons didn't deserve to live under these conditions, the staff definitely didn't deserve to work in them. The threat of violence in the air, the constant blood from self-injury. Yet there was no support for the staff, either. They were expected to walk into this war zone day after day and stay normal, stay sane.

The POA union – formerly the Prison Officers' Association – represents over 30,000 prison staff. Its 2020 survey, prior to the Covid-19 pandemic, found that working in prison is having a detrimental impact on the health, well-being and safety of its members. Reported mental health problems are higher than many other lines of work and one third of officers surveyed have been diagnosed with work-related stress since starting work inside.[13]

The results of the survey make for depressing reading.

While the outside world becomes more understanding of the need to look after our mental health, prison staff are expected to just 'man up', suck it up and pretend that all of this is absolutely normal. These officers feel unable to discuss stress with their managers and instead rely on the support of colleagues. Most report they have 'difficulty "switching off" from the worries and concerns of their job'.[14] One officer summed it up perfectly in the report when they said, 'the price you pay for spending too much time with very damaged people is not covered by the salary'.[15]

We accept the madness behind the walls as the normal outcome of a broken system. Staff hang up their keys and radios every night and then bury the things they've seen for fear of terrifying their loved ones with the reality of their world behind the walls. And every night, behind their cell doors, prisoners are left to their own thoughts. All these mental health issues grow and worsen, a stain spreading through the prison estate, intensifying as the weeks and months go by. Trauma and suffering exacerbate trauma and suffering. Both prisoners and officers benefit if we move towards the example set by Norway. It's insanity to think the current system is acceptable.

It's true that our prison system aggravates psychological issues. Yet for most of the crims I worked with, the first seeds were sown in childhood.

CHAPTER 9

In Loco Parentis – Care to Custody

I can remember the moment the penny seemed to drop for Jimmy. That morning in the group session, we'd returned to a catchphrase I'd picked up from Mickey a few months before. I'd scrawled on the whiteboard: *I learn what I feel when I hear what I say.* It was meant to be a clarion call to encourage new group members to speak their feelings out loud, to surprise themselves with what they actually felt. In my experience, that slogan brought out some of the most poignant life-changing moments. You could see it in his eyes: the light-bulb moment when a crim started to speak his truth and was shocked by the content of his thoughts.

We hadn't had group in five days. The prison had been in lockdown after a tip-off had uncovered a stash of knives and weapons hidden in the laundry on E wing. The place had echoed with the barks of the search dogs and the grunts of officers tearing cells apart one by one in search of more contraband. It had taken them three days to spin every suspicious cell in the building. Meanwhile, we all pretended to ignore the lines running in and out of every window, up and down the whole length of the building, as if they weren't being used to move drugs and phones and weapons out of reach of the search teams.

On day four, when the crims were tentatively opened up

again for association, Taylor had immediately jumped on the mess net, unable to control his anger and frustration at being locked up for three days with a cellmate who was likely harassing and bullying him. After just ten minutes out of their cells, everyone was put back behind the door and staff like me were banned from the landing as the officers first cajoled and then finally wrestled him off the netting.

They wouldn't open Taylor up the next day, knowing that the wing was looking for retribution. Everyone was strung out as group began. Frayed nerves from too long behind the door, trapped with another man, trapped with their own thoughts.

Jimmy shuffled into the room. He inspected the damaged and dilapidated chairs – a ragbag mix of plastic school seats and torn and broken office swivel chairs. He eventually decided on a plastic bucket seat and dusted it with the back of his forearm before sitting down. He took the Pot Noodle tub that he was using as a mug from its resting place on top of the gurgling radiator and settled. Then, emerging from his thoughts, he looked up at the board. I saw Jimmy notice it. I saw him mouth the words to himself as he read them out loud – *I learn what I feel when I hear what I say* – and then I saw his brow furrow. I watched him withdraw as others tried to catch his attention, asking for tobacco.

I saw him rolling the words around in his mouth, testing out how they felt on his tongue. His head nodded back and forth as he got his mind around their meaning.

Every morning, the group would do a check-in. We would go around the circle and everyone would introduce themselves, explaining how they were feeling that day. It was a way of figuring out the mood of the room, getting to know new people and coming up with ideas for our discussion that day. When it was Jimmy's turn, he pointed towards the board.

'What's that meant to mean, then?'

I explained that sometimes we bullshit ourselves so much, we don't actually know what we think or feel until we start talking. Sometimes, our thoughts have been racing around so much in our head that we've been unable to make any sense of them while they remain trapped in our brain.

'Sometimes, we can surprise ourselves with our feelings. Sometimes, Jimmy, it's just good to talk.'

Jimmy nodded, accepting this explanation. He went quiet.

'Do you want to talk today, Jimmy?' I asked gently.

He was tentative. His eyes were wide and his ears alert to risk. He looked like a gazelle at the water's edge, aware of the ever-present danger lurking.

His voice faltered at first. He coughed and corrected himself. And then Jimmy started speaking his truth for the first time in his life and, as he did, he started to understand how he felt and why.

'I suppose I find it hard to trust people,' Jimmy mused, testing the theory. 'It might have something to do with being moved around so much as a kid?'

It wasn't a statement, more a question, checking whether or not it was truly how he felt, whether or not it felt 'right' as he spoke out loud.

The room was silent, giving Jimmy the time he needed to take those Bambi-on-ice first steps into this new journey of getting real with himself. He looked at me for reassurance. He looked at me with imploring eyes, hoping that he'd come to the right conclusion about why he found it hard to trust people.

'I suppose it's because my parents used to beat the fuck out of me?'

I looked him square in the eyes. 'I guess that would do it.'

His voice got stronger after that, as if all he'd needed was the validation. Jimmy had never understood his emotions because, throughout his life, he'd always been told he was wrong and bad. He was wrong when he cried when his dad beat him, he was wrong when he fought back in prison when officers restrained him, he was wrong when he self-harmed because it was the *only way* to feel anything. He was wrong when he ran away from care homes and he was wrong when he stayed and was abused. But in that moment, when Jimmy spoke his truth out loud, he suddenly realised the weight of what he'd kept hidden for so long. He was finally starting to understand and acknowledge why he felt the way he did, why he was always on high alert, always angry, always scared; why he lashed out and hurt others before they got the first dig in. In articulating how he'd always felt, Jimmy began to take back the power and control that had been out of his grasp his whole life.

As Jimmy opened up, regaling us with the near constant flow of trauma, I started to remember a client I'd worked with years ago, out in the community. I rarely worked with women. I seemed to have found my niche dealing with anger, substance misuse and psychological mental health. This work usually focused on men because, more often than not, it was the men who presented as angry and violent. But before I found myself in prison, I did work with some women. Unfortunately, what made them 'complex and chaotic' was usually a very violent male partner.

Beverley had been referred to me because she had substance misuse and mental health issues. She also had a boyfriend who repeatedly beat her, pimped her out and threatened any support worker who went near her. Beverley's home visits were deemed 'high-risk' because of Derek, the violent pimp/ boyfriend who always hung around. They had children, and social services had been involved with the couple for years even before they were born. A host of agencies had worked with both Derek and Beverley in the run-up to the births. Contrary to the popular belief that social workers are trigger-happy in their removal of children from families, the law they operate within actually states the opposite very clearly. Social workers have a duty to promote the upbringing of children within their birth families, even if the family home is a shitstorm of drugs, alcohol, sex work and violence.[1] The state's care of children is shockingly woeful and it's a sad indictment of the social care system when the law acknowledges that a family home like that is preferable to being looked after by the state.

For a few years, Derek was banged up and Beverley managed to raise the children with intensive support and regular monitoring. Sometimes she'd relapse and the kids would be carted off to foster care for a couple of months. When she got them back, they'd be anxious and withdrawn. Social workers and community organisations supported her. In the late 1990s, Sure Start centres started opening, providing support to parents in deprived communities. Beverley was able to make the most of the health, education and childcare services they provided.[2] The family had muddled through.

But by the time I started working with her, the children were long gone, placed with some faraway foster carers. Budgets were constantly being slashed in social care. Their workers were carrying even bigger caseloads, unable to spare the time the family needed to remain as one unit. Voluntary organisations had tried to plug the gaps but they, too, were being financially squeezed. Then Derek's release from prison brought such a cacophony of violence back to the family home, it became apparent that even with the best will in the world, no one could guarantee the safety of the children.

Beverley and Derek were still technically granted monthly contact with them. But Derek didn't give a shit and Beverley's mental health had deteriorated to such an extent since they were removed that she couldn't begin to consider the insurmountable task of travelling four hours across the country to arrive on time at a contact centre.

My colleague, Paul, tossed her casefile across the desk to me. As a novice, I took my superior's advice and dutifully scanned through the information, trying to build a picture of Beverley before we drove to the estate on the outskirts of the city for a joint visit. She'd just been discharged from a stay in a psychiatric hospital. She'd already called the office saying she'd relapsed and was drinking again but agreed to stay sober enough for us to go round and check on her. 'Sober' is a loose term when working with addicts in the community. If you can string a sentence together and aren't falling over, we'll take that as a win.

Beverley was reminded of the agreement that she'd made with my team: if Derek was around, we'd meet in a café instead, not at her home. She assured us Derek wasn't in, so Paul and I left the office and headed out.

Paul's Ford Fiesta was filled with the detritus of a life constantly on the move, driving from one estate to the next, writing up case notes on his lap while slurping on an oversized takeaway drink for energy. I swept a crisp packet to the floor and pocketed a couple of pens from the seat as I clambered in. He clasped the old work Nokia mobile phone in the same hand he held the steering wheel and shouted towards the microphone our location and the time we expected to be finished by. Should the office not hear from us by this time, they were to call the police and send them round to the address. It was standard protocol in community work. You had to trust that the admin who took the message didn't go on their lunch break and just forget about you.

Paul and I discussed our plan of action. We'd see quite how drunk Beverley was before encouraging her out of the house to collect her benefits from the post office. We'd then take her food shopping to get some basics before dropping

her off back at home. We agreed that if there was any sign
of Derek, we'd leave and ask that Beverley come and meet us
later in the week at the office.

We arrived at her house. The front garden was overgrown,
with broken toys in the bushes, tinnies cascading out of the
overstuffed bin, a cheap vodka bottle on the doorstep being
used as an ashtray. Cat shit on the path.

Paul knocked loudly and I stood slightly behind him.
These were the days before I was brave enough to stand in
front of a three-man unlock as a cell door was cracked.

The house was quiet.

Paul knocked again, bending down to holler through the
letter box.

'Beverley, it's Paul. Are you coming to let us in?'

We waited for a second, then heard rustling. A drunken
slur replied.

'Brilliant, we'll wait right here,' Paul said and then, just for
extra reassurance, asked, 'Derek isn't here, is he?'

Beverley answered the door barely dressed. She was still
pulling a nightgown over her bare breasts but had got it stuck
round her arm and she was struggling. I instinctively stepped
forwards as Paul instinctively stepped back and looked away.

'Come on, Beverley, let's get you sorted.' I took the lead
and helped her to pull her nightdress down.

Without realising, I was now closest to the threshold of
the house and was the first to enter. The corridor was narrow,
only wide enough for one person. It was dark and smelled of
smoke and alcohol. It didn't feel right. That intuition, that
drop in temperature, those subconscious signals. The skills
that I honed over the coming years in order to navigate prison
life safely came into full force in that moment and I turned to
Paul, holding my arm out behind me to stop him in his tracks.

He hovered on the threshold, sticking his foot against the
door to keep an escape route free for me. A shadow moved

across the living room wall. Only for a second – blink and you'd miss it – but I was certain I saw movement.

'Beverley,' I said as assertively as I could, fear coursing through my veins. 'Beverley,' I shouted again when she ignored me the first time. 'Who else is in this house?'

As I said it, I started slowly stepping backwards, inching towards the sunlight and the open door. After events like this, I would try to break down what it was exactly that forewarned me of danger. What was it that sent my body into high alert that day, even before I saw the shadow move across the wall? It felt like a primal response when it happened, something I couldn't know rationally.

Whatever it was, that feeling had me slowly, slowly, so as not to cause alarm, edging back towards the relative safety of Paul. It was as if everything that happened next crashed together and took place at exactly the same time. I saw Derek's arm sweep Beverley out of the way as he came striding towards me. I took off running, never turning away from him until both Paul and I were safely at the end of the driveway. Paul had yanked the door shut as soon as I'd made it out, slowing Derek but not stopping him. He opened the door and chased us down the street, screaming curses.

We ran down the road and back to the car. Paul slammed it into gear and we screeched off, pulling to a stop around the corner. My heart was beating in my mouth. Paul and I looked at each other.

'Beverley's fucked,' he said, while reaching in his pocket to call the police to an immediate response.

I'd started working in prison because I thought it would get me closer to the root of the problem. I remembered Derek's aggression towards me, towards Beverley, and had thought that if I could get behind the bars and do some serious rehabilitation work before release, things might have been different.

If I'd been honest with myself, a move into children's services would have been more useful. I'd have been able to work with men like Jimmy while they were still kids. But children's services terrified me. Social workers were damned if they did and damned if they didn't, resources were non-existent and I didn't have the stomach for working with highly traumatised children.

The irony isn't lost on me that I thought prison was a better option, as if waiting until these kids turned eighteen, then waiting a few more years until the trauma really kicked in, would be a much more appropriate time to intervene and try to change their trajectory.

As the memory of the fear I had felt that day crept icily down my back, I looked over at Jimmy, wondering how many times he'd felt that way during his childhood. How many times had he run out of houses or stayed and taken the beatings? I thought of Beverley's children and wondered how long it would be before they ended up in here, attending the group. I looked around the room, watching everyone nodding along as Jimmy spoke, with a knowledge of his childhood I could never begin to comprehend.

Jimmy spoke matter-of-factly about a life I could objectively say I understood. I'd heard these stories and witnessed homes like Beverley's enough times. But I could never truly appreciate the reality. Just like I could say I knew what doing time must've been like, I'd never had a cell door slam closed behind me and listened to the key turn.

I suppose what shocked me the most was that Jimmy had never considered his shitty childhood could have led to his emotional problems in later life. I wanted to scream at the group, 'You do know that this isn't how life is supposed to be?' But a normal childhood would have been as alien to them as their lives were to me.

I didn't need to look at the statistics to understand what

childhood experiences led men here. After my first client, my tenth client, my hundredth client, I could guess at the depressingly obvious upbringing they'd had. Their backgrounds blurred into one as I listened every day to the horror of failed children, who became failed adults.

Some 41 per cent of the men on the landings had witnessed violence in the home, 29 per cent of whom had experienced abuse. Of the eleven men sat listening to Jimmy speak, statistically, at least three of them would have had first-hand experience of the violence he talked about. I took in their faces one by one and realised that in this group, the number was even higher. These fucked-up experiences upped the odds that as the child grew into adulthood, he would become a repeat offender, develop substance misuse issues and mental health problems. The men in the room ticked all those boxes, desperately trying to unpick the damage done years ago.[3]

Some 18 per cent of inmates reported that when they were growing up, a family member had alcohol problems, and 14 per cent stated a family member had a drug problem.[4] They grew up surrounded by crack pipes and needles and pills and powders. As children, they cared for parents covered in piss and vomit, passed out from drink. As children, they became used to strangers in the house and the acrid taste filling the air as their parents got a fix.

As Jimmy told us more about his life, I imagined his mother as Beverley and wondered how any child was expected to cope in a home like hers. His mum had loved him, he told us. But when she relapsed, Jimmy and his brother cleaned the house and brushed her hair. It was the children who knocked on the neighbour's door asking for money for the meter. The children who tried to keep their shit together so they wouldn't be taken away, trying to pretend to increasingly concerned social workers that everything was still OK. On the nights she left them alone, they had to feed themselves and stayed up clinging to one another in the darkness, wondering if she'd ever come home. They cleaned the blood from her face on the nights she returned from a violent client. I thought of Beverley, and then I thought of Jimmy in that house, tiny and scared.

I looked into his haunted eyes and tried to imagine even an ounce of what he experienced. And I wondered if anyone could be expected to come through a childhood like that unscathed. The confusion between desperately loving his parents but witnessing violence and getting beaten himself. The fridge always empty and the house always cold.

There's no easy answer to whether or not a child should be removed from the family home. However chaotic, there's often a strong bond between parent and child, and separation heaps additional trauma onto both. But hearing Jimmy speak, I felt relieved when he finally came to the part where he was removed by social services, even though the care system was a far cry from the stable, safe place he needed.

Fully 24 per cent of those banged up at Her Majesty's pleasure at any moment in time have been in care at some point in their childhood.[5] The care-to-custody pipeline is steep and slippery – and the most obvious example of how these men are failed from day one. Children who end up in the care of the state aren't bad. They're not destined to be criminals. The majority are removed from their family because of abuse or neglect, not their own behaviour. It's true that those who have experienced abuse or neglect may act out, their behaviour may be challenging. But when we don't address the reasons for that behaviour and we instead criminalise them, we're failing the young victims. Yet children in care from the ages of ten to seventeen are five times more likely to become involved in the criminal justice system than children who live in their family home. While only 1 per cent of children are looked after by the state, they make up 50 per cent of the children we incarcerate.[6]

Removing kids from the home isn't the wrong thing to do. When circumstances have got so bad, then it's necessary. But after we've done that, we shouldn't skimp on a single resource to support these children to overcome the adverse effects of their childhood.

We currently spend £2.5 billion each year on foster care and care homes. When we pay taxes for social care, we believe this money is being used to provide suitable accommodation and support for children who have already had a difficult start in life. Instead, during the latest inspection of 171 care homes, twenty-seven were deemed inadequate and fifty-two required improvement to be good.[7] We could blame the parents, say it's their fault the kids are in care in the first place. But this doesn't excuse the fact that children from very damaged backgrounds are being hauled away from the only flimsy security they've ever known and dumped into homes not fit for purpose.

For those kids lucky enough to be matched with a foster family rather than placed in a home, things aren't much better. For half of all placements, the social worker involved reported that they had no choice of carer for the child. They were unable to consider matching the needs of the child to an appropriate adult. They got what they were given. This is cited as a 'supply' issue.[8] Of the 78,000 children placed, one in three children can expect to move placement at least once in the year.[9]

We're paying the cost of a failed care system the minute these men land in custody. We're shutting the stable door after the horse has bolted. It's pointless to try to paper over the cracks with thousands of pounds when they've already entered prison. This money needs to be channelled into care services that are fit for purpose, fixing the root of the problem.

Children in care have needs that cost money. They're more likely to have psychological and mental health problems than the general population. Their special educational needs dwarf those of their classmates.[10] These are expensive and time-consuming issues, but if they were our kids, wouldn't we find every spare penny we had to help them? Wouldn't we argue that placing them in an 'inadequate' care home would only happen over our dead body? Wouldn't we refuse to accept the possibility of a descent into the criminal justice system?

Jimmy didn't have parents fighting for him. For him, the idea of one day ending up in prison seemed likely. One in three crims on the wing had a family member in prison as they were growing up, as if incarceration was as normal as Uncle Pete being away on a business trip. Prison walls cast a shadow over their childhoods in a way that made their ultimate incarceration seem, if not an inevitability, then an extreme possibility.

There's never an easy answer about whether or not children are better in the home or in care. Social workers grapple with these life-changing decisions daily. Yet they increasingly do so with limited budgets and resources. The government has taken a machete to youth services, justice and children's centres, with a 56 per cent reduction in spending from 2010 to 2018. Council spending on children's centres has been slashed by 62 per cent over the same eight years.[11]

There are reports from social workers that certain areas have tightened the definition of a 'child in need', which results in fewer children who are eligible for social care support or care placement. Councillors report they lack the resources to meet their statutory responsibilities to protect vulnerable children.[12] Meanwhile, social workers face wage freezes as they attempt to cover a burgeoning caseload, filled with the clients of colleagues off on long-term sick leave.

At their peak in 2009, there were 3,600 Sure Start centres providing parents and children with free support in their own community.[13] The parenting classes, health screenings, healthy living courses, breastfeeding support and countless other services were seen as unimportant by the government. Although the only lifeline for some isolated parents in deprived communities, the government didn't see the value. Years of austerity saw their function chipped away at until in 2019 only one third of the centres remained, providing limited services. Yet finally, after the decimation of Sure Start is almost complete, empirical research from the Institute for Fiscal Studies shows the millions the centres saved the NHS.[14] There will be other, as yet unmeasured, outcomes, I'm sure.

I'm sure because I knew it had taken Jimmy months to feel safe enough to speak out loud about his suffering but, when he did, it transformed his life.

For the first time in his life, Jimmy had found a space where he could be vulnerable. A group of people he wasn't scared would disappear, like the dozens of foster parents. The group created the safety Jimmy had never experienced throughout his life. There's no data to show the true impact of this work. It can take years to unpick and reprogram behaviours that have been learned in order to survive violent homes and the care system.

Positive changes in behaviour were often slow to come and rehabilitation wasn't linear. But I'd seen Jimmy grow in strength and watched him find purpose articulating his feelings in our groups, understanding himself and finding the self-respect he needed to turn things around. Jimmy's progress felt tangible to me.

And then the swingeing budgets cuts that all but annihilated community services came inside the prison, too. With no money to spend, thousands of staff were made redundant in a matter of months. Across the whole prison estate, resources dwindled and prisoners like Jimmy started spending even longer periods behind their door. There were fewer officers available to unlock them, fewer nurses to medicate them.

Civvies like me were expected to spread ourselves thinner across a growing prison population. Cost-cutting meant crims like Jimmy could no longer be given the unstructured space and time to listen to their feelings.

Days were spent on full bang-up. Officers were unable to unlock the crims for group. Half of the skeleton staff had called in sick, too overworked and underpaid to drag themselves in. So instead, I'd slip a worksheet under the door for Jimmy, asking him to figure out his feelings all by himself in the silence of his cell. I ploughed on, running the group as often as I could, hoping that the reduced regime wouldn't be a setback for him.

When we did manage to get together in the classroom, I asked him why he was working so hard to stop using drugs.

'Why are you trying so hard to better yourself? Why are you doing all this work on your feelings when it's obviously so painful? Isn't it easier just to keep doing what you've always been doing?'

Jimmy fiddled with the bracelets he'd taken to wearing, struggling to make eye contact with me or anyone else. Eventually, he cleared his throat, looked up and answered with the realest truth I'd ever heard in group.

'Because I want to live,' he said.

And I noticed Titch wipe away a tear at the depth of Jimmy's words.

He cleared his throat again. Just like the first time he spoke up in group, he seemed to become more confident, surer of his feelings, as he spoke them out loud.

'Because I've wasted so much of my life trying to fucking kill myself, poisoning myself, fucking hating myself that I owe it to myself to live every single possible day I have left.'

Every one of the crims looked down at their feet as they let the truth of what Jimmy had said sink in. He let out a huge sigh, as if he'd been holding on to these feelings for his whole life. He breathed in, filling up his lungs, like he was desperate to inhale all that life he'd already missed and wasted.

Creating the culture of our group sessions had taken time and commitment. It's easy to look at this as a luxury that we can't afford when resources are limited. But the cost of not investing in these services is higher. From the community to custody, our government is failing to look at the bigger picture as it pulls more and more funding from the services that save money and lives in the long-term.

There are now 4.3 million children in Britain living below the poverty line, with an additional 200,000 children falling into poverty between 2019 and 2020. The Trussell Trust gave out 700,000 three-day food parcels to children in that period.[15] If it wasn't clear before, the government's callousness towards struggling families and children couldn't be ignored when free school meals were fought over as if spending one pound more on them would bring down the economy. All while politicians continued to claim expenses for subsidised four-course dinners.[16]

There is money available. Cuts to politicians' expenses can be made. Non-violent prisoners can be released. We can think long-term and invest in our children and their families so the criminal justice system doesn't end up footing the bill years down the line. Yet more money must be found and spent, too. We must accept that. Reforming our society so every child has a fighting chance won't be cheap. But if we go back to imagining the children, those kids who had the shit kicked out of them, or found needles in their living room, or were sexually abused in care. Or any other horrific, traumatic experience the majority of us couldn't even comprehend.

And if we look around my classroom and imagine that at least half of the group were once one of these poor little kids. And then look at the data and the long-term savings economists report when we invest in community services, and compare this to the maths of the cost of incarceration and how one in four of the cons has been in the care system, then we know what we must do.

And then if we say, 'Fuck the money,' and imagine how we'd move heaven and earth for our own children – how we'd give up everything to make sure they had the best start in life. There are 78,000 children a year in the care of the state. That means we, the people who make up the state, who pay our taxes towards its continual functioning, should be fighting for these children with just as much ferocity and determination as we would for our own. And if we do, one day, just maybe, the kids of Beverley won't be sat in Jimmy's place, trying to figure out how the fuck to build a life out of the hand they were dealt.

Lacking the belonging and security of family was commonplace. And while some used drugs to deal with their situation, many of the young men I worked with searched for meaning and structure in gangs.

CHAPTER 10

Can't Drive a Lambo around the Exercise Yard – Gangs, Youths and Race

Jamal was from my neck of the woods, a northerner who'd found himself down south. He'd been moved across the country because of his affiliations. But even in a prison so far from home, he was surrounded by danger. He couldn't come to my group classes because he couldn't move freely around the prison. He was at high risk of being attacked in one of the warren-like tunnels that had no CCTV cameras. Youths who wanted to make a name for themselves would happily try to kill him.

Jamal trusted no one. One day, the builders came to erect metal cages around the five-storey stairwells on the wings. The purpose of these cages was to prevent prisoners from being thrown over the sides when they were moving up and down the landings. Jamal watched in dismay.

'They're dangerous, miss.'

I didn't understand what he meant; they were building them to *stop* people from being thrown off the stairwell.

'They trap you,' he said. 'You need to be able to jump over the side. What if you get cornered on the stairs? You could get stabbed from the front and the back and there's no escape. It's like fucking Hillsborough.'

I shuddered.

Jamal risk-assessed everything he saw. He'd scoped out all escape routes. He wasn't working out how to escape from prison, but how to escape the violence that follows young men from certain postcodes both inside and out. As his eyes darted up and down the wings, he was making a mental note of all the places he was vulnerable.

Jamal wore a comb in his hair when it was brushed out. The rest of the time it was tightly braided to his head. His hairstyle usually depended on whether or not he was having visitors that week. Once a month, his mum would make the long and expensive journey, setting off before sunrise, to visit her son on an eight-hour round trip. She was involved in the Church and dressed in her best when she visited. He'd been in prison before he'd turned thirteen. He was twenty-four now. He was released once but breached his parole by staying in contact with some old associates, so had been brought back in for at least a further five years.

I wasn't naive enough to think that everyone I worked with wanted to change their lives. Some of the men were just bored and fancied an hour or two off the wing chatting to someone different. They knew it'd look good on their file when they went for parole if they'd been actively engaging in work or education to tackle their 'offending behaviour'. But Jamal wanted help and, up until that point, no one had given him any.

He referred himself to me, although I had no idea why really. There were no mental health or substance misuse risk markers on his file. I was tasked with signing him up to the anger management group I was running, yet when I met him, I never saw a hint of aggression or a flicker of frustration. He smoked a lot of weed, which might have explained the chilled-out vibes, but he never seemed spaced out. Just calm. Yet he was doubly incarcerated. Not only was he locked in prison, but he was also locked on this one wing, never able to go to the gym or the library or to pray.

He talked openly about the trauma he'd experienced with a disassociation that was disconcerting. His needs had been missed during the initial assessment into the prison, but there were clearly issues that he wanted to address. This echoed a larger pattern across the prison estate. The Lammy Review found clear evidence that youths from BAME backgrounds were missing out on support in prison because upon initial reception, they were:

> less likely to be recorded as having problems, such as mental health, learning difficulties and troubled family relationships, suggesting many may have unmet needs. All this hinders efforts to tackle the root causes of offending and reoffending among BAME prisoners, entrenching disproportionality.[1]

In fact, the only area where BAME youths were over-represented was regarding concern about the risk they posed to other young people.[2]

Jamal was perceived to be a gangster, nothing more. And the perception that gangsters don't have substance misuse issues or mental health problems or thoughts of self-harm meant he was left to figure out how to get through his stretch alone.

Jamal had committed some really bad crimes back in Liverpool. Crimes so bad that they had been reported as front-page news, his mugshot spread across the country. He couldn't lie low and do his time quietly. He was infamous in prison. He'd carried crack rocks around the estate in his mouth from the age of eleven. He'd seen his best friend die in his arms before he was sixteen. He'd watched stabbings and shootings over nothing but drugs and money and respect and all the other things that I found it so difficult to comprehend. He'd been attacked himself, multiple times. But the man sitting in front of me now seemed so far removed from his crimes of nearly a decade earlier.

He was clever and quick-witted and seemed just too damn normal to be trapped in this decrepit and collapsing shithole. We spent hours talking about how he could maintain his Zen master calm. We also spent hours talking about whether or not he'd be able to maintain his composure when, one day, he'd be released back into the outside world, and back onto unforgiving streets.

Jamal had been earmarked for anger management group, but he told me he couldn't come because mass movement was too risky for him. If he didn't die on the way to my classroom, he'd certainly be injured. How do you teach someone 'anger management' if they have to run a gauntlet, literally, to even start the lessons? We were trying to replicate the class one to one, but Jamal didn't really need anger management. He had flashbacks and nightmares, smoked more and more to calm his thoughts. He had mental health problems and substance misuse issues. But he was a youth, and Black, so all he was really seen as was a gangster.

I'd doubled down on my group activities after Norway, providing support that was changing lives. But working with Jamal made me realise this whole swathe of the prison population – the youths – were getting sweet fuck all and lots of it. And it seemed so counter-intuitive, because it was the youths causing havoc on the landings, running drugs around the prison and stabbing, shanking and beating the shit out of each other with increasing regularity. Just like Kai, Jamal was being contained on his wing, the perceived threat mitigated, but it didn't mean he was changing for the better. He wasn't getting the help he needed. I wanted to do more. Jamal was ripe for rehabilitation, but the only thing that I did that I knew really worked magic was group therapy. If he was too high-risk to come along, I didn't know what else I could offer him.

I remembered Christian in Norway telling me about how work should be evidence-based and research-led. I still had a large chunk of my funding from the Churchill Fellowship left over. With Jamal in mind, I had the bright idea that I would go and visit some gangsters on the South Side in Chicago, learn how they were rehabilitating and then come back and replicate the work here. I dragged one of the biggest officers in the establishment along with me for moral support.

The weekend we arrived, it felt baking hot. The humidity made it hard to sleep and the city seemed restless. That year, there would be 2,900 recorded shootings and 468 murders in total.[3] Some people died on the streets in their own blood, others died in the ambulance that had to drive across the city to get them to the better-equipped hospital. Despite the South Side having more shootings than anywhere else in the city, it had no trauma centre, so gunshot victims routinely died on the journey to the hospital that sat in the richer, whiter neighbourhoods further north.

Before leaving the UK, I'd made contact with an organisation that served as a halfway house. All residents were on electronic tag and expected to attend group sessions like the ones I ran. They were also expected to work a food bank that served the local community.

Roy, the centre manager, was like an American pastor. All booming voice and infectious energy. He told me he'd been a resident here many years ago but had now been working straight 'for ten damn long years'. He didn't care about rules and regulations, so said we could come and work the food bank shift then attend groups the next day. No security checks, no paperwork to fill out.

'You think you can lift heavy weights, girl?' he asked me as I glanced over at my friend.

'I think I can, sir,' I replied.

'You better, cause I'm gonna work you two damn hard tomorrow.'

He laughed and slapped my friend hard on the back.

'Wear comfortable shoes, you two, cos we're gonna be making you run laps of this place,' he carried on, chuckling to himself.

The sun started to rise as the train took us further south. The coffee kicked in and we arrived ten minutes early for the start of our 7.30 a.m. shift. Roy waved us over as we entered the building.

'This way, my English new recruits. Come meet your team!'

We were led into a canteen, where our tired-looking team-mates slumped back in chairs, sipping on strong black coffee. The male and female residents slept in separate parts of the building and they had special group activities that catered to each. But those who worked down in the food bank worked side by side. By the sound of it, Roy needed the people working the food bank to be physically fit and all of them were young. Although right then, they barely looked awake.

He introduced us to the group. A couple of the guys raised a hand to say 'hi', too cool to get up and say anything more to us.

There in the canteen, none of them looked too threatening. From a distance, they were just like a group of tired-out college kids hanging around before class. They seemed to do as Roy said, not scared of him but grudgingly respectful.

As Roy led us down into the warehouse, though, I got closer and I saw the gang tattoos on faces and necks. The scars on the arms from knives and guns. The gold teeth reflecting back in the half-light of the warehouse.

Shit, I thought. *These are proper American gangsters, like in films.*

After taking it all in, I had a quiet word with myself. *Treat people how you want to be treated. Be respectful and just act normal.*

We made small talk. I turned to the man next to me. His hair was cut tightly to his head, showing off scrapes and cuts that had turned to scar tissue. Round his neck he had elaborate writing tattooed. I couldn't make out the words without staring and it would have been rude, maybe even dangerous, to look too closely. On his face were prison tattoos: teardrops, crosses, more writing I couldn't make out. Four teeth in a row all solid gold.

'Thanks for letting us come along today.'

I introduced myself and asked if he was OK to answer some questions. No teenage grunting from him like I got at this time in the morning from the youths back in England, just pure enthusiasm. On a cigarette break later, I found that the excitement and openness that followed was because he'd never met anyone from England. He was keen to show us the work he did and confused and intrigued as to why we gave a shit about what they were doing down here.

'Nobody in our own city cares about us, it's cool that you guys have taken the time to come down here. To come and see and listen to us,' he told me later.

I asked him how long the food bank had been running.

'I been here for six months, but they been feeding the community for years now. Roy used to be like me, with the bracelet on fifty years ago,' he said, pointing at the electronic tag around his ankle.

'Ain't no electric bracelets fifty years ago, fool,' one of the girls who had been listening into our conversation chimed in.

'How old you think I am, boy?' Roy's voice boomed from the front of the crowd.

Everyone laughed. I could manage this. I was good at the

balance between seriousness and humour required in a place like this.

'Well, you just tell me what needs doing and I'll get to it,' I told the young man. I was there to watch and learn.

Roy was right when he said it was physically demanding. Me and the boys hauled sacks of potatoes onto our shoulders and carried them from the warehouse in the back to the front food bank area. Back and forth for over an hour carrying kilos and kilos of carbs out front.

Once all the food was laid out, Roy said we could have a ten-minute break before we had to get to group therapy. We all headed outside. I went to cross the road to stand in the shade.

'We can't go there, we gotta stay on this side of the road,' the kid with tattoos reminded me, pointing at the tag. 'Have to stay on site.'

We sat on the sidewalk in the sun, sweat dripping from the exertion of the morning. We spent the next few minutes trading English and American swear words. Them asking me about English prisons, me asking what the American justice system was like.

They told me how they first got 'stop and searched' when they were still in junior school, that their first response to a police car pulling up would be to turn and face the wall, hands up. That Black people in America learn as children how to interact with the police, knowing they could be killed if they took a misstep. They told me how American prisons work for profit, so there's no incentive to ever help anyone stop committing crime. How there's no air conditioning in the prisons and they've known men die from the heat.

They told me how on The Out, they couldn't vote, couldn't return to their old addresses and had to check a box on every job application if they'd ever been found guilty of a felony.

I listened, horrified by their experiences. But a lot of it sounded scarily familiar.

Roy tapped me on the shoulder.

'You do know it's worse in England. You think we're racist? You lock up Black people more than we do,' he laughed.

They explained that the halfway house offered them hope, that Roy understood and truly cared about them. They were learning useful skills living in there. I told them that in prison, I ran groups like the ones they attended in the halfway house. I told them how I wanted to do better work in my prisons and that's why I was travelling the world, seeing how other countries did it and seeing if I could learn anything.

'So come along to our group,' they said.

After we'd completed our shift in the food bank, I watched as Roy held together an unruly group of ten youths, first listening to their complaints before focusing them on talking deep. It was a replica of the group I ran back in the UK, except here in America everyone was under twenty-one and no one had a diagnosed substance misuse or mental health issue. The topics covered, from guilt to trauma, from drugs to block out feelings to drugs that drove them wild with anger, were almost exactly the same as the things we talked about back home.

'The youths don't get help with these issues,' Roy told me later. 'Everyone thinks they're just violent and aggressive, but don't forget they got souls just like you and me. They need the same help everybody needs.'

Back on B wing, I told Jamal excitedly about the group I'd attended in Chicago.

'It was a room full of youths, sat talking and opening up,' I explained. 'Do you think it would ever work in here?'

Jamal was dubious.

'How are you going to keep us safe? Most of us want to kill each other,' he replied.

We have staff in the prisons who map out postcodes and

use the police's database to try to figure out who's at risk from whom inside. If street violence is going to spill over into prison violence, where the hell can we house all these young men and give them a fighting chance?

There are two possible ways of dealing with this. The first is to overhaul an institutionally racist criminal justice system and reverse the years of austerity that have seen our poorest communities get even poorer. Black children are more than twice as likely to grow up in poverty than their white peers.[4]

You fund the organisations that are running street gyms, community centres and peer support tirelessly every day out on the estates. Like Roy's facility, in the UK there are people who are doing the work, the real work, needed to engage young people and help them to escape or avoid the wrong path. They're plugging a hole but can't hold back the torrent alone.

You redesign the education system so that there's true equality of opportunity for children regardless of race or class. Black and mixed ethnicity boys are more likely to be permanently excluded from school and arrested as a teenager than their white classmates.[5] You follow every one of the recommendations of the Lammy Review, which demonstrates how racism and unconscious bias permeates the way youths are dealt with throughout their criminal justice journey. If they do end up banged up, you then engage them in wraparound support that views aggression as a symptom, not the cause, of their issues.

Aggression is the tip of the iceberg, where underneath there are learning difficulties, mental health issues, illiteracy, unstable upbringings, drugs and alcohol, abuse, trauma and all the other problems it becomes so fucking tedious to list because they're just so normal it seems unnecessary to continue to repeat. As Lammy succinctly put it, 'prisons may be walled off from society, but they remain a product of it'.[6]

Or, because it's cheaper in the short-term and we haven't got any staff, you just segregate the youths and separate them instead. D wing becomes a proxy wing for one area, E wing gets its own postcodes, that sort of thing. Who ends up in a particular prison depends largely on which court feeds into the establishment. Each court deals with a specific geographical area and so the prisons overflow with the problems from the streets, the road issues. Each prison inherits its own wars and soldiers from one area. Stick them on a wing, don't let the ones like Jamal off and then stand back congratulating ourselves that we've solved the gangs issue.

Still, holding the hope that had been inspired in me in both Norway and America, I continued to look for ways to rehabilitate and change the world from within the system. I started to put feelers out to run some sessions on smoking weed, violence and youth mental health. Jamal agreed to support me, and Daryll had finally got out of seg and could be guaranteed to agree to anything that got him out of his cell. I didn't mention the word 'gangs', knowing that no one with an ounce of drugs or an ounce of sense would engage with groups that highlighted their affiliations.

In the UK, we love a certain sort of gangster. The Krays and the Goodfellas and the Godfathers. All hard-working, idolised, admired for the way they stuck it to the Man. But Jamal wasn't that kind of gangster. He was the kind of gangster the papers referred to as 'feral', one of the 'illiterate swaggering thugs'.[7] When 'white chavs' become involved in violence, they are accused of 'becoming black'.[8] The racism drips from the page, souring public opinion against any young person who looks a certain way.

Any article that even hints at knife crime is usually illustrated with the image of a Black youth, hood up, scowling menacingly into the camera. Black, Asian and people from a minority ethnic background aren't more criminal, but we lock them up as if they are. The UK is 86 per cent white, yet white people make up only 75 per cent of the prison population.[9] Not because white people break the law less, but because even when other factors are accounted for, BAME defendants are far more likely to receive a custodial for drug offences than their white counterparts.

I hadn't believed Roy when he told me we lock up more Black people than America. We're better than the States. We haven't got racism like them. There might be pockets of it in our country, but nothing like the widespread inequality in America. I was wrong. Very wrong.

There's greater disproportionality in our incarceration of Black people than there is in America.[10] BAME men are more likely to go to high-security prisons for the same crimes as white prisoners. For those in on public order offences, 417 Black offenders and 631 Asian offenders are placed in high-security prisons for every 100 white crims.[11]

Black people are nine times more likely to face stop-and-search than white people.[12] Section 60 of the law, which allows stop-and-search without reasonable suspicion, was used 18,081 times in 2019. Only 4 per cent of these interactions between the public and the police led to an arrest.[13]

There's a horrible, perpetuating cycle that means the more BAME people you stop and search, the higher proportion will be arrested comparatively. The view of a criminal becomes that of a BAME youth. And then, whether unconsciously or not, racial profiling leads to more stops, more arrests, more disproportionality in our system.

American data shows us that if white people were stopped and searched at the rate BAME people are, they'd be found with drugs to a far higher degree.[14] Yet drugs aren't really a problem if they're shoved up noses at dinner parties or used on university campuses by white people destined to be our next cadre of politicians. So the police target the people they think look like criminals and we end up where I am now, in a classroom with four youths who are Black British Caribbean, one British Pakistani youth, two white British boys, an Irish Traveller and a lad from Somalia. The BAME proportion of youth prisoners has risen from 25 per cent to 41 per cent in the decade 2006–2016.[15] These kids turn eighteen and are shipped into my place, to survive the landings with the adults.

Daryll was excited to come to the new group and there was more interest than Jamal or I had expected. I later learned this was because BAME inmates statistically get less time out of cell and have more reduced access to interventions than white inmates.[16]

And so, my first youth workshop involved putting rival postcodes into one room and then trying to figure out what the fuck I was going to do with them when I got them there. I had officers on standby. I had to clear each name with the head of security before I was allowed to get this experiment off the ground. Jamal would be escorted over to the class alone, outside mass movement time. I pulled a radio that morning, double-checking it had a full battery. Never before had I felt more in need of that emergency button at my waist. I was worried I was creating a situation where I was putting the crims in danger. At lunchtime, before the group started, I spoke to the officer who had been in Chicago with me.

'I'm on radio call sign Hotel 22. You hear that, you come fucking running and save me.'

I'd put together a rough outline of the topics I wanted to cover in the group but, to be honest, I was just hoping we could get through the hour and a half without someone getting hurt. I'd been working with Daryll and Jamal for the month beforehand and I was relying on them to keep the peace and the conversation flowing.

We were in as big a classroom as I could find, away from the main prison building. Everyone needed as much space as possible so as not to feel at risk from the others in the room. We were spread out, more than a fist's reach away from each other.

'Thanks for coming,' I started. 'Have any of you ever done group therapy before?'

Daryll raised his hand. There were nine of them, one of me; two who had worked with me, seven who had never done anything like this before.

'All right. The way it's going to go is that we're here for an hour and a half. If you decide at the end that you want to come back next week, and we keep it on a level this week, then we have the afternoon over here with a coffee break in the middle from next week on. We'll keep it going so long as you think it's worth it.'

There were nods around the room.

Daryll's hand shot up. 'Will there be biscuits, miss?'

Others rolled their eyes, laughed.

The youth next to me said in a calm tone, 'Nah, shut up, man.'

I smiled. No matter which prison, or which wing, biscuits were always a priority.

'If biscuits are what it takes to get you boys to change your lives, there will be fucking biscuits, I promise.'

Daryll's eyes lit up. 'Sweet, miss.'

'We start with my basic rules, then we do a check-in. This is where we go around the room, telling everyone who we are, how we're feeling today. If you have anything you specifically want to talk about, you can tell us during check-in and we'll all try to agree on the topic. If you're not sure where to start, there are some things I want to talk about. Everyone ready?'

Again, uncertain nods, no eye contact yet, most of them staring at the floor.

I'd written three lines on the board:

Just Do You

Show Respect
Be Honest with Yourself

'Just for today, I'm going to tell you what I think all these rules mean. To me, "Just Do You" means that prison and the system and all the other people in here can wind you up at times. But we have this hour and a half a week to try to work out our own stuff. We're not going to spend this time complaining about everyone and everything else that's beyond our control. In this time, we need to focus on ourselves and what we can control. We're going to take responsibility for our own actions. We're going to focus on doing our own time, no one else's. Does that make sense?'

The group mumbled an agreement.

'To me, being respectful means that if anyone in here is brave enough to talk, we're going to listen. If you don't agree with what someone says in here, you can challenge them, but don't make it personal. You can disagree with him, but that doesn't mean you can attack the person.'

I stood up and moved to the front of the classroom, trying to reiterate my point.

'If anyone gets real in here, we keep everything they say private. We don't take anyone's private lives back to the landing and use it as gossip.'

I paused for effect.

'Finally, the most important one.'

I'd stolen this one from Mickey. Ever since he'd given his speech during Shaun's first group, I'd been using his words to set the tone in every group I ran.

'Be honest with yourself. It doesn't bother me whether you come here lying or telling the truth. I get to go home at the end of the day. But you'll be wasting your own time and everyone else's time if you aren't honest. I'm not going to sit here and tell you that drugs are bad or violence is wrong, but I want you to be real with yourself about where these things can lead. Are you happy spending your life in this prison? Is this the life you want?'

Silence.

'OK. Let's get to work. Daryll, do you want to start with the check-in?'

'Daryll, twenty-two,' he said, before adding the name of the estate where he'd grown up. He raised a hand to wave at the rest of the group.

I hadn't asked them to say where they were from. He chose to add this because he thought it was important. Either important because that was how he identified himself or important because he'd worked out quite quickly that this group had something to do with those postcodes. I hadn't advertised it that way, but he knew the other faces in the room.

We went round the rest of the circle. Taking the lead from Daryll, everyone told us where they were from, as well as how they were feeling that day. Jamal was as cool as usual, keeping the energy calm as we listened to the others declare their rival postcodes. The last kid finished speaking.

He told us how he felt then said, 'Cool, let's get this group going, then.'

'Wait, wait, wait. I've not done my check-in yet!' I said to him.

'Ah, miss, I didn't know you do one, too,' he apologised.

'My name is Ange, twenty-seven, Manchester.'

They started howling, laughing, shouting over each other.

'Manchester! Manchester, miss? Gunchester. It's rough up there though, innit.'

Every youth in the prison called me 'Manc' from that day forwards.

We'd broken the ice. Now, we started trying to do the hard work. Session one: the pros and cons of dealing drugs.

'It's bad, you get me. It's not a nice thing to do,' Daryll started off.

'Don't tell me what you think I want to hear – tell me what you actually think,' I countered.

'All right, fuck it.' He started giggling. 'Bet I make more money than you though, miss. You've not got gold chains.' He laughed and fist-bumped the kid next to him.

'OK, who wants to write up in the "pros" column "making lots of money"?'

Daryll stood up. 'Throw me the pen, miss.'

I passed him the marker and he wrote on the board: *making money.*

Again, everyone started laughing. The mood was light in the room. It was a good vibe. It felt like I could challenge them and they could challenge each other, if we managed to keep it like this.

'Anyone want to argue against Daryll?' I asked, wincing at myself as I said it, hoping they knew I meant only verbally.

Jamal raised his hand to shoulder height, asking for his turn to speak. I nodded.

'Doesn't matter in here, though. Can't drive a Lambo round the exercise yard,' he said, deadpan.

Laughter and fist-bumps followed.

'Go write it up there, Jam,' I encouraged him.

He wrote it up in the 'cons' column word for word. The group was loud and raucous and, as he finished, I shushed them.

'OK. I want you to tell us more of what you mean by that, if you can?'

'What I mean is, money doesn't mean shit if you haven't got your freedom. We're sat in here rotting, miss. I've not got my family, my girl. I get told what to do all the time. Have to wait once a month for visits, ask a fucking guv for toilet roll. Nah, money is nothing in here. I'd rather be poor and free. You're happy, miss. And you earn fuck all. But you get to go home and see your family tonight, you get me?'

The laughter had stopped. We were all looking at Jamal, faces sombre.

'For real,' Daryll muttered.

'I hear that,' said the youth next to me.

'I get you,' I replied. 'Family, freedom, happiness. Worth more than gold, I reckon. Can't drive a Lambo round the exercise yard,' I repeated, smiling.

During the time we met as a group, not one of the youths was involved in an assault. They all stayed out of seg for the duration. It wasn't changing the world, but it was certainly changing something. It had felt like there was finally something good happening again inside the walls.

It didn't last.

A couple of months later, the groups were pulled from the schedule. It was decided that there weren't enough staff available to get these kids out of their cells all at once. When there were barely enough officers to open a landing and get everyone fed twice a day, the youth groups were an added extra the prison couldn't afford. They were a non-essential part of the prison regime that was too costly and time-consuming. The prison was now running on a restricted regime. Staff sickness was draining resources, funding for the prison was being pulled tighter and tighter, the drones flying drugs over the walls were causing chaos we couldn't keep under control.

The groups were working – as much as anything could in this place – but as the wings became more volatile, time behind the door stretched on and sentences were served on constant bang-up. There would be no more sessions with rival youths in one room. They all went back to the wings, back to their madness. I watched as all eight of them reverted to what they knew best and the prison estate continued rolling towards its own special sort of hell.

The prison budget couldn't stretch to cover actual rehabilitation. The short-term cost saving was put above the long-term benefit of reducing assaults on officers, on other inmates, and reducing reoffending rates after release. These intelligent young men could hustle and graft hard. They had drive and passion. They could have used those skills towards bettering themselves, with the right support. The budget cuts demonstrate that we don't believe it's worth the time, effort or cost to make our communities safer and their lives better. From that point on, the priority had to be keeping them apart as a short-term strategy to stop them from killing each other.

Even that failed. Two months later, I answered a code red and ran to a wing where a trail of blood stretched 30 feet from the start of the landing to the showers. I held a wad of bandages to one youth's head while we watched the nurses desperately working on his friend who lay on the shower block floor. They worked valiantly and saved the youth. They had more stomach than me. He'd been stabbed so deeply I could see bone. I walked back to the office with the nurses, smearing red footprints as I went. The following year, a prisoner was killed on the wing.

The destruction of community services during Britain's decade of austerity meant more and more young people recruited into gangs. Lammy says that 'there is a settled narrative about young BAME people associating in gangs, but far too little attention is paid to the criminals who provide them with weapons and use them to sell drugs'.[17] We pull out the funding for the support that keeps kids out of gangs and then spend very little time and attention on the higher-ups, the glamorous gangsters, who orchestrate their madness. This approach leads to BAME youths being locked up in disproportionately high numbers. Meanwhile, the very community services that could reduce these risks are being squeezed into oblivion. The restorative justice and mediation services get little time and less attention. Yet there's still enough money in the pot for the police to continually employ stop-and-search. There's enough money to warehouse these kids in custody.

I think back to how we failed the kids in care who ended up in prison, how Jimmy was once looked after by the state and with a tragic inevitability ended up in custody. Then I think of the institutional racism that sees those ethnicities that are in the minority on The Out in Britain become over-represented behind prison walls. And I wonder how a system that actively works against certain groups of people in our society can ever be relied upon to keep them safe.

Because once they're swallowed by the system, so many of the men I met are there to stay.

CHAPTER 11

When Life Means Life – Imprisonment for Public Protection

Titch had been a youth like Jamal decades earlier. But now he was like the wise old convict you see in films except, despite pushing fifty, his skin was clear and when he wasn't taking drugs, his lively eyes sparkled white. He also spoke much louder and faster than that old-time lag in fiction. We often talked politics and I learned that when he was passionate about a topic, he boomed.

There were a couple of times I had to reassure a concerned officer we were just having an animated debate and, no, he didn't need to go back behind his door. So, although he didn't look or sound like the stereotype, he was the crim on the wing more clued up than most on the inner workings of the criminal justice system, having served decades behind bars. Yet he wasn't a murderer or a sex offender. In fact, when we started working together, he'd been back inside for six months because he told his probation officer he'd relapsed and requested help to get clean again. He was serving time even though he hadn't committed a crime. He hadn't hurt or robbed anyone. All he did was use drugs. And yet he didn't have a release date.

'I didn't even fail a piss test. They didn't even catch me using. I told them because I needed rehab, I needed help,' he said.

I didn't believe him. Didn't think it was possible to lock someone up indefinitely because they'd used. Titch took it upon himself to educate me about the reality of the criminal justice system. As I ran around the landings, he'd beckon me over and pull a newspaper from his back pocket. He'd hold out that day's latest headline to me, shaking his head in disgust.

'They're banning books in prison now. Books!' He enunciated the word so it echoed around the landing.

He was right, of course. They did ban books being sent in, and he'd been locked up indeterminately for a relapse. He was one of the men given one of those Imprisonment for Public Protection (IPP) sentences I mentioned. A sentence category that's seen people serving years beyond their tariff behind bars, often longer than rapists and murderers for lesser offences.

IPPs were brought in under the Criminal Justice Act in 2003 and crims started getting sentenced to them in 2005. IPP changed the court's powers when dealing with 'dangerous offenders'. For specific offences, the judge was obligated to give out an IPP without discretion. Like a life sentence, after conviction the crim must serve a minimum tariff before he can be considered for parole. Only when his tariff has expired and the Parole Board is 'completely satisfied that the risk had sufficiently diminished' can he expect to be released.[1]

Back in 2005, Titch had beaten the shit out of someone in a drug-fuelled rage. He pleaded guilty and he served his time for the offence. After six years, his tariff expired. He waited another nine months for his first parole hearing because of the backlog in cases. When he did get in front of the Parole Board, they were satisfied that he'd dealt with the addiction and violence. He was released under supervision onto a life licence. One slip-up, one shoplifting charge or, in his case, a relapse on drugs and he could be recalled to prison immediately for an indefinite amount of time.

IPP was brought in at a time when the government wanted to show how seriously they took crime and punishment. They were going to be tough on crime. It was assumed that less than 1,000 IPPs would be given out, yet as this ill-conceived law was implemented, the prison population ballooned and nearly 9,000 people were sentenced in this way.[2]

The law was also so badly written that a judge was required to give a life sentence for quite minor offences if the crim had a historic violent conviction that he'd already served time for in the past. As the waiting list for a parole hearing grew and Parole Boards continually knocked back release, robbers and assaulters served longer than murderers and rapists.

IPPs caused even more pressure on an overcrowded prison estate and then these prisoners found themselves in a horrific catch-22. They had to engage in education, therapy, groups like mine to prove they were rehabilitated. But there were too many prisoners and not enough courses. They ended up stuck in local remand prisons that didn't offer the accredited programmes the Parole Board would accept as proof of their rehabilitation.

Our local remand prison didn't run the three-month substance misuse course that Titch had been asked to complete prior to appearing before them. He'd already put in requests to transfer to the prison that ran the course, but they were full. Hundreds of inmates were applying for the same programme in the same prison up north, after their Parole Board had requested they complete it, too.

Instead, Titch looked around at his options, spotted me and then begged to work with me. We spent the next six months preparing for the board – his only shot at getting out that year. If we failed to convince the panel of middle-class, middle-aged strangers that this working-class, self-educated gobshite was fully rehabilitated and would never relapse again, he'd be inside for another twelve months until his next chance at parole.

The Parole Board would be made up of three individuals, drawn from a pool of 246 members of the independent body. Supported by about 120 staff to help with the admin, these 246 people would be referred 25,000 cases per year by the Ministry of Justice. During the hearing, they'd assess the risk Titch posed to the general public using oral evidence and a collection of reports relating to his history and current behaviour in prison. In 2018/2019, these individuals carried out 5,380 oral hearings, of which 38 per cent were refused, 49 per cent were released and 13 per cent were recommended for a move down to cat D conditions.[3]

The sheer volume of hearings they carry out implied that they wouldn't be spending too much time looking into Titch's case in detail. The Parole Board website likes to point out that only 1.1 per cent of those released or sent to open conditions reoffended in the first year.[4] It also implies that their decisions come from a place of risk aversion. This wasn't good news for Titch, who had been released once and started using again.

Still, we got down to work. He had two initial motivations for coming to the group. First, he was clever and wanted some conversation that was deeper than the bullshit gossip and grafting on the landings. Secondly, at least to begin with, he thought it would look good for the Board.

But regardless of his motivation, I was glad he started coming. He was a valuable group member who could always be relied upon to get the conversation flowing. When he grew bored of listening to his fellow inmates complain about being in prison, he would roll his eyes. Then politely, but defiantly, he would start his monologue. 'You can't change the situation. Right now, you're stuck here. The only thing you can do is change the way you feel about it.'

I'd heard it so many times, but I always asked him to elaborate for the benefit of the other crims. Titch had more reason than most to be frustrated and angry at the system. He loved it when he could talk freely to the room.

'Some days I manage better than others. Some days I want to burn this place to the ground. But I can't. I've got to keep believing that I will one day get out, and I will one day have a good life.' He eyeballed the others then took a breath before getting to the main thrust. 'Prison is shit and I hate it here, but here is where I find myself, and I can't change that. This fucked-up criminal justice system. I just can't let it live rent-free inside my head, you feel me? It's already got my fucking body. The only thing I can change is how I feel about it. I decided that I'm going to use this time to milk the system for all it's worth.'

Deano gave a little 'hear, hear' and Titch stared him back into silence.

'I'm going to get an education. I'm going to get to know myself and better myself in these groups. I'm going to leave here the best version of myself possible. I can't change my situation – I can only change the way I feel about it.'

It was amazing when the crims did my job for me. I was starting to see the value in peer support, in hearing this advice from a fellow con rather than the worker sat at the front of the classroom. Titch didn't disappoint. He came to every group I ran and in group he was the perfect assistant. But one to one, the stress of the upcoming Parole Board was taking its toll. Everyone else had a release date to work towards, something to focus on, something that could keep him hopeful. Titch had nothing but the parole hearing and he was becoming increasingly worried that he'd be knocked back, with no future release date in sight.

In his open way, he'd remind me over and over again that however good the group was, it wasn't the course he'd been told to complete. He and I might have seen the value in it, but he was convinced that the Parole Board would laugh him out of the room, send him back to his cell and back to another year of uncertainty. And all because he'd relapsed.

We focused him on coping inside and put plans together so he could survive without using on The Out. He always said he was angry, but I didn't see it. He was just passionate about the injustice of it all. I'd talk to him about plans for when he got released.

'If, miss, not when,' he'd correct me every time.

When the day came and I walked with him down the landing, off the wing and into an office especially assigned for us at the other end of the prison, we were silent. He had one chance to fight for his freedom and, instead of clinging to the certificates that the Parole Board wanted to see, he only had me to report on his engagement and progress.

We sat across the desk from a panel of three. Their faces as white as expected, their plummy accents caustic as they asked questions devoid of empathy or understanding. They asked whether or not I was sure Titch would never use again. I bit my tongue, fearful I'd scream back at them.

'You do know we'll be releasing him with a once-a-week check-in with an overworked, unsupported substance misuse worker? You do know he'll be getting no psychological support whatsoever? You do know that no one employs anyone on licence?'

If Titch could have left that day and somehow magically stepped into one of their lives, perhaps I could have assured them he wouldn't relapse. But I knew the reality of the world he'd be released into and the support he required and wouldn't receive. Surely they knew this too, but in the moment, I saw them as part of the system that slashed and burned that support and then blamed the individual if he couldn't make it on his own. We all knew community services were decimated. We all knew the odds were stacked against him.

Titch was no danger whatsoever when he was clean, but his relapse had been criminalised and instead of receiving treatment in a facility designed to address substance misuse, he'd been thrown onto the violent, drug-filled landings and expected to figure it out for himself. He'd been left to rot in a local remand prison that didn't run the programmes he needed to complete as a tick-box exercise to secure his release.

No, I couldn't guarantee he'd never use again upon release, but then I couldn't guarantee he wouldn't use again in here, either. I knew the prison was rife with drugs and I knew that he'd kept clean the whole time, attended group every day, begged for extra work that would show how seriously he was taking the whole thing. The group might not have been the one parole had asked him to attend, but we'd worked some magic in that classroom, addressing every issue under the sun. We'd worked hard to equip him with the tools he needed.

I did my best to show them just how much effort and dedication he'd brought to the work we did together. I told them how his engagement in group had been limitless. I tried to explain the plans we'd developed to keep him straight on The Out. They dismissed it all; they dismissed him, dismissed me. We were asked to leave the room. For minutes that seemed like hours, we sat next to each other in the corridor, waiting to be returned to the wings. I knew better than to show my feelings, but really, I wanted to cry. We sat side by side, with our heads arched against the wall behind us, looking towards the skies that existed just beyond the ceiling. He kept his head back to stop the tears from falling.

Provided with the right substance misuse support on the outside, Titch might have made it. Instead, he was falling apart, inside on a life sentence for a relapse. It was a waste of taxpayers' money to lock him up and throw away the key because he'd used. But more than that, it was such a waste of a life. Without any hope for the future, without any glimmer of possibility to work towards, I never saw that sparkle in his eyes again.

Titch had shown admirable spirit in the face of an uncertain future, but his engagement with me and his efforts to better his life didn't get him released. Over time, he became despondent. I suspect that he started using drugs in prison again after the knock-back.

The days and weeks and months of intensive work he'd done to make something of himself had seemingly meant nothing. Before the knock-back, Titch had been a huge asset to the groups. He challenged other people. He was loud and sometimes unruly, but everything he said raised a discussion point. He was so alive, so engaged, so ready to fight for himself. After that day, his eyes started to glaze over. His skin became sallow. The energy had gone.

By the time of the hearing, the use of IPPs had been outlawed, yet this wasn't applied retrospectively. It's a step in the right direction that no future inmates will suffer the cruel punishment of being sentenced without an end date, of serving more time for less serious crimes. But by 2020, 1,895 IPP inmates remained in custody beyond their tariff end date, having never been released. And like Titch, another 1,357 inmates were recalled by September of the same year.[5]

And it's not just us care bears who rail against these sentences. The main man himself, the champion of IPP David Blunkett MP, said in 2014 that he 'very much regrets' the injustices of the sentence.[6]

The officers and prison staff who have to deal with the inmates who are unable to sign up for the courses they need, and who feel hopeless without a release date, also argued vehemently against IPPs. When senior prison staff, with an average time in the service of twenty-one years, were each asked about IPPs, they reported it was 'poorly planned and implemented and resulted in unjust punishments'.[7] Interviews conducted with 103 of these highly skilled prison officers found that 92 per cent reported that 'IPPs decreased staff job satisfaction as they undermined staff credibility . . . and often meant staff were unable to assist prisoners in progressing through their sentences.'[8]

Of all the inhumane, money-wasting facets of the prison system, IPPs are probably the only one that prison staff, politicians and crims all agree should be abolished. And the sad truth is that it was abolished in 2012, but those who were swept up in the initial convictions still remain behind bars to this day.[9]

Titch and I still had our political debates on the landings, but I never again felt able to defend the criminal justice system to him. We both knew it to be fundamentally flawed. I had believed that common sense would have prevailed. I should have listened to this old-timer.

While, mercifully, IPPs only make up around 2.5 per cent of the prison population, by 2021 12 per cent of inmates were those held on remand, awaiting trial.[10]

CHAPTER 12

Freedom's Just Another Word for Nothing Left to Lose – Remand

Callum was a first-timer, a wrong-place, wrong-timer. He didn't have the usual close-cropped hair of the criminal masses but rather, long waves that he'd tuck behind his ears repeatedly when he got nervous. A self-soothing tick I witnessed multiple times during his first unsteady weeks inside.

There was nothing specific about his behaviour that made me worry. His stylish hair, his unblemished skin, apart from the slight wrinkles of any forty-year-old, made him look more like a solicitor than a crim. He wasn't aggressive or violent. He wasn't a crier. Never emerged from his cell in the morning with bloodshot eyes. When he was too warm, he unthinkingly rolled up his sweater sleeves, unembarrassed to show unscarred arms. He appeared calm. Too calm. And in a place like this, normality seemed abnormal. He moved around the landings slowly with an unassuming gait that drew my attention. It was as if he was doing his best not to be noticed, which made me instantly suspicious.

'What's your pad mate about?' I asked Jimmy casually during a regular one-to-one session.

'He's all right, miss. No trouble, like.' And then, without prompting, Jimmy called down the landing to Cal and was soon introducing us. 'This is my worker, Cal. The one I was talking about. Runs those groups.'

Callum automatically stuck his hand out to shake mine as he said hello. He didn't have the accent common to the rest of the prison population. A softer drawl than I'd become used to.

'Nice to meet you, miss. Jimmy keeps saying I should come to these groups.' He looked at me hopefully.

Up close I could see his eyes darting furiously around the wing, trying to take in every detail. Shining and alert. Up close, it was obvious he wasn't calm. He was terrified.

'Everyone's welcome,' I reassured him. 'Me and Jimmy are just finishing up. We can fill in the referral form now if you like?'

As I'd become more comfortable with the paperwork, I could get it completed in less than twenty minutes. I knew how to ask 'how many units' and 'which types of drugs' and 'what diagnoses' he had, all without it sounding too tick-box. But the first few questions were always prescriptive. The facts about court dates and release dates and cell numbers and age.

'Status?' I asked, my pen hovering.

'Innocent,' he replied.

'No, don't worry, I don't need to know that. Just are you remand or sentenced?'

'Remand.'

After five minutes, we were finished. All the sections that were relevant and usually covered in notes were left blank. No substance misuse, no mental health, no learning difficulties. He didn't even have any particular issues with the prison regime. Jimmy had helped him to organise his phone credit and showed him how to book time down in the gym. I looked at him quizzically, wondering if the fraud charge he'd told me about was a cover for a more sinister offence that he didn't want to admit.

I paused, trying to think of a way to politely ask him what the fuck he was doing here and what exactly he thought I could help him with.

Finally, I tactlessly blurted out, 'So what's the problem, then?'

He looked at me like I'd spoken a foreign language. His eyes stopped flitting for a second and he stared at me as he said, 'I'm innocent.'

'When's your court date?' I asked him hopefully.

A brief flash of anger ticked across his face and his body tensed. I instinctively pulled back, a defensive gesture I disguised by putting my pen behind my ear.

'I shouldn't be here,' he muttered.

I learned that Callum had a life on The Out. A proper life, that he was desperate to get back to. He had a mortgage to pay, a wife who was working full-time while raising their children. His eldest was getting ready to start her GCSEs. The youngest was going to big school soon. He smiled as he told me how excited his middle boy was about the holiday they'd booked next month to Portugal. He had to make the final payment, shop for new swimming costumes. His car was due an MOT. He had clients and deadlines. They didn't know where he was and all of their contact details were stuck in his mobile phone locked in the prison reception. He had work that needed to be done and emails to be sent.

Callum told me about the day when he'd been feeding his kids breakfast and two police officers had knocked at his door. The day his ordinary life collapsed. The day they held out a warrant for his arrest and forty-eight hours later, with no warning, he'd ended up here.

I couldn't make sense of what he was in for, what he'd been charged with. He was trying to put together the pieces himself. Hoping that by recounting the details to me, it would become clear to him, too. There was something about a car, not his car. An uncle's car. No tax. But insured to Callum's address. The uncle had stayed on Callum's sofa a few months earlier for a week or two. Bills had started coming through in his name. Unsecured loans that Callum didn't know anything about. There was a phone call from the bank about unusual activity on his credit card.

'Nothing to do with me,' he said.

The uncle was back at the house with gifts. A new TV and PlayStation as a thank you. Thought nothing of it. Until the police were at the door. Stolen goods. Credit card discrepancies. Need you to answer a few questions down the station. A magistrates' appearance. Possibly has the means to abscond. Significant sums of money. Flight risk. Remand.

Bail had been refused because the court felt the amount of money involved made this crime a serious one and if he was hiding that money, there was a risk he might try to run away and wouldn't turn up at court.

Most of the men I worked with were in for either petty or violent crimes. They got bail knocked back because they'd either been refused it in the past or they didn't have anywhere to be bailed to. Their lack of suitable accommodation meant the courts and police wouldn't have been able to keep track of their whereabouts and there was a risk they were so chaotic, they wouldn't show up for court when it was time for the trial.

Like the 3 million other people globally,[1] or the 72,877 in England and Wales that year, Callum had had his liberty taken away before he'd been to trial.[2] He was not guilty – not yet guilty, at least. Therefore, he was innocent, just like 15 per cent of the whole prison population at any one time. And his life on The Out was turning to chaos as he tried to mount a defence to the charges with only five quid of phone credit and one visit from his solicitor in the past fortnight.

After only a few years behind the walls, I was already becoming cynical to protestations of innocence.

'It doesn't matter to me if you're guilty or innocent,' I started to say, but Callum interrupted me.

'I'm innocent. Seriously. And it *does* matter to me! This is my life!'

While cynical about the guilt or innocence of the men I met, I was still woefully naive when it came to the criminal justice system. I'd studied law at college. I knew that the golden thread of the presumption of innocence was weaved throughout our system. Whatever Titch had tried to teach me, I knew that normal people living normal lives don't just get arrested one day and then refused bail. You only go inside if you're dangerous or there's overwhelming evidence. Things like this don't happen to people who live law-abiding lives. Over the next five months, as I watched Titch's and Callum's cases unfold, they took a hammer to my naivety and smashed it to pieces.

At Jimmy's insistence, Callum started coming to group. My tactlessness during our first meeting hadn't put him off too much. The promised time out of cell probably allowed him to overlook it.

Half of my caseload was made up of remand prisoners, the group of inmates most likely to self-harm or kill themselves. Half of all self-inflicted deaths in custody are of people on remand.[3] These inmates who, although receiving some perks like getting to wear their own clothes, in reality are likely to spend more time banged up behind their door than convicted inmates.[4] Like Callum, people on remand are overwhelmingly likely to be held in local prisons – the ones that are older and more overcrowded. Therefore, the conditions they live in are often worse than those experienced by sentenced prisoners.[5] They're also less likely to be accepted for education and training courses that depend on course completion to secure funding. If a remand prisoner isn't sure how long he's going to be in for, it's unlikely that he'll be accepted on any of the longer programmes or apprenticeships. My group, therefore, with its open-door policy, was one of the only things Callum was eligible to attend.

During group, he opened up about how desperate he was to see his wife and kids again. But he was reluctant to expose them to this environment. No one he knew had ever been to prison. He didn't even have any points on his driving licence. He spent the first month of his time on remand phoning her as often as he could, reassuring her he was all right, and fending off her suggestions that she come and visit. Like me, his wife still had confidence in the criminal justice system. Although her husband had been arrested and locked up on remand, she believed the courts would soon realise they'd made a terrible mistake and he'd be on his way home.

She didn't understand that a remand prisoner gets thrown onto a wing with all the other convicted criminals. She didn't know that an innocent man, once behind the walls, wouldn't be differentiated from the guilty and would be treated exactly the same as everyone else.

She'd been researching online and knew he had rights that the convicted didn't have. Theoretically, he was allowed to access a laptop computer to get ready for trial. He was allowed to wear his own clothes still. He was allowed more visits. If he would just let her visit, she'd make the journey immediately across London to see him again. He didn't want to worry her. Didn't want to correct her when she assumed he was on a small unit with the other innocent men awaiting trial.

I imagine that as he sat in his cell at night, writing letters to his solicitor and the police, begging them to try to contact witnesses to support his defence, even he couldn't help laughing out loud when she suggested he could ask the governor for a computer.

Likewise, although he was allowed to wear his own clothes

inside, she hadn't completed the paperwork for the delivery accurately and his belongings sat in the prison reception, unprocessed. He couldn't stand the thought of her knowing that had happened. He couldn't face seeing her if he had to wear the prison tracksuit.

He was attending group regularly, but increasingly an officer was popping in to pull him out of the room and into a video conference with his legal team or for a video court appearance. Each time this happened, he returned the following day looking a little more beaten, as if the air were being sucked out of him. Bail applications were refused, the case was moved up to the Crown Court. The trial date pushed back.

'It's a complex case,' the prosecution would say.

More time was needed to pore over his financial records.

Remand prisoners can be kept in custody for 182 days before the case gets to court. For fraud trials like Callum's, there was the possibility this could be extended further. Six months. Not too problematic if he was found guilty, because these days would become time served. But he wasn't guilty. And he was desperate for his day in court to prove his innocence.

His solicitor warned him that he was in for the long haul. He needed to sit tight for six months and not expect to be out any earlier than that. When it finally sank in that he'd miss his anniversary, his kids' birthdays, his holiday, Callum cracked.

Eventually, he decided that no matter the emotional consequences, he had to have a visit. He had to see his kids. Unaware of how traumatising a prison visit could be, his wife had been ecstatic when he'd agreed they could come.

He didn't live on this side of the city and it was a long trip for her. Getting the money together wasn't easy. She was struggling on her own on The Out with Cal stuck inside.

Her income didn't cover the cost of living without his wage coming in and she was starting to rely on friends and family to help her out. She had to get public transport, and it would take about three hours of hopping on and off buses and trains with the children before she'd make it to the front gate.

She'd relied on Callum for a lot on The Out. He'd always driven them everywhere, so she was nervous about navigating across the city, scared of getting lost or missing a connection. Callum told me she was planning to leave with hours to spare, just to make sure she'd arrive on time. She'd never been to a prison before and didn't really know what to expect from the visit. On the day I saw her, she was dressed smartly, as if she were going for an interview. His eldest was hunched over her phone, wishing herself away to anywhere but there.

Cal had been in his cell that morning, doing everything he could to make himself look smart, too. He'd swapped some tobacco for a haircut and asked to borrow an iron from the officers. He'd spent half an hour making sure he got the creases out of a borrowed shirt. He'd doused himself in aftershave and I could smell him immediately as I walked onto the landing. His visit was that afternoon and I wished him luck before I headed off for my lunchbreak. A spark of positivity and excitement on an otherwise grey afternoon. The other crims were excited for him, too. He was well liked on B wing and we all knew how much this visit meant to him.

As I headed out of the prison, I saw them waiting nervously in the visitors' centre. He'd shown me pictures of his family, so I knew it was them and they were so early, there was no one else around. I smiled to myself. It was heartbreaking to see children having to go through the security checks, but the joy of seeing kids reunited with their dads was worth it.

I finished for the day and thought nothing more of it. Cal would be in the group the next morning and he could tell us all about his visit then.

'How you doing, Cal?' I asked when it was his turn to check in the next day.

'Yeah, you know. It is what it is. Hopefully, I'll be out soon enough anyway,' he said with a sad smile.

Cal's wife had forgotten her ID. Without it, she wasn't allowed in to see him. He'd sat in the visits' hall watching the door, waiting for their arrival. He hadn't known during that time if she'd made it to the prison at all. Eventually, after pleading with an officer to call through to the other side, he found out about the forgotten ID and that his wife was there in tears on the other side of the wall. He hadn't been able to see her or the children.

She tried again a week later, suffering the humiliation of being searched. The younger children had been terrified of the drugs dogs, with their teeth bared and straining at their leashes. They'd already started crying before they'd even entered the visits' hall. Their hour together had been fraught. She'd brought bad news with her. The bank had been on the phone about her falling behind on mortgage repayments. She'd spoken to the Citizens' Advice Bureau – they'd suggested she look at selling up and moving somewhere smaller.

Callum looked down at the table in shame, only noticing then that she wasn't wearing her wedding ring. The engagement band that usually shimmered and shined was missing, too.

'I had to sell them,' she whispered as she bounced their youngest on her knee and glanced over at their eldest. 'It doesn't mean anything,' she said quickly as his eyes asked more questions than he dared to speak. 'I'll fetch us some coffee,' she said, putting the child down and moving towards the small area that sold drinks and snacks.

Callum's children stared at him in silence.

Over 200,000 children a year in England and Wales go through the experience of having a parent incarcerated and

10,000 visits like this are made to prison by children every single week.[6] His eldest, usually so focused, was struggling at school. She was having nightmares. Not sleeping properly. There had been a referral to a support service, but his daughter couldn't help but absorb the worry that hung over the household. The weekly therapy sessions she was now attending did little to alleviate her anxiety. Just like the research suggests, her mental health was deteriorating owing to Cal's incarceration.[7]

Since he'd been arrested, her risk of having antisocial behaviour and mental health issues were twice as high as they had been.[8] She hadn't told anyone about her dad being locked up. She'd been too ashamed.[9] Research says this is normal, too. Children who have parents in prison can become withdrawn and isolated as they try to hide their experience from friends and peers. The isolation fed the mental health issues she was experiencing and Callum could do nothing but look on hopelessly as his daughter became another victim of his remand in custody.

His hair grew longer as the days ticked by. He caught a nicking for a mobile in his cell. Later, he told me he'd been so desperate for contact with his family that he thought it was worth the risk. He couldn't face the snatched ten minutes each morning on the landing phone with cons and screws hovering and listening to his marriage very publicly breaking down. Objectively, it seemed rational. But this breach of prison rules cast a shadow over Callum and seemed like an omen of things to come.

The house sale went through three weeks before he finally got to trial. The children were pulled out of their schools as the family upped sticks and moved back to the Midlands. His wife was no longer convinced that the truth would come out. She was worried she'd be left to raise the children by herself for the next ten years. She was preparing herself to do it alone and she needed to be close to her family.

He started rolling his sleeves down, even on hot days. An ACCT was opened. Callum was another addition to those self-harm statistics as he started to contemplate the reality that he was losing everything.

His final group session was on his 181st day in custody. He'd never wavered in maintaining his innocence. He'd opened up in group about his children's problems, his family's financial struggles. Every week, he'd have another catastrophe to report. His mother had had a stroke and was in hospital or his daughter's grades had dropped even further. His wife hadn't answered his calls for the past two days. And I wondered even if he did get cleared in court, what exactly would he be going out to?

Of the 72,877 people remanded into custody each year, 35,257 are either acquitted or given a non-custodial sentence. Almost half of those who are dragged into prison, away from their homes and their jobs and their families, should never have been in prison in the first place. Back when Callum found himself banged up, £240 million of taxpayers' money was wasted on those 35,257 people.[10] Since 2014 this has only increased, as the time spent awaiting trial has gotten longer and the cost of incarceration has increased.[11] That money could pay the wages of 10,000 nurses per year.[12] Meanwhile, the financial and psychological cost to the individual and their family is unmeasurable.

Callum was one of those tens of thousands released immediately from court, after the case was thrown out owing to lack of evidence on the first day of trial. He'd spent six months in custody. He lost his home, his business. His wife and children suffered the impact of his incarceration. He lost six months he'd never get back.

And since the pandemic, things have only got worse. It was recorded that 3,608 people on remand had been held beyond the legal time limit of six months, and 2,551 people had been held for eight months and counting.[13] These were people who weren't guilty, who hadn't had a trial. People who were innocent. Almost half of them, like Callum, would be acquitted or receive a non-custodial sentence by the time they got to court.

He walked out of court a free and innocent man. I don't know if he wept or cheered. He'd escaped the nightmare of custody, but next he'd have to rebuild the devastation that had been wrought on his life and the life of his family. He was entitled to no practical or financial support. He was handed a plastic bag containing his belongings that had been taken from him six months earlier. A mobile phone on a contract he'd still been paying for. A wallet full of credit cards his wife had had to max out. I don't know if his family attended court that day, driving down from their new home miles away. If they didn't, I have no idea how he made it home, because the court doesn't give compensation for tearing apart an innocent person's life. They don't apologise. They don't even offer the usual measly £46 discharge grant that a convicted offender gets upon his release from prison.

I used to think that justice prevailed within our system, that innocent people didn't get remanded, that there's no smoke without fire. Maybe those 35,000 people who go to prison innocent and are released immediately when they finally do get their day in court felt that way at one time, too.

I said I wouldn't tell the sensationalist tales of Britain's most notorious criminals. Callum's story is even more horrifying than theirs. Callum's case shows that anyone – any one of us – could so easily become one of these 35,000 people. Callum's case shows that our prisons aren't crammed full of dangerous and violent offenders. They're packed with innocent people. Innocent people who suffer harsher conditions, more overcrowding, less time out of the cell, less access to work and activities. It's no wonder the remand prisoners were the ones who I ended up working with. It's no wonder they were the ones most at risk of suicide.

And the situation has got worse, not better. The number of remanded inmates within our prison system has increased by a third since the pandemic hit.[14] Coronavirus has caused huge backlogs and delays in the already bursting court system. Instead of rapidly adapting the court system through funding and reform, the government has just changed the law on remand. It's now legal to hold an innocent person awaiting trial for 238 days instead of 182.[15]

If conditions were bad when Callum was inside, they've only deteriorated during the Covid-19 crisis, which has further limited time out of cells, social interaction, education and group activities. For sure, my groups would no longer be running in that small, airless classroom that allowed for no social distancing. Imagine trying to survive eight months of this pandemic in there, knowing you were innocent, knowing your life outside was falling to pieces.

There's growing concern among legal professionals that innocent people are pleading guilty, because they're doing the maths and realising that they'll serve more time on remand even if they're eventually found innocent at court. Tens of thousands of those in custody get a sentence of less than a year and are expected to serve half of their sentence incarcerated. With trial dates now sometimes being set for years in the future, it's becoming increasingly convincing for an innocent person to plead guilty, get his time served and get out.[16]

Those who stick to their principles, serving the time on remand because it matters to them to maintain their innocence, must not only survive the psychological impact of prolonged bang-up. They must also survive the virus. Inmates can't control their personal space, they don't have showers in their cells, they have to double up. A person locked up in prison is at 'substantially greater risk' of dying from Covid-19 than the general population.[17]

A growth in remanded prisoners, longer waits until trial, a lockdown regime within the normal lockdown of prison and greater risk from the virus. I used to believe that in our system, you were innocent until proven guilty and treated as such. I now know the system is not only failing convicted criminals and the victims of those criminals – it's also failing the innocent.

Callum still believed he could salvage his life outside of prison. He was desperate to get back to his family and rebuild what his time on remand had taken from him. But for a significant minority, life beyond the prison walls could be even more difficult than doing time. For these men, the day of release brought with it the reality of homelessness and rough sleeping.

CHAPTER 13

There but for the Grace of God Go I – Homelessness

I'd seen Clifford at the train station a couple of days earlier, stopped to see how he was doing.

'Even the emergency night shelters are full, miss,' he told me, clutching a super-strength cider as I sipped an overpriced coffee, both of us fighting off the cold in our own ways.

It was impossible to avoid men I knew from the wing. Outside the coffee shop, Ashley would be begging for spare change. The clack-clack of Ryan's crutches behind me as I turned onto the high street. Doorways piled high with the belongings of men who would soon be breaking the law to follow me inside for a few weeks of respite from the cold and the damp. As Callum was fighting to get out, there were some men desperate enough to want to come back in.

While I was living the big city dream, the releases from the prison existed alongside the gentrifying ex-council houses and artisanal bakeries, moving through the same spaces but only visible if you looked, instead of nervously averting your gaze for fear of making eye contact.

The voluntary soup kitchens and sock drops and rough sleeper counters were out in force. A man had died after being released from prison a week earlier, hypothermia kicking in as he bedded down for the night. I didn't know him, hadn't worked with him, but I walked past the spot where he must have slept every day on my way home from work. Only a few days earlier he'd been in prison, warmer and safer.

I promised Cliff I'd ring the phone line to report rough sleepers, get an outreach worker to him to try to get him into a bed.

'I'm not going to last the week,' he said as I handed him all the spare change I had.

I left him to his exquisite misery of bedding down under the railway arches, knowing that however hellish the near constant Christmas bang-up was for the cons like Callum, for men like Cliff, at least in prison he'd be fed and protected from the elements.

When Cliff arrived on the wing two weeks later, he looked worse than I'd ever seen him. Skin and bone, hollowed cheeks and blackened eyes. His neck sported a nasty set of scratches. He'd started fitting in police custody as he came off the drink and smashed his face into the wall.

Over the winter months, the prison would pick up the men failed by the meagre community services. Men who committed petty crimes to survive the cold. Men who would get their head down for six or eight weeks, avoiding the worst of the weather, before slipping away from the gates as the temperature rose.

Withdrawals were brutal and could be deadly. Clifford would be medically detoxed on a Librium prescription as he fought off the shakes and the vomiting. There was no psychological support in that first week as the alcohol left his body, just a single focus on surviving the detox. If Cliff had ever tried to give up drinking alone, out on the streets, he'd have died. Alcohol ravages the insides, but it clings on tightly and stopping outright can shut down organs and kill a man.

Back on the wing, he was sharing with Tommy. Best pals both inside and out, they'd ride their bang-up together, pull each other through the first few worse days and look after each other when they landed back on the streets in the springtime. For the first week Cliff barely left his cell, too weak to get further than the meds queue each morning. I'd go up to his locked door as I rounded up the troops for group, a gentle tap and a smile just to make sure he was still alive. Tommy assured me they were fine, just detoxing, but I worried about him.

He was vulnerable in prison. Not a criminal, just a homeless man who had weighed up his options through an alcohol-fuelled fog and rationally decided it was too cold to be outside. There was nowhere for him to go. He was freezing and too tired to walk across the city to try to hunt down one of the precious spare beds for the night in a hostel. He'd stuffed his pockets with the turkey sandwiches and a bottle of Baileys left over from Christmas at the Tesco on the high street.

The arrest had been a blessing, the warmth of the police car thawing him out. It was only when he got to the police station and the tremors began that the feeling of terror at the fast-approaching withdrawal took hold.

Cliff didn't want to stop drinking, or at least couldn't imagine living his life without. The streets were unforgiving, too harsh to face sober. I didn't disagree. We both knew that he'd leave in a few weeks, still homeless. The prison stay would do nothing to alter the course of his life. Just a stopgap, a reprieve, a break from the worse conditions outside. He'd gain a little weight, get some strength back, avoid the worst of the weather and I wouldn't see him inside until things got desperate again. The short custodial would hopefully save his life and then he'd join the 100,000 people released between 2015 and 2018 into accommodation that was either not tracked by authorities, usually because it didn't exist, or classified as 'unsettled' – a euphemism for the lost sofa surfers and street dwellers who fell through society's fragile safety net.[1] He would become one of the one in six inmates going through the gate to rough sleeping or other, more hidden forms of homelessness.[2]

But he wasn't improving. If anything, he was looking even worse than when he arrived. Ten days into his detox, Cliff should have been getting stronger, but he was struggling more than ever. Tommy and Cliff knew the drill, had followed this same routine of in and out together for years. But they weren't coming out to wash, they were barely eating. Cliff might have come off the alcohol, but he was on something and he looked like a fucking zombie.

Usually, he'd at least show his face in group, enjoy the team spirit of it. But this time, my gentle encouragement couldn't get him to budge. He wasn't going to Alcoholics Anonymous meetings, even though there were always guaranteed biscuits from the men who came in from the community each week to host the sessions. He'd looked in better condition when I'd seen him out on the streets. I was on high alert. Something bad was coming.

The normal association noise was pierced by the death wail of a dying animal. I crashed from my seat, throwing the release paperwork back towards the crim across the table, shouting a promise over my shoulder that we'd finish it later. I launched myself up the metal stairs, jumping two by two as the code blue alarm sirens filled the wing. Fear powering me up, slamming through gates, the locking and unlocking slowing me at every landing. Grabbing the meds bag, the defib, the oxygen, hauling myself back down the stairs.

Human instinct tells you to run from danger. Yet prison staff get the alarm telling them there's an emergency and we run towards it. It could be a riot, a death, an assault. You don't know until you get there and as you're running down the landings as fast as you can, you're secretly hoping not to be the first on the scene, terrified of what will greet you.

But I knew as soon as I'd heard that blood-curling sound which cell I was heading towards.

'Spice attack on the ones, miss,' Deano shouted, trying to

be helpful, as I blazed past him carrying the equipment for the nurses who were already arriving.

'I can fucking hear it,' I snapped back at him over my shoulder as I reached the growing crowd of healthcare and officers and crims craning their necks to get a better look.

The nurse was already there, his sleeves rolled up and his tie tucked in. It was the third code blue of the day.

I handed over the meds bag, waiting to see if they needed me to fetch and carry any more equipment – equipment that always seemed to be stored at the opposite end of the prison to the emergency unfolding.

Cliff was on the floor, fitting and bucking as if he'd been shot. The whites of his eyes were huge and pleading, bulging, and he gasped as if he were taking his final breaths. My guts twisted. I was certain he was dying. The noises coming from him weren't human. They echoed around the landing, drowning out the officers who were shouting everyone else back behind their doors.

There had been a bumper delivery of spice over the New Year and the artfully named new strain, Man Down, was doing exactly what it said on the tin. Every hour, someone was collapsing. Crowds of inmates watched, laughing at the dying man on the floor. I stood helplessly, writing down the vital signs that the nurses shouted out at me. The uncontrollable noise coming from his frothing mouth was fear in its purest form.

But he lived. The nurses shoved meds inside him and worked their miracles and roused him back to life. He was able to sit up and talk before that fucking alarm blasted again and the healthcare team were pulled to a cell just one landing up. Cell doors rumbled with the sound of kicking. Hollers echoed through prised-open hatches. There was barely any time out of cell any more. When there was association, it was cut short because someone had gone over on spice.

The constant bang-up in filthy cells, the missed visits and

phone calls to loved ones over the holidays, was bringing out the worst possible tendencies on the wing. Where once there had seemed to be a camaraderie between cons, now I was seeing sneers on faces as they sniggered 'Better run faster, he's not looking too bright' to the nurses, who were holding back an apocalypse with sticking plasters and hope.

I stayed with Cliff as the nurses ran off to the real work of saving another life on the landing above us. Tommy and I knelt down by him. He was weeping now, apologising to Tommy. He clung on to his hand and Tommy quietly kept reassuring him over and over again that he was safe.

Over his best pal's head, Tommy told me how scared he was. Cliff was the only family he had. I passed him his tobacco and he started to roll as he spoke.

'We used to have family, other people. It's all just gone to shit.' He looked around the cell, taking it all in within seconds and realising quite how bad it had become.

I slumped to the floor, leaning against the frame of their cell door so I could stay and talk to Tommy. The adrenaline was leaving my body and I felt shaky. I wished I could smoke, too. I quietly watched him roll the paper, light the cigarette. From my position at the edge of the cell, I could still hear the drama of the overdose upstairs. I had to strain to hear Tommy as he talked.

'He used to be normal, you know. I've known him since school. We joined the army together when we were eighteen. Our girlfriends were best friends, too. They looked after each other when we were away. We weren't rich, but we weren't poor, you know?'

I nodded, too exhausted to speak.

'We went to serve. We didn't know how it would end up. You're not ready for that. We were kids. Then we came back and we've got nothing. No help.'

He shook his head mournfully. 'We gave up years to go

and fight. You can't talk about it. No one understands. We've been left with nothing,' he repeated. 'A head full of nightmares. Pockets so empty we have to come here for a fucking roof over our heads.'

I didn't know Cliff had been in the military, didn't know he'd not always been like this. He'd once had a family, a home. He'd had a job and a life travelling the world.

'We both suffered,' Tommy said. 'Flashbacks. Just these fucked-up thoughts. You start to think different.'

When he found he couldn't manage his mental health any longer, he drank to keep the memories quiet. With nothing there to catch his fall, once his girlfriend kicked him out, he'd ended up homeless and begging on the streets, relying on food banks to eat.

'Cliff let me stay on his sofa for a while, but I dragged him down. Both of us drinking every day. Soon we were both out on our arses,' he said.

'You need to stop the fucking spice,' I said flatly, uselessly, unsure what else I could ever say or do to make their lives any better.

Cliff went over on spice again and again after that day and Tommy's words kept filling my mind every time the emergency alarm went off. Without a safety net, without help and support, we're all just a few short steps away from the chaos of Cliff's life. We're all just one mental breakdown, one missed rent payment, one bad choice away from it.

Cliff didn't deserve homelessness and he didn't deserve the addictions that were destroying him. A decade before, he'd been one of 'Our Boys', revered and respected. Once his life started to collapse around him, he became just another alcoholic in a doorway, no longer 'ours'. Not our problem. He was responsible for his own downfall.

My anger surged, knowing that we're all only one small stone's throw away from being like Cliff, weeping on the floor of a filthy prison cell. The community safety net that should have helped him, protected him, saved him, has been torn to pieces by cut after cut. A decimation of community services that's destroyed lives. A shift in attitude towards individuality that implies he's at fault for the bad luck and disaster that's befallen him. If only he'd worked harder, been stronger, then he wouldn't be here now. And the shared responsibility we have for all members of our community has been blown apart by a narrative that's turned our focus away from the real culprits in power and turned us against one another.

In a three-month period in 2019, 626 people were received into prison reporting they'd been in the armed forces.[3] After comparing multiple studies, the British Royal Legion puts the figure at 2,820 veterans in custody at any one time.[4] Men like Cliff, men who were once 'Our Boys', our source of pride.

When did we start buying the bullshit that there isn't enough money to support the most vulnerable members of society? I wonder when did it become us versus them? Who drew the battle lines between the poor and the poverty-stricken, turning the lens from government, from those really responsible? When did it become acceptable to let anyone spend a single night on the streets?

And as Clifford's release date beckoned, I wondered who the fuck thought it was acceptable that a man needed to come into prison to survive the cold of winter? Who thought that it was acceptable to release him after eight weeks back onto the same streets, to the same fate? For all the nightmarish conditions, for some, prison is a salvation and a saviour. The staff inside picking men up from the floor and bringing them back to life when they should never have needed to be there in the first place.

We'd released a man to die on the streets at the start of winter. And yet no lessons were learned, his death barely registered. Of those released, 14 per cent go out homeless each year. Nine thousand individuals. This increases to one in five of those serving a sentence of less than six months.[5]

By coming into prison, Cliff was classified as intentionally homeless and so not eligible to join the growing list of people waiting for housing. There was no duty on the local authority to secure a roof for him. He was on his own, left to repeat the endless, inescapable cycle. He couldn't scrape together his own money for a few temporary nights in accommodation because he couldn't sign on or claim benefits. You couldn't do that until you were actually released. On his final day, Cliff collected his discharge grant of £46 and a one-day train ticket to get him back to whichever doorway he chose to call home that time around.

With all the endless criticisms of the custodial system, it's easy to forget that prison could be a lifesaver for some people. But it shouldn't need to be. Prison should be reserved for those who have committed dangerous offences and remain a danger to society. Prison shouldn't be a warehouse to keep people warm while the government ignores its responsibility of protecting our most vulnerable citizens, stuck in a cycle that they have no way of escaping.

As the pandemic struck, suddenly news reports were filled with homeless people being moved into hotels, money appearing, as if out of thin air, to put a roof over people's heads. Suddenly, the cash was available, as if all that had been stopping us from housing homeless people before had been the lack of political will. We were all being told to stay home, stay indoors, for the safety of ourselves and the nation. For those with nowhere to go, it seemed the government would finally step in to deal with a homelessness crisis that should never have existed in the first place.

Having survived the winter months on the streets, from March 2020 onwards, London alone placed 1,700 people into these hotels.[6] Yet at exactly the same time, in the six-week period from 23 March 2020 to the end of April 2020, 840 men, 89 women and 85 young adults aged eighteen to twenty-four were released into rough sleeping or other forms of homelessness from prison.[7]

And as the initial first wave of Covid subsided, these hotels quietly closed their doors to our homeless population and returned to their normal business.[8]

The cherry blossoms were just starting to push through when I next saw Cliff. The air was getting warmer. He'd survived another winter. But he was high on spice and still clasped that super-strength can in his shaking hands. The thought of rehabilitation was laughable. For Cliff and the other one in six inmates released homeless, the only thought is survival.

I gave him all my spare change again and as he wandered slowly away from me, I said a silent prayer. *There but for the grace of God, go I.*

I started to go through the gate with as many of my clients as possible, escorting them back out into the community upon release, securing them the support and housing they desperately needed. Going through the gate with an inmate was one of the only tangible ways I could see my work making a difference. But with groups across two prisons – on the detox unit, with the youths and anger management – it wasn't often I had the time to spend the whole day with just one crim. When I did, it had to be with men who at least had a fighting chance. I could never have escorted Cliff. Where would I have taken him? To a doorway or railway arch? Bumping into him on The Out regularly, at least I knew he was still alive. But he wasn't living.

I'd never hear from the ones who made a success of it. Never knew how they were getting on. Whether or not they were staying safe. Once released, silence was usually the only signal I got that they were doing OK. Once, I was asked what success looked like in my line of work.

'The absence of disaster,' I replied seriously.

CHAPTER 14
Time Served – Release

It was still dark outside when I woke up. I rolled over in bed, wondering why the alarm was set so early, then jolted awake, remembering that it was Timms's release day. It was going to be a long one. As I rushed to get ready for work, I knew he'd be going through the rituals of a final day of incarceration. He could be released at 8.30 a.m. or late in the afternoon, but he'd have been up since 6 a.m., too.

It was Friday before the first May bank holiday. Early summer sun warmed the pavement as I made my way to work. In just a few hours, I'd be riding the train in the opposite direction with Timms, escorting him home. The sky was cloudless and there was the promise of a beautiful day. It was going to be a scorcher.

He'd done eighteen months inside for actual bodily harm (ABH) and although most men tried to get recategorised and moved on to do their time in a comfier cat C prison, Timms wanted to stay close to home so his family could keep visiting. He'd fought off transfers to other prisons, sometimes literally. Refusing to move to one of those new-build cat Cs out of the city seemed like madness to most of us, but he'd focused his rehabilitation efforts around his family. They were his motivation and he relied on their visits. So he'd stayed put in our shithole and was now preparing to see out the remaining eighteen months of his sentence in the community,

under the supervision of a probation officer. There were strict
stipulations to his release and if he breached any of them, like
Titch, he'd be recalled straight back to prison.

He was determined to get it right, no chance of using. Get
the first day out set up perfectly so he could just get on with
rebuilding his life. Every day, dozens of men left that place
with the same intention. Around 60,000 inmates returned to
the community every year.[1] Some scored the moment they left,
some made it back to their local area before a relapse. Some
only made it as far as the train station when they were distracted by the unavoidable off-licence. And still, some walked
with their heads high and never looked back. No matter how
many times I went through the gate with an inmate, I never
knew how the day would play out. Some ran, some paused in
the car park feeling the sun on their free face, some cowered
next to me as we walked up the busy main road, fearful of
the fast-moving cars.

Getting the first day out organised was often easier said
than done in a system that was intent on setting crims up
to fail, so we'd worked hard to plan as much as we could.
The first condition of his release was that he had to engage
with drug services. This was obvious. He was on a methadone script and needed someone to prescribe it to him. The
appointment with the community drug team was our priority. If he relapsed on his first weekend out, nothing else would
matter and he'd be back in before I was back to work on
Tuesday. He was expected to go to the chemist every morning
to take the methadone in front of the pharmacist, queuing up
in much the same way he had inside.

Every day of his first few months out would start with this
ritual until he was trusted enough to take a few days' supply
home at a time. Fuck knows what he was ever meant to do
if he got a job. No employer would have given him an hour
off every day to go and score his prescribed opiates from

the pharmacy. Lucky, I suppose, that no one really expected ex-offender addicts to be employable. It was enough for us to have found somewhere for him to live, a community worker who agreed to help with his benefits applications and a drug team ready to assess and prescribe him. Employment was an added luxury neither of us had considered possible.

I'd tried to convince him to apply for a place in rehab, but he'd done his year and a half, built his weight back up and reduced his methadone script. He wanted to go to rehab, but not immediately, not then. He couldn't stand the idea of going straight from custody to three months in a facility in the north of England, away from his family and friends for even longer. I suggested that ninety days was nothing, if it meant he'd be with his family forever after that, but Timms wasn't convinced. He was feeling strong, needed his family more than he needed the rehab. He wanted to go home.

His next condition was to engage with his probation officer and attend his first appointment by 3 p.m. on his day of release. We'd met her once before, when she'd spent the day in the visits' hall doing paperwork for all her latest charges coming close to release. Timms had asked me to come along to the meeting.

'She doesn't like me. I'm going to need your help,' he'd said.

The probation officer had been fine. I gave her a little leeway, as I'd seen the procession of offenders she was meant to be supervising and watched how in turn, over the course of an afternoon, each one had given her another problem to try to deal with. But she was curt and when Timms explained that we might end up being late for the 3 p.m. appointment she was proposing, she cut him off.

I tried to intervene, explaining how slow the prison was to release men in the morning at the moment, but she had her diary open on the desk and I could see she had a nice week of annual leave booked to make the most of the bank holiday. She'd be clocking off at 5 p.m. and would be fuming if it was Timms who held that up in any way.

There were a thousand other things that needed arranging. On his first day out, we needed to start his benefit claim or at least hand the task over to the voluntary support worker who had agreed to help him. While in custody, he'd got himself a sponsor from Narcotics Anonymous who'd want to check on him at some point over the weekend, too. And then there were his children, and his family and all the people who were getting excited for his release. But we couldn't plan for any of that, couldn't fit it into the limited time frame where the methadone and probation officer had to be the priorities.

A Friday release just before the bank holiday meant that time wasn't on our side. Although Timms had had two days knocked off his sentence because prisons don't release at the weekend, it meant that almost all community support services would be closed for the following three days. To have any chance of staying drug-free and free from arrest over the weekend, Timms had the next eight hours to take three trains across London and make both appointments on time.

On his final night in custody, he cleared his cell and packed up the few belongings he owned. He gave away what spare bits of chocolate and toothpaste he had to friends on the wing. He lay awake most of the night and as the light started shining into his cell, he got dressed quietly so as not to disturb his cellmate. He didn't eat his breakfast pack. Too nervous to choke down the child-sized portion of cereal and UHT milk. He left it for his cellmate.

Timms had been quiet in the week before his release, fearing the gate as much as he wanted it. He was curling in on himself, silently trying to build his reserves of willpower for the big day. He'd promised himself that this would be his final last day in prison. He didn't want to ever go through a release day again. The knotted stomach, the bouncing, agitated legs. He wanted out that final time.

We'd spent weeks preparing for this. He'd assured me that he hadn't thought about using, hadn't already relapsed in his head before making it out of the gate, but anything was possible on release day.

And as I arrived at the prison, there was a familiar sight that could've fucked up the whole day before it'd even started. There were four police officers leaning against their car, gossiping idly in the morning sun. Relaxed and happy, content with an easy assignment. They were there to gate-arrest someone. Their job that morning was to let an inmate step out of custody having served his sentence, give him a couple of seconds of freedom, then slap the handcuffs back on for another offence.

The police would argue that they gate-arrest because they don't have the evidence to make an arrest any earlier. But there's also another logic to their approach. If a crim gets charged with another offence while he's serving a sentence, it's likely that the judge will run his convictions concurrently. This means, overall, he'll serve less time than if the sentences were consecutive.

A gate arrest means his convictions can't be stacked up. He'll do a separate stretch for each separate offence. The police can do this to keep him off the streets for longer. It can work, in that it means a prolific offender is kept from committing possible future crimes because he's always banged up in HMP. But it serves to show that the police have no faith in the rehabilitative powers of prison. If they thought prison worked, he'd be rehabilitated after his first sentence. The fact that they're desperate to chuck him back inside to incapacitate him shows how all that taxpayers' money is being wasted time and time again. Sentence after consecutive sentence.

It's always seemed a brutal way of policing to me. The

crim they've come to arrest today has been locked up for God knows how long. There was plenty of time to come into the prison and charge him, take the case to court, even get a conviction. Why wait until his day of release, let him physically step out of the prison, taste the freedom and then snatch it away from him? It felt like fucking with people for the sake of fucking with them. Like someone was enjoying it, wielding this power over another person.

I headed towards the reception, trying to guess if the gate arrest could possibly be for Timms. Surely that probation officer would have given me a warning? We had spoken last night to confirm his appointment today, wouldn't she have told me if there was a new warrant being issued for his arrest? I started to panic. Even if they weren't there for Timms, it could royally fuck up how quickly, or slowly, he'd be released.

The prison reception sits inside the prison walls and is the place where every inmate is processed before entering or leaving. Timms had already been brought down and was waiting in a holding room with the twelve other men being released that day. Fridays were the busiest release day. All of the crims whose sentences finished over the weekend got to leave that day, too. It made going through the gate with Timms more difficult for me. If just one of those other men decided to have a dealer waiting for him or went to the off-licence, it would be hard for Timms to resist. It also made it more dangerous for me. While I'd risk-assessed Timms and felt safe in his company on The Out, I didn't know anything about the twelve other men who might end up catching the train with us back to his home borough.

We had safety procedures in place, just like when I used to work out in the community and visit people like Beverley. I called the office when we left the prison. I checked in with them after an hour, and I called again when we arrived safely at the drug and alcohol team. But in reality, once I was outside with Timms, I was on my own.

The air was tight with nerves. Everyone had gate fever. Everyone was desperate to get their paperwork signed off, their property handed back to them, and be out for the long, sunny weekend. Even those who were terrified of what life held for them on The Out just wanted to get the waiting over with. Timms hadn't received his methadone and there was confusion as to who should bring it down to reception for him. While the crims were bouncing, among the staff there was no sense of urgency. The governor would be needed to sign off each release and he was still in the morning meeting. If there were any problems in the prison that day, it'd be hours before he had the free time to come and sign everyone out.

I entered the holding room, trying to catch Timms's attention over the twelve other men. My heart sank when I saw Deano in the corner fiddling with a dog-end, trying to make a roll-up. I had forgotten it was his release day today too. He beamed at me and I smiled back, but I knew immediately that he was exactly the kind of repeat offender the police would love to gate-arrest. The kind of nuisance to the community who could be chucked back inside for a few more months. I was relieved, knowing for certain that Timms was going home tonight, but I cringed at my own duplicity as I wished Deano luck and escorted Timms into a separate holding cell. Away from the other crims, I pushed a cup of tea across the table to him. He nodded a thanks at me. Watery eyes dulled from too many hours inside that seemed too grateful for the small kindness.

He was trying to hide the tremble in his arms by sitting tightly on his hands but when he reached for the cup I saw the shakes. He cradled his tea gently in cracked grey hands, trying not to spill it. His methadone still hadn't arrived and he was starting to feel the withdrawal already.

The ends of his jumper were frayed, but he didn't have any other clothes to change into. The T-shirt he was wearing when he got arrested was covered in blood and taken as evidence. Because he consistently refused to get on the transfer bus, he'd never made it to enhanced prisoner status, so couldn't ever have his own clothes to wear. I wondered if the sleeves of the prison sweater would roll up over his forearms. He was going to be boiling out there.

Asking Timms how he was feeling was a stupid question, but I said it anyway. We went through our release agreement, the rules we had in place to keep both of us safe while we spent the day in the community together. No drink, no drugs, no aggression. Although he was in for ABH and had fought with the officers over his transfers, his risk to me wasn't too high. He could try to rob me, but apart from the pouch of tobacco I'd started smoking again and a shitty work phone, I hadn't really got much worth taking. Besides, I'd worked with him for six months by then and we'd built the release plan together. I wasn't worried. I felt that I was as safe as I could be in this job.

For the past few months, Timms had only been outside in the fresh air for a maximum of one hour per day. Freedom beckoned. Yet his first day out wasn't going to be relaxed or pleasant.

Inside, Timms worked hard on his substance misuse issues. He was focused on his kids and attended parenting classes, securing extra visits with the children. The drugs had torn him and his family apart enough times in the past. All he had to do was stop using. But if it was that easy, he'd have stopped years ago. It takes hard work, failure and trying over and over again. This time, he had to put everything he'd ever learned into practice on The Out, avoid the patterns of behaviour that had defined his life for the past fifteen years and make a real go of it. That's why I was there, to change the pattern of that first day of release he'd had so many times before.

We didn't secure any housing for him before release. His family had managed to collect his belongings from the flat he'd been living in before his arrest, but his conviction meant he was classed as intentionally homeless. They took his accommodation from him and, once out, he'd again have to go through the bureaucracy of applying for housing that he wasn't even eligible to access.

He was one of the lucky ones, though. Timms had an uncle who'd agreed he could crash on the sofa for the next couple of months until he found his feet. Although his children's mother had visited regularly while he'd been inside, she didn't trust the promises to change that he'd already made a million times. She'd let him visit the kids, but she didn't want him back living with them, risking the relapses and the knocks on the door from social services that she'd had to face in the past.

Still, a sofa at an uncle's house was better than nothing. I knew that most of the men getting out that day had no idea where they'd be spending the night. Like Cliff, most of them didn't have anywhere to go, anyone looking out for them. Those who would have to sleep on the streets tonight were lucky that at least the weather was good. A summer release meant a better chance of survival, but it also meant that there were no emergency cold weather night shelters open to offer safety.

The image of Cliff danced through my thoughts. Waving goodbye to him, knowing that he'd spend the night wandering the streets, unable to secure a bed. Those days lay heavy on me. At least today I could say goodbye to Timms knowing he'd have a front door of a house to close behind him. I'd be with him until five o'clock, but after that, he was on his own until his next community support meeting on Tuesday.

After checking in with the team at my office, I left the prison, dropping off my keys, radio, collecting my backpack from the locker room.

There's a waiting room outside the prison walls. An area for family and friends to loiter before visits begin. I went inside and tucked myself into a corner, smiling kindly at the women and their children. I wondered who was there for the releases and who was waiting to go inside, into the visits' hall, counting down the days until it would be her man who would be walking free.

The police officers came in and used the coffee machine, feeding twenty-pence pieces in one at a time. They chatted loudly, as if they owned the place. The women sneered at them. Gate arrests felt low. A real low blow. They didn't notice or didn't care about the venom being directed at them in dirty looks and sideways glances.

I watched *The Jeremy Kyle Show* distractedly, while always keeping one eye on the gate, looking for signs of movement. The prison gate is a huge metal structure to let the vans through. But for release, the crims are walked over and a small door inside the gate is opened for them.

It was possible that the prison could release all thirteen men at once, but they rarely did. Instead, usually three or four men were escorted out at a time, the releases coming in half-hour waves throughout the morning. The gate arrest meant the process would be even slower, the men being sent out two by two because the police needed to be able to identify their man and get the cuffs on with minimal fuss. I hoped that Timms would be in the first batch but knew that these things never seemed to happen how you wanted them to.

I saw the shift in light and the shadows moved. The gate was opening. One of the women rushed outside, convinced it was her man coming out. I stood too, hurriedly slinging my backpack over my shoulder, and headed towards the gate.

The morbid curiosity of how Deano would behave took over me.

The minute it swung open, Deano and the other con registered what was happening and hesitated on the threshold. Neither of them trusted the police, and both were trying to work out what offence they could have been caught for now. They looked at each other, trying to figure out if they were the unfortunate one, and then stepped forwards together, out into freedom. I watched the police move towards them in unison, unsure whether or not their man was going to try to run. They fanned out, blocking Deano's path, ready for a fight, but in the end he went peacefully.

'Fucking scum,' the woman waiting for her man hissed, tossing her hair and lighting another cigarette.

I made a noise that acknowledged her feelings.

I watched the police car drive away. The woman crushed the cigarette under her heel and we both went back inside, hoping it wouldn't be long before the gate opened again. I called into the office and asked admin to get Deano's file out for me. I needed to write up what'd happened, then prepare a fresh set of paperwork to start all over again with him on Tuesday morning.

Timms finally stepped out at 12.37 p.m. with three other inmates. He blinked against the sun, paused, then slowly walked towards me, smiling. Although Timms was now officially an ex-offender, he didn't look like one as we moved through London back to his home borough. He was in his prison tracksuit and had a see-through bin bag emblazoned with the HMP logo to carry his few belongings.

He moved the bag from shoulder to shoulder as I rang the drug and alcohol team, letting them know we wouldn't be there until 2 p.m. I tried to get hold of his probation officer, but she was on her lunch break. I did the mental maths – the timings weren't adding up and we were going to struggle to fit in those vital appointments before the end of the day.

The drug team promised to be ready to start his assessment the minute he arrived. They knew that we were going to be rushed. For our safety, I'd usually try and wait until the other men left the area, but we didn't have time. Instead, we all walked together to the train station. I kept them all in my peripheral while trying to speed up the pace.

At the station, I left Timms smoking outside while I went to the ticket office. I needed to exchange the voucher the prison had given him for a travel card. Timms could have done this himself, but experience had taught me how frustrating this process could be. The ticket office staff always acted like they'd never seen a prison-issued voucher before, even though dozens of men were released every day and made this journey home. I could barely keep my cool with them, so I saved Timms the hassle and tried to deal with it for him.

They were closed for lunch, anyway. We couldn't wait for them to return at 1 p.m. and I counted on my smooth-talking if we got into any trouble. I knew that having me, an upstanding member of society with him, would protect Timms from ticket inspectors or the transport police or almost any other problem we might encounter.

There were no barriers at the station, so we hopped straight on board. Timms stayed standing, staring out of the window, smiling to himself. Two of the other three men released were on the train too, heading in the same direction as us. They sat in the same carriage but kept a little distance from one another, trying to avoid looking like the menacing crowd of ex-cons that they were.

We switched trains smoothly, the timings working perfectly for once, and were back in the borough before 2 p.m. Only then did we stop for a moment. Timms asked permission to go into the newsagent and I followed him inside. He walked straight past the alcohol and to the fridge at the back, pulling out an ice-cold can of Fanta. I smiled, relieved that he hadn't picked up a beer.

'What do you want, miss?' he asked.

The shopkeeper raised an eyebrow at the 'miss' and clocked the HMP bin bag, but he didn't say anything. Having me next to him gave Timms some protection from the judgement of the public, too.

I'd have loved a can, but I held up my bottle, shook it from side to side.

'I'm all right, cheers. I've got my water.'

He'd saved up a bit while he was inside working a wing cleaning job. The £46 the prison gave him to survive on until he somehow managed to get some more money was topped up with £38 of his own savings. Practically a millionaire. Even though he was now on The Out, it would have been unprofessional to accept anything from him. But more than that, it would have been brutal to spend a quid of his money when he had so little.

That money was meant to last him until his first benefits payment kicked in, but that could take six weeks. I calculated the cost of a travel card and realised that the prison discharge grant wouldn't even cover the travel to and from his appointments at probation and the drug team for the next month.

I felt positive that he'd make the best of it on The Out, but as I watched him count out his money on the counter, I was unsure why I held such optimism. With the best will in the world, the odds were stacked against him.

As the doctor at the drug team assessed Timms, I made a brew in the staffroom of the run-down office and popped into the car park at the back for a cigarette. A group therapy session was on break, the men smoking in the sunshine with their coffees, too. I saw some familiar faces and smiled.

'All right, miss! What you doing here?' hollered a face I knew I knew from inside but couldn't place.

I exchanged pleasantries with the group for a few minutes, asked how their recovery and life on The Out was going, before it was time to scoop Timms back up and chaperone him to the chemist. Timms's methadone hadn't arrived by the time he was allowed to leave the prison, so he needed that fresh prescription he held in his hands desperately.

The pharmacist seemed kind and friendly, but he looked frazzled, desperately trying to prepare the correct doses for all his patients before the long weekend. He kept us waiting for twenty minutes while he served the old dears queuing up for their inhalers and diabetes medication. I spent the first ten minutes pretending to browse the expensive moisturisers and the second ten minutes making phone calls, where I mentioned loudly to colleagues just how rushed we were. The pharmacist didn't notice, or if he did, he didn't care.

Eventually, he handed over a bottle of green liquid. Timms knocked it back quickly, in full view of the judgemental queue. He flashed his tongue and we turned for the door. This first day out wasn't the fun and family-filled one he'd longed for from his cell for months. The first day out, if a crim wanted to stay out, was long and boring and full of assessments and answering the same questions he'd been asked a million times before. He wanted to linger in the sun, wander round the borough and see what'd changed over the past year and a half, but we didn't have the time. It'd be 4 p.m. before we made it to probation. I tried calling his officer again and left a message for her, explaining the situation. Timms had bought a £10 phone top-up from the newsagent and charged his phone while he talked to the doctor. If he'd have been on his own, maybe he'd have called probation himself and explained why he was running so late. I doubt he'd have been believed. It helped that I was there. Other professionals believed me when I spoke. They wouldn't have believed him.

He tried to call his uncle, but there was no answer. He

texted instead, then tried to call his kids' mum. She was at work, though, and rushed him off the phone. Release day always seemed a let-down.

At probation, Timms introduced himself to the receptionist, who asked him immediately why he was late for his appointment. I stepped forwards, official prison lanyard swinging obviously around my neck, and did the talking for him. With no call back from his uncle yet, Timms was winding tighter by the minute and a rude receptionist could be all it took for him to blow. Any sign of aggression, any raised voice, and he'd be fucked. He still had eighteen months on licence in the community. He could be recalled for the smallest infraction.

The receptionist softened as I explained the situation, but her tight lips didn't break into a smile. We were forgiven for our lateness, just about, but it felt like she was taking a mental note of Timms and vowing to keep an eye on his timekeeping in the future. I smiled as winningly as I could, started to make small talk, but she went back to her computer, obviously not wanting to be disturbed by us anymore.

We waited quietly, sitting next to each other as I geared myself up for the goodbye. I never knew what to say, what to do. It's the kind of goodbye where you hope you'll never see the person again, even though you really, really wish them well.

'You going to be all right?' I asked him in a whisper.

His mobile pinged and he smiled.

'Look . . .' Timms held the phone out to me and I read.

The uncle was all ready to pick him up from here in an hour, his bed had been made up and he'd been promised a takeaway that night. I breathed a sigh of relief I didn't realise I'd been holding in.

'All right, then. This is it.' I went to stand.

Timms stood, too. We had spoken to each other every

week for six months and now I hoped I'd never see him again. I held out my hand and he shook it, firmly, looking me square in the eyes.

'Thanks, miss. For real. I couldn't have done it without you,' he said, his voice quiet and serious.

I pumped his hand hard and shook my head.

'Nah, you've got this. I believe you've got this.'

It was a poignant moment and the seriousness of it felt heavy.

'All right, then,' I said again, smiling. 'In the nicest way possible, Timms, I never want to see you again.'

He nodded, made promises he wouldn't be back and I turned towards the afternoon sunshine. I looked up to the sky. It was so beautiful out there that day and the long weekend ahead made it even better. I'd done everything I could.

My biggest success stories are the ones that just fizzle out. Timms went to all appointments with his community support worker for the next six weeks. I rang every Friday and checked on his progress. He'd managed to get his benefits set up and was stable on the script. The probation officer had warmed to him. He was getting on well with his uncle and the living arrangement seemed steady. He was seeing his kids. And then my work with him was done. Case officially closed. I never heard from him again. The best result possible.

Timms's exit from prison was as positive as they come. But the hoops and hurdles, the sheer difficulties of connecting custody to community, mean for the majority, those first few days are a million times harder than they need to be. Going straight is a fucking drag and may just make many think it isn't worth the effort.

He couldn't expect to find work. We pointedly ignored the box on his support plan titled 'employment'. Both of us knew that the benefits and the methadone and the probation officer would take up all of his time. We knew that most employers would look at him the way that shopkeeper did. He may have done his time, but the sentence was never really over.

No, he couldn't work. Not if he had to go down to the pharmacy every day to take his methadone. Not with his record. He couldn't even sign on, couldn't access the benefits that were necessary to bring in a bit of money while he found his feet. That process couldn't be started while wasted hours ticked by in custody. With only his discharge grant in his pocket, Timms was expected to walk away from a life of crime and attend appointments every week he didn't even have the money to travel to. Thank fuck he had that uncle looking out for him. Without him, Timms would have been following Clifford onto the streets or into a crack den.

The uncle put a roof over his head because the local authority had no legal duty to do so. He'd been in prison. Forfeited his right. Punished once more, upon release, for his crime.

The story of Timms was some positivity in the darkness, but just because he somehow cobbled together the willpower and support network to help him through those first unsteady weeks didn't mean the system was working.

Of the twelve other men released with Timms that day, I saw eight of them again. One was begging on the high street. He recognised me. Called me miss. And as usual, I asked the stupid question 'How are you doing?' as I fished in my bag for some spare change. He said he was OK, surviving. I told him about the Narcotics Anonymous meeting that happened around the corner, softly suggested he check it out. He nodded, looking down at the pathetic coins I'd placed in his hand.

'Stay safe,' I offered as I left him to spend a night on the streets.

A second I saw moving fast down the street early one Thursday morning as I smoked out of my flat window. He was on a mission. Out grafting hours before most of us even started thinking about work. I listened to his footsteps as they disappeared into the distance, wondering whether he had a fighting chance of ever leaving this lifestyle behind.

The other six men returned to the establishment. One lasting a week before breaching his licence and got recalled. One staying out for eleven months until he rejoined us inside HMP.

I could only go through the gate with certain inmates because funding was patchy. Through-the-gate support isn't a service the prison or the community have a duty to provide. Instead, the majority of meet-at-the-gates were carried out by volunteers. Alcoholics and Narcotics Anonymous came into establishments, running groups in their own time, giving back to the peer support organisation that once saved their own lives. These men and women were the ones who then loitered at the gate, providing the service that reduced more relapses and reoffending than we could ever measure.

Sometimes, the drugs worker would come along on release day and take the prisoner back out into the community. Most of them weren't funded to carry out this vital service. The individual workers juggled their own caseload, working unpaid overtime to get the rest of their admin finished because they knew that the first day out was where the risk of relapse would be greatest.

An inmate has almost nothing to do to kill time while he's inside. The assessments, paperwork and applications that become urgent as soon as he leaves the prison could have been completed before release. If the law was changed, his benefits could hit his bank account on that very first day, making it possible for him to at least breathe a little easier, be able to afford phone credit and food and a night in a hostel. The lack of continuity of care makes the process immeasurably more difficult than it needs to be. For men trying to escape chaotic lifestyles, this can often prove too much, too hard to navigate, and criminality and drug use win out.

Deano was brought straight back to us after the gate arrest. Crestfallen, defeated and cursing the system. His anger carried him through the first few weeks back in custody. He was dragged down to seg for fighting. But finally, he calmed and started making plans for his next release.

'Will you go through the gate with me, miss?' he asked one day.

I'd have loved to have said yes. But the truth was, funding only covered me to do that first day out with crims from one borough. The cons that fell under any other local authority would have to make their own way without me. I tried to explain to Deano that funding wouldn't stretch to support him on release day. He stared at me with that blank expression on his face.

Eventually, he said, 'That's fucking stupid.'

Yes, it is.

CHAPTER 15

Permission to Leave the Net? – Suicide

I walked up to the key cabinet and my stomach lurched. The 'death in custody' (DIC) notice was printed on A4 in black and white. There were smear marks from where the page had been photocopied multiple times so it could be stuck to the front of every cabinet. My eyes darted back and forth along the words, searching out the name. I beat my fist so hard into the wall that the skin grazed. Leaning my head back, breathing deeply, trying to stop the tears coming. No, no, no.

The room was empty. I was early for work and alone. I allowed the noiseless tears to fall. I pulled my head back to continue reading to the bottom of the DIC notice. He'd been found in his cell on Sunday. A ligature. I threw my fist into the wall again. This time, it bled.

I'd been able to hold it together through all the violence, the overdoses, the stabbings and the assaults; cancelled groups, parole knock-backs, life sentences and failures. This was too much. I'd never wanted to turn and run so much in my life. I'd never wanted to use drugs to block out the thoughts and feelings as much as I did in that moment. I'd never wanted to hurt someone, or hurt myself, as badly as I did when I learned from a sheet of paper pinned to the key cabinet that he was dead.

The work I did was just a temporary fix. The system had

failed. I had failed. Let the whole place burn to the ground, let them riot and rebel. Let them fight and hurt each other and hurt themselves until the politicians finally open their eyes. In that moment, I no longer believed in the idea of reforming the prison estate. It had sunk too low. It needed to be torn down.

It was 7.30 a.m. No one else would be in work for another hour. His electronic file would now be sealed and anyone who tried to access it would be questioned when the case went to court. I sat in the office in silence, staring at the blank screen of my computer desperately trying to figure out what it was I could have missed. What sign did he give me that he wanted to die? I'd spent Thursday with him, he'd been excited and happy about his upcoming release.

He told me he'd spoken to his family that day and they were planning to come up and visit before he got out. He'd been worried about some of his belongings that he'd left at a hostel. With the help of the priest, we'd pulled in some favours with community workers and had found out that all his things were being kept safely at the local church.

He wasn't going to kill himself that Thursday. He didn't display a single sign or symptom or signal that had given me cause to worry. I thought back to the medical phrases, the professional vocabulary I'd learned to describe the demeanour of inmates: he'd been engaged and engaging, well-kempt, focused, neither distracted nor perplexed. He didn't appear to be responding to auditory or visual hallucinations. He'd verbalised strong future planning. And now he was dead.

Overwhelmed by the sadness, in the back of my mind I was praying that I'd written up my notes from that final day with him, because I knew I was going to be facing Coroner's Court. I knew if I hadn't written all of this down in the rush of a busy day, I'd be fucked.

I sat staring at the blank screen, desperate to be able to scan through his file and notes to see just what could have happened in those few days between him being excited and hopeful for the future and having been found hanging, alone.

The next few hours were a blur. My manager arrived and granted me access to the file. I had written everything up. Every group he'd attended, every one-to-one. Our plans for his release. My notes had been the last entry until the hurried shorthand of vital signs and chest compressions and desperate attempts at resuscitation that were scrawled down on Sunday. No medical member of staff had noted contact with him since the Thursday. Then he was dead. None of the records explained what happened. No one could tell me. He'd left no note.

I was briefed by my manager that I'd be assigned legal advice and that I'd get support through the inquest. I drank tea. I couldn't face going out onto the landings. I ran my hands through my hair in a desperate attempt to calm and organise my thoughts. I read and re-read every single note I'd made on his file in all the time I'd known him. I looked at all that work that had come to nothing. Because now he was dead. He was the first man I'd worked with to die by suicide.

There were 354 DICs in 2016. Three of those deaths were homicides. A hundred and twenty were suicides, the highest figure since records began in 1978, and twelve people who died by suicide were under twenty-four years old. Deaths were more likely to happen in overcrowded establishments and more likely if the inmate was on remand or had been recalled to prison from licence.[1] Between June 2013 and September 2016, seventy-nine deaths were linked to the use of spice; fifty-eight of these were self-inflicted.[2] A death from natural causes is a tragedy, a suicide is a travesty and a murder, inside a prison, is fucking inexcusable.

I had to face the crims and as I walked back onto the landing a day later, there was an eeriness in the quiet. I rapped gently on each of their cell doors.

'Group's on, guys. Get a brew, let's go,' I quietly told them.

I got to the end of the landing and hovered outside his now empty, sealed cell. It would only be a day or two before the overcrowded prison would have to put someone into his pad again but, for now at least, it remained unoccupied.

On the way to the classroom, I went to speak to the officers, but none of them could give any answers, either. No one would tell me what happened on Sunday – or no one knew exactly what had tipped him over the edge. This Tuesday morning, the wings were busier than normal. The rumours of short staffing over the weekend seemed to be true, because all of a sudden there was a hell of a lot of overtime on the wing. Everyone would be getting exercise and association this week at least, until the initial investigation had been completed. Then it would be back to business as usual and everyone would pretend they were shocked when someone else killed themselves the following month. The prison knew the inquiries that would be made after a DIC and knew that staffing levels would be questioned. Staffing shortages that were a direct result of government cuts.

The guys filed in one by one – no small talk, just handshakes and a few pats on the back. They were all staring, looking at me to make it better, make it right again. I'd stayed awake for hours the night before planning how to talk about this death that would impact us all. But as we sat there looking at each other, I was lost for words.

I shakily started the check-in.

'I feel sad. I feel confused. I feel angry. Today, group is going to be about giving each and every one of you the chance to speak about how you feel and then making sure you're all OK before we go back to the landing. Today, I won't finish this group until I know you've offloaded these emotions and you're safe and well enough to go back behind your doors. Does everyone understand?'

'Yes, miss,' they said in unison.

We talked for hours. We talked about him. They talked about how he'd started smashing up his cell early on the Sunday and how he'd demanded medication. They talked about how they'd had almost constant bang-up all weekend. Too few staff had come into work. There had been almost no time out of cell.

I thought about it for a long time afterwards. What could have driven him to take his own life? I was sure that he hadn't meant to – he hadn't even left a note. But then I thought of him in that cell alone, counting hours and days and slowly deteriorating behind the door. How scared he must have been. How low he must have felt. We are barbaric. We allowed this to happen. I allowed this to happen. I'd worked to keep my crims just about sane enough to not kill themselves or anyone else. And I hadn't even managed that.

Then there was Coroner's Court to contend with. As this had been a death in custody, a jury was summoned. I continued to work until the court date and then was called to the stand. My decision-making was questioned and I felt attacked in front of the jurors. None of them had any idea of the complete chaos behind the walls. They trusted that prisons were working, that they were safe. They didn't know that we were trying to keep men alive and communities protected with no resources, with no staff, just good luck and good intentions. The austerity cuts that decimated mental health and substance misuse services both inside and outside the prison for a decade were never called into question. Instead we were challenged, the individual staff, and the efforts we'd made. No amount of dedication or hard work could ever counteract this lack of resources, the unsanitary conditions and the acceptance that anything short of a complete psychotic episode would have to be dealt with on the wings.

The jury didn't know, nor were they ever told, that the

prison had been on progressively tighter and tighter lock-downs, bang-up a near constant throughout the summer months as staffing levels dropped further and violence esca-lated. They didn't hear that things were so bad that the Prison Officers' Association was about to go on strike, stating that 'the continued surge in violence and unprecedented levels of suicide and acts of self-harm, coupled with the recent (alleged) murder and escapes, demonstrate that the service is in meltdown'.[3] And that was just in my establishment. The whole estate was going crazy.

They didn't know that spice was being flown over the walls by drones night after night or posted in on soaked paper. They didn't know that inmates were using more and more to try to deal with the bang-up. They didn't know it was causing the healthcare team to race up and down landings four times a day saving life after life after life.

They didn't know that the staff toilets had blocked and flooded my whole classroom in human excrement the week before. They didn't know that instead of having our group session, the cons were tasked with mopping up shit. It was a poignant metaphor.

They didn't know that coming to prison had made him intentionally homeless in the eyes of the local authority and, for all of his efforts to change, his future remained uncertain, his release a terrifying prospect.

They didn't know that the government's policies of pri-vatisation and mass incarceration further overcrowded an estate that's been bursting for decades. They didn't know that the buildings we worked in, the buildings we tried to keep men alive in, were infested with rats and cockroaches. They didn't know that the government was well aware of the data that shows prison doesn't work and yet they still throw non-violent people, or innocent people, or addicted people, or mentally unwell people, to rot on 23-hour bang-up.

I went back to work. The radio on my hip crackled every hour with emergency call signs: code red would be followed by code blue followed by 'all available officers' followed by the order for all officers to 'stand fast' immediately and conduct a 'roll count' of all the inmates. The wings were jumping.

I'd promised these men that however many times they slipped up, I'd still be there. I'd promised that I'd be a constant in their lives, never judging them no matter how many times they fucked up. I'd spent years building trust with them, showing them that no matter how many times they tested the boundaries, I'd never condemn them. But I couldn't bear witness to the horror any more. My job had been to support these men to thrive. In this environment, I'd failed at even keeping them alive. Mickey was dead. I had nothing left to give.

I hung up my keys, held the radio to my mouth and asked for the last time, 'Permission to leave the net?'

CHAPTER 16

A Change Is Gonna Come . . .

My final days inside were marred by constant bang-up. I said goodbye to the men I worked with through locked doors. The situation hasn't improved since.

The Prison Officers' Association went on strike in November 2016, declaring the estate in 'meltdown'. Their action was deemed 'unlawful' and all staff were ordered to go back to work. A situation that would have been darkly comical, if it wasn't so serious. The officers all law-breakers too, now.[1] Justice Secretary Liz Truss branded the actions of staff and the association 'unnecessary and unlawful'. She went on to say that the strike would make prisons 'more dangerous', as if those involved were having a toddler tantrum rather than trying to highlight quite how low our prisons have sunk.[2]

HMP Birmingham started rioting in December 2016 and officers from all over the country were hauled to the Midlands as 500 inmates took control of four landings. The riot was filmed on mobile phones, the news was awash with high and drunk inmates dancing around in seized riot gear, tearing the place apart. The subsequent inquiry reported that 'we formed the view that staff had, over the preceding year and . . . the preceding few months, become worn down by the chronic staffing shortages at HMP Birmingham, caused by a combination of high levels of sickness, attrition and disorganised deployment'.[3]

Tensions in HMP Swaleside also blew in December 2016, then HMP The Mount in Hertfordshire joined the rioting in the summer of 2017.[5] Shortly afterwards, Birmingham went off again.

The government scrambled to reverse the staff cuts that lit the fuse on the powder keg of our prisons and £100 million was spent recruiting 2,500 new officers.[6] But the damage had been done. Staffing levels remained low and the experience of officers on the landing decreased. By March 2017, the proportion of prison officers with two years' service or less was 24 per cent.[7] The new officers were leaving as quickly as they could be recruited.

The number of self-inflicted deaths was brought down from 120 in 2016 to eighty by the end of 2019, but self-injury increased again to a record high of 63,328 incidents, with more people self-harming than ever before.[8,9]

Assaults on staff and inmates continued to hit record-breaking levels until they showed a slight decrease in 2019. Perhaps we can celebrate only 32,669 incidents and 9,995 assaults on staff.[10]

Then, suddenly in March 2020, we were all told to stay home, stay behind our walls, stay in lockdown. Comparing our own experience to being in prison would be naive and insulting. We still had access to the internet, were able to go outside for exercise. We continued to engage in work from home, giving ourselves purpose and meaning. For all the difficulties of home-schooling, we were able to maintain contact with our children. Most of us weren't locked in with a violent housemate. We weren't confined to an 8ft x 12ft cage. We had access to showers and soap. We were able to manage our own hygiene and maintain social distancing to keep ourselves safe.

In HMP Coldingley in Surrey, nearly 400 men live without any in-cell sanitation.[11] They're still, in 2021, slopping out. In the middle of a global pandemic. The cruelty of these conditions could never be likened to our own luxurious bang-up and comparisons risk diminishing the horror of a prison system under quarantine regime.

But the pandemic did highlight how quickly mental health can suffer when our lives are turned inside out, when we become socially isolated. There's growing concern over the psychological impact of quarantine with post-traumatic stress, anxiety, obsessive-compulsive behaviour and insomnia all likely outcomes for a significant minority of us.[12]

Just like the crims, on The Out, we turned to substances to manage the lockdown and the toll it took, with 21 per cent of people surveyed reporting drinking more during lockdown than ever before.[13]

No, lockdown was nothing like being incarcerated. Sure, it gave a sneak peek of how substance misuse issues or mental health problems could easily manifest for any one of us. It didn't, however, give us any notion of the 23-hour bang-up that's now normal behind the walls. The imprisonment within a prison. It didn't allow us any understanding of having no contact with other people, of not being able to engage in therapeutic groups or education or employment, not even over Zoom. It didn't allow us to understand the fear of feeling like a sitting duck, waiting for Covid to strike, unable to manage our own hygiene, unable to distance from the man snoring on the bunk below.

Thankfully, the Covid pandemic brought with it the promise of a reduction of the overcrowding by releasing non-violent offenders. But while plenty of other countries in the world managed to do this successfully,[14] in the UK we fucked it up, released a couple of the wrong people and then pulled the scheme. After only 275 prisoners were released, the plan was quietly shelved.[15]

We had the real opportunity to reduce the problems of

overcrowding, the problems of a prison estate full of non-violent, drug-related offenders. Instead, court backlogs meant that remand prisoners, the innocent until proven guilty, now faced an even longer wait before they got their day in court.[16]

Years earlier, following Strangeways and the biggest prison riot in English history, Lord Woolf reported that overcrowding was 'a cancer eating at the ability of the prison service to deliver' effective education, tackle offending behaviour and prepare prisoners for life on the outside.[17] Nothing has been learned in the decades after Strangeways, which left 194 injured and two dead.[18]

Our attempt to house the homeless in hotels during the pandemic was another sign that sensible policies could trump rhetoric when a global crisis forced the government's hand. However, over 1,000 prisoners were still released homeless in the six weeks when the rest of the country first entered lockdown.[19] Meanwhile, on The Out, 70,000 households found themselves newly homeless in the first year of the pandemic.[20]

We had the opportunity, and we still have the opportunity, beyond the pandemic to really consider our approach to crime, punishment and incarceration. What we're doing now isn't working. We have the most expensive prison bill in Europe and our reoffending rate, only twelve months after release, is 48 per cent.[21]

It's easy to turn a blind eye to horror if it's hidden. My hope is that hearing the human stories of the men I worked with will mean we can no longer look away. We're all victims of a system that runs sex offender treatment programmes that lead to more recidivism. Longer sentences that don't reduce crime. Short sentences that actually increase offending.

No one benefits when we criminalise the addicted, spending ten times more on incarcerating them than treatment would ever cost. Or when we allow prisons to operate for profit, where the owners and shareholders actively benefit from moving along problem prisoners rather than rehabilitating.

We disrespect both cons and screws when there's no psychological input for mental health issues. Inmates display behaviours like cutting, swallowing bleach, tying nooses, headbanging. Then we have staff, who aren't trained in mental health, trying to manage this behaviour with no clinical supervision or support.

We, the state, fail in our duty when one in four of our prison population has been in care. Then we fail again when we allow a system riddled with institutional racism to continue to function.[22]

We mustn't look away from the barbaric IPP sentences that were outlawed in 2012, still impacting the lives of inmates. Or the reality that remand prisoners are now waiting eight months in prison before getting to trial.[23] Our disgust should be palpable when human beings are released to spend the night on the streets. We should be horrified that the police are so cynical of the rehabilitative powers of prison that they gate-arrest. Then we have suicide. So much suicide.

Reforming and rebuilding the whole prison estate won't be easy and it won't be cheap. There will be huge spending needed initially to construct buildings fit for purpose and give the staff the training and support they require. Yet this is an investment we must make. The long-term savings, the long-term benefits to society, will repay the money spent tenfold.

Our drug-addicted should be diverted to rehabilitation facilities. The reduction in reoffending would quickly offset any initial cost.

Those with mental health issues should be treated in hospitals and secure settings where intensive psychological and psychiatric support is provided. Just like Norway, we need to shift our thinking radically if we're to make our society safer and fairer for all. We have a duty to fight to end the mass incarceration of the mentally unwell and the addicted.

We must reform our community services, so prison isn't the only option during the winter months for those sleeping rough. We must pour money into our social care system, bring back the Sure Start model and then keep spending, to haul the 4.3 million children in our country out of poverty.[24] We must give community children and family teams the funding and resources needed to do their jobs.

We must only remand people to custody in the most high-risk circumstances. Locking up the innocent shouldn't be seen as the norm. This could be any one of us one day. We must refuse to accept the notion that putting remand prisoners on wings with convicted inmates is ever appropriate.

We must utilise community orders, the kind that actually reduce crime compared to incarceration, for petty and non-violent offenders. They're cheaper and more effective than prison. Not using these sentences is insanity.

Once we've removed those who require substance misuse support, mental health support, the majority of the remand population and those with non-violent convictions, we'll have more than halved the prison population in an instant.

Yet there are thousands for whom prison is still necessary at the moment. For these dangerous and high-risk offenders, we should transfer every single one of them out of the old Victorians and into buildings fit for purpose. Buildings where showers and toilets aren't seen as a luxury. Into cells that don't have to be shared.

We flood the wings with education specialists, learning disability specialists, therapists and psychologists. Then we provide proper training, funding and wages to the men and women whose job it is to keep them locked in and alive. We don't allow a single officer to go into a workplace filled with vermin and cockroaches. We provide clinical and psychological support for our staff. We train them in mental health, we give them appropriate supervision to manage the horror they face on a daily basis. We recognise and thank them for the work they do. We don't cut their numbers just because the prison population has reduced. We give them the proper resources and staff numbers to do the job safely and effectively.

This may all seem like an impossible dream, but our Scandinavian counterparts have done it successfully. Staff turnover is minimal, they rarely suffer assaults or staff sickness owing to trauma and stress. The cost saving of having a stable, healthy workforce shouldn't be ignored.

And finally, once staff are trained and supported, working in clean and sanitary buildings, we start the long process of rehabilitation of people with criminal convictions. We provide meaningful work and education opportunities, allowing our inmates to build their CVs ready for the outside world. We ensure a continuity of care from the inside out, creating a statutory duty that anyone released from prison should be housed and receive intensive support during their first few months back in the community. We run community services that link up with the prison and remain open every day of the week. We change legislation so it's possible to arrange all the paperwork and benefit claims while awaiting release. We no longer accept a revolving door of offending behaviour and we investigate what failed every single time an inmate returns to custody.

Norway spends generously on rehabilitation within its prisons, but this is counterbalanced by having one of the lowest recidivism rates in the world. Not only does this make the country one of the safest, but it also means the taxpayer doesn't foot the bill for the incarceration of a constantly reoffending prison population. The rehabilitated Norwegian inmates go on to secure employment and financially contribute to society too, creating more wealth across the whole country.

The need for a new approach isn't an attempt to ignore the very real damage these people have done to society. They've caused untold trauma through the crimes they've committed. They must, and should, take responsibility for the pain they've inflicted on individuals and communities. Yet we must try to step back and look unemotionally at the data: punitive punishment of offenders doesn't reduce crime. It may make us feel better in the moment, but it doesn't make society safer.

There are the statistics and the data, and then there are the people. The stories I've shared, the men I've introduced you to, weren't born bad. They were built and shaped by our shared society. They're more than their crimes, they're better than their worst behaviours. So, the next time you read that prison is a holiday camp, remember Taylor begging for a toilet roll. Or when someone says that released crims don't deserve a roof over their heads, know that Cliff used to be one of 'Our Boys' and is spending tonight trying to survive on the streets. When the latest swaggering politician spouts a sound bite about building more prisons, remember Callum, an innocent man, and Titch, who'd already served his time. Then know that these are the people who will fill those new wings.

I want you to remember the abuse and trauma and neglect that Jimmy and Kai and Jamal faced and how Smithy would have received psychological support, if only he'd been imprisoned in Norway. I want you to remember how Shaun found some mad levels of superhuman strength to kick the drugs from inside prison and know that he did it in spite of his sentence, never because of it. And I want you to remember the deaths. The desperation of Mickey. The tears I cried.

And when you hear the lie, repeated so often that it's seen as fact, that prison works, remember Deano, his bagels and his blank stare when I asked him what he was in for.

Prison is made up of tens of thousands of people like them. Like us. And we must do our best to avoid reverting to our own worst tendencies of revenge and retribution, even when in the midst of the suffering caused by offenders. If we're able to check the data rationally, then check our humanity, we know that there's no option but a complete overhaul of our system of incarceration.

We'll need to support difficult, politically unpopular decisions to make our world a safer, kinder place. We must show courage. We must show compassion. We must commit to systemic change. We must be firm in our resolve to believe in the good in people. Because to refuse to do so would be criminal.

APPENDIX

What You Can Do

- Subscribe to *Inside Time*, the national prison newspaper. It gives an honest look, from the inmate's point of view, of current conditions and issues behind the walls. insidetime.org
- Donate to the Samaritans, who train up inmates as listeners and save more lives than we could count every single year. samaritans.org/how-we-can-help/prisons/
- The Howard League for Penal Reform often hosts events and panel discussions on some of the topics raised. Sign up on their website at howardleague.org/
- If you're an employer, actively promote that you'd like to receive applications from ex-prisoners. Reach out to your local establishment and see how you can link up with men and women preparing for release. Timpson, the shoe repair and locksmith retailer, do this brilliantly, as does Combat2Coffee. Check out their work at timpson-group.co.uk/timpson-foundation/ex-offenders/ and at www.combat2coffee.co.uk/ and see if you can support them.
- Just give some money to a homeless person, without judgement. You're not Henry VIII – there aren't 'worthy' and 'unworthy' poor. There are just people sleeping

rough who can choose to spend your change in the way that aids their survival in that moment.

- Search for meet-at-the-gate volunteering opportunities in your area. Get yourself signed up to visit the individual in custody and then go through the gate with him or her on their first day back out into the community.
- Volunteer with The Shannon Trust, an organisation that goes behind the walls and supports people in prison to learn to read. shannontrust.org.uk/about-us/
- Contact your local MP to challenge the continued use of IPP sentences to keep inmates beyond their tariffs. parliament.uk/get-involved/contact-an-mp-or-lord/contact-your-mp/
- Then contact your MP again to complain about the increased amount of time innocent remand prisoners can be kept without trial.
- And contact your MP again to demand to know why all Lammy's recommendations to stop institutional racism haven't been implemented yet . . .
- And one more time, to ask why profits are being made by their pals in business from a prison system that fails on every metric.
- Realise that any social justice issue that's a problem in our community is probably amplified in prison. Don't forget these men, women and children in your campaigning for a fairer society on The Out.

ENDNOTES

1. What Are You in For?

1. Ministry of Justice, 'Offender management statistics quarterly: October to December 2019 and annual 2019', updated 8 June 2021. Available at: https://www.gov.uk/government/statistics/offender-management-statistics-quarterly-october-to-december-2019/offender-management-statistics-quarterly-october-to-december-2019-and-annual-2019 [accessed: 08.11.21]

2. Prison Reform Trust, 'Prison: the facts', summer 2019, p. 3. Available at: http://www.prisonreformtrust.org.uk/Portals/0/Documents/Bromley%20Briefings/Prison%20the%20facts%20Summer%202019.pdf [accessed: 08.11.21]

3. Ministry of Justice, '2013 Compendium of re-offending statistics and analysis',11 July 2012. Available at: https://assets.publishing.service.gov.uk/government/uploads/system/uploads/attachment_data/file/278133/compendium-reoffending-stats-2013.pdf [accessed: 08.11.21]

4. Ibid.

5. Prison Reform Trust, 'Prison: the facts', p. 4.

6. Ministry of Justice, 'Offender Management Statistics Bulletin, England and Wales, Quarterly: October to December 2020'. Available at: https://www.gov.uk/government/statistics/offender-management-statistics-quarterly-october-to-december-2020/offender-management-statistics-quarterly-october-to-december-2020-and-annual-2020--2 [accessed: 10.12.21]

7. Prison Reform Trust, 'Prison: the facts', p. 2.

8. Ibid.

9. Dr K. Edgar et al., Prison Reform Trust, 'No life, no freedom, no future: The experiences of prisoners recalled under the sentence of Imprisonment

for Public Protection', 2020. Available at: http://www.prisonreformtrust. org.uk/Portals/0/Documents/no%20freedom_final_web.pdf [accessed: 09.12.21]

10. Ibid.

11. National Audit Office, 'NAO Briefing for the House of Commons Justice Committee, February 2021: Comparing International Criminal Justice Systems', March 2012. Available at: https://www.nao.org.uk/ wp-content/uploads/2012/03/NAO_Briefing_Comparing_International_ Criminal_Justice.pdf [accessed: 08.11.21]

12. Dr N. Loucks, 'No One Knows: offenders with learning difficulties and learning disabilities', Prison Reform Trust, 2007. Available at: http:// www.prisonreformtrust.org.uk/uploads/documents/noknl.pdf [accessed: 08.11.21]

13. Prison Reform Trust, 'What we do: Projects & Research – Race'. Available at: http://www.prisonreformtrust.org.uk/WhatWeDo/Projects-research/Race [accessed: 08.11.21]

14. Shelter, 'This is England: A picture of homelessness in 2019, the numbers behind the story', 17 December 2019. Available at: https:// assets.ctfassets.net/6sxvmndnpnos/1QzOPPJcoPD2R5OzhUNJUo/ cbe3cco28eaed31d333645d892006b3c/This_is_England_A_picture_of_ homelessness_in_2019.pdf [accessed: 08.11.21]; J. Elgot, 'Thousands of ex-prisoners likely to be sleeping rough', *Guardian*, 13 August 2018. Available at: https://www.theguardian.com/society/2018/aug/13/thou-sands-of-ex-prisoners-likely-to-be-sleeping-rough [accessed 08.11.21]

15. See, for example, Children in Poverty Action Group, 'Child Poverty Facts and Figures', updated March 2021. Available at: https://cpag.org. uk/child-poverty/child-poverty-facts-and-figures [accessed: 08.11.21]

2. Doing Time – The History of Prisons

1. 'England and Wales spend more on prisons than all of Europe except Russia', *Independent*, 8 April 2021. Available at: https://www.indepen-dent.co.uk/news/uk/home-news/prison-spending-england-wales-eu-rope-russia-b1828396.html [accessed: 08.11.21]

2. Ministry of Justice, 'Economic and social costs of reoffending – Ana-lytical report', 2019. Available at: https://assets.publishing.service.gov. uk/government/uploads/system/uploads/attachment_data/file/814650/ economic-social-costs-reoffending.pdf [accessed 08.11.21]

3. 'One in seven prisons in England and Wales of "serious concern"', *BBC News*, 25 July 2019. Available at: https://www.bbc.com/news/

uk-49110327 [accessed 08.11.21]

4. F. Zhengyuan, *Autocratic Tradition and Chinese Politics* (Cambridge [England]; New York: Cambridge University Press, 1993).

5. M. Wood, 'Anglo-Saxon Law and Order', BBC History, 18 September 2014. Available at: http://www.bbc.co.uk/history/trail/conquest/wessex_kings/anglosaxon_law_05.shtml [accessed: 08.11.21]

6. H. Meyers (1950), 'Revisions of the Criminal Code of Japan During the Occupation', *Washington Law Review*, vol. 25, p. 105. Available at: https://digitalcommons.law.uw.edu/wlr/vol25/iss1/9 [accessed: 29.11.21]

7. D. Leatherdale, 'Trial by ordeal: When fire and water determined guilt', *BBC News*, 9 February 2019. Available at: https://www.bbc.co.uk/news/uk-45799443 [accessed: 08.11.21]

8. Ibid.

9. J. Fishman (2005), 'Encouraging Charity in a Time of Crisis: The Poor Laws and the Statute of Charitable Uses of 1601', SSRN, p. 6. Available at: https://ssrn.com/abstract=868394 [accessed: 29.11.21]

10. Crime and Disorder Act 1998. Part II Criminal Law – Racially or religiously aggravated offences: England and Wales. Available at: https://www.legislation.gov.uk/ukpga/1998/37/contents [accessed: 08.11.21]

11. Sexual Offences Act 2003, Part 1 Sexual Offences – Preparatory Offences, Section 61. Available at: https://www.legislation.gov.uk/ukpga/2003/42/contents [accessed: 08.11.21]

12. Ministry of Justice, 'Costs per place and costs per prisoner by individual prison', 29 October 2020. Available at: https://assets.publishing.service.gov.uk/government/uploads/system/uploads/attachment_data/file/929417/costs-prison-place-costs-prisoner-2019-2020-summary.pdf [accessed: 08.11.21]

13. J. Bentham et al., *The rationale of punishment* (London: R. Heward, 1830).

14. National Justice Museum, 'The "Bloody Code"?', 29 July 2019. Available at: https://www.nationaljusticemuseum.org.uk/museum/news/what-was-the-bloody-code [accessed: 08.11.21]

15. J.J. Tobias, *Crime and industrial society in the nineteenth century* (Harmondsworth: Penguin, 1967).

16. W.A. Coffey, *Inside Out, or an Interior View of the New-York State Prison (1823)* (New York: Kessinger Publishing, 2010), p. 69.

17. Ibid.

18. Great Britain and Gladstone, H.J.G., 'Departmental Committee on Prisons, 1895: The "Gladstone Committee" – report and minutes ...'

(London: H.M.S.O, 1895).

19. The Howard League for Penal Reform, 'History of the penal system', 8 April 2016. Available at: https://howardleague.org/history-of-the-penal-system/ [accessed: 09.11.21]

20. G. Sturge, 'UK Prison Population Statistics', House of Commons Library, 29 October 2021. Available at: https://researchbriefings.files.parliament.uk/documents/SN04334/SN04334.pdf p. 7 [accessed: 09.11.21]

21. J.B. Knowles, *The Abolition of the Death Penalty in the United Kingdom: How It Happened and Why It Still Matters* (London: The Death Penalty Project, 2015), p. 21. Available at: https://www.deathpenaltyproject.org/wp-content/uploads/2017/12/DPP-50-Years-on-pp1-68-1.pdf [accessed: 09.11.21]

22. Ministry of Justice, 'Prison population figures: 2019', updated 10 January 2020. Available at: https://www.gov.uk/government/statistics/prison-population-figures-2019 [accessed: 09.11.21]

23. Knowles, *The Abolition of the Death Penalty in the United Kingdom*, p. 21.

24. V. Bailey, *The Rise and Fall of the Rehabilitative Ideal, 1895–1970* (London; New York: Routledge, Taylor & Francis Group, 2019); The National Archives, 'White Paper on Penal Reform; Penal Practice in a Changing Society – Aspects of Future Development (England and Wales)', 1958, p.13. Available at: https://www.butlertrust.org.uk/wp-content/uploads/2015/07/RAB-white-paper-1959.pdf [accessed 09.11.21]

25. For example, see The May Inquiry, 'Prison Services: The May Report', 4 December 1979, vol. 403, cc624–79. Available at: https://api.parliament.uk/historic-hansard/lords/1979/dec/04/prison-services-the-may-report [accessed: 09.11.21]

26. Clinks, 'Supporting positive relationships between prisoners and their families', 1 June 2016. Available at: https://www.clinks.org/publication/supporting-positive-relationships-between-prisoners-and-their-families [accessed: 09.11.21]

27. I. Drury, 'Prisons are accused of running "holiday camps" after report reveals young inmates are allowed to make Skype calls to friends and family', *Mail Online*, 20 February 2018. Available at: https://www.dailymail.co.uk/news/article-5410821/Prisons-accused-running-holiday-camps-inmates.html [accessed: 09.11.21]

28. A. Selby, '"Holiday camp" prison with most escapees in UK lets lags out for weekly fun-run', *Mirror*, 14 September 2019. Available at: https://www.mirror.co.uk/news/uk-news/holiday-camp-prison-most-

escapees-20063017 [accessed: 09.11.21]

29. S. Williams and T. Airey, 'Strangeways riot: Ex-inmates recall siege, 25 years on', *BBC Inside Out North West*, 23 March 2015. Available at: https://www.bbc.com/news/uk-england-manchester-31750112 [accessed: 09.11.21]

30. J. Weightman, Independent Monitoring Boards, '"Slopping Out?" A report on the lack of in-cell sanitation in Her Majesty's Prisons in England and Wales', August 2010. Available at: https://www.justice.gov. uk/downloads/prison-probation-inspection-monitoring/In-Cell_Sanitation_Report_V2_Aug_10.pdf [accessed: 09.11.21]

31. M. Bulman, 'Prisoners disposing of human waste via cell windows due to "degrading" sanitation system, finds report', *Independent*, 26 September 2019. Available at: https://www.independent.co.uk/news/uk/home-news/prisoners-forced-dispose-human-waste-cell-windows-finds-report-a9120176.html [accessed: 09.11.21]

32. Nelson Mandela, quoted by The United Nations. Available at: https://www.un.org/en/events/mandeladay/mandela_rules.shtml   [accessed: 09.11.21]

33. Prison Reform Trust, 'Prison: the facts', summer 2019. Available at: http://www.prisonreformtrust.org.uk/Portals/0/Documents/Bromley%20Briefings/Prison%20the%20facts%20Summer%202019.pdf [accessed: 08.11.21]

34. J. Grierson, 'Longer sentences will not cut crime, say prison experts', *Guardian*, 27 January 2020. Available at: https://www.theguardian.com/society/2020/jan/27/prison-experts-longer-sentences-will-not-cut-crime [accessed: 09.11.21]

35. Ministry of Justice, 'Economic and social costs of reoffending'.

36. R. Davies, 'G4S fined £44m by Serious Fraud Office over electronic tagging', *Guardian*, 10 July 2020. Available at: https://www.theguardian.com/business/2020/jul/10/g4s-fined-44m-by-serious-office-over-electronic-tagging [accessed: 09.11.21]

37. 'Serco fined £22.9m over electronic tagging scandal', *Guardian*, 3 July 2019. Available at: https://www.theguardian.com/business/2019/jul/03/serco-fined-229m-over-electronic-tagging-scandal   [accessed: 09.11.21]

38. Ministry of Justice, 'Prison population figures: 2019: Latest prison population figures for 2019', 10 January 2020. Available at: https://www.gov.uk/government/statistics/prison-population-figures-2019 [accessed: 09.11.21]

39. Prison Reform Trust, 'Private Punishment: Who Profits?', January 2005. Available at: http://www.prisonreformtrust.org.uk/portals/o/documents/private%20punishment%20who%20profits.pdf [accessed: 09.11.21]

40. N. Cowen, Civitas Crime, 'Comparisons of Crime in OECD Countries', 2010, updated by N. Williams, 2012. Available at: https://www.civitas.org.uk/content/files/crime_stats_oecdjan2012.pdf [accessed: 09.11.21]

41. S. Boztas, 'Why are there so few prisoners in the Netherlands?', *Guardian*, 12 December 2019. Available at: https://www.theguardian.com/world/2019/dec/12/why-are-there-so-few-prisoners-in-the-netherlands [accessed 09.11.21]

42. 'How Norway turns criminals into good neighbours', *BBC News*, 7 July 2019. Available at: https://www.bbc.com/news/stories-48885846 [accessed: 09.11.21]

43. M. Alexander and C. West, *The New Jim Crow: Mass Incarceration in the Age of Colorblindness*, revised edition (New York: New Press, 2012).

44. R. Cookson and P. Chamberlain, 'Inside the sell blocks', *Guardian*, 9 September 2009. Available at: https://www.theguardian.com/society/2009/sep/09/prisoners-cheap-labour-major-companies [accessed: 09.11.21]

45. Dr K. Edgar, et al., Prison Reform Trust, 'No life, no freedom, no future: The experiences of prisoners recalled under the sentence of Imprisonment Public Protection', 2020. Available at: http://www.prisonreformtrust.org.uk/Portals/o/Documents/no%20freedom_final_web.pdf [accessed: 09.11.21]

46. Z. Conway, 'David Blunkett "regrets injustices" of indeterminate sentences', *BBC Newsnight*, 13 March 2014. Available at: https://www.bbc.com/news/uk-26561380 [accessed: 09.11.21]

47. Great Britain and National Audit Office, 'Ministry of Justice, HM Prison & Probation Service: improving the prison estate', 7 February 2020. Available at: https://www.nao.org.uk/wp-content/uploads/2020/02/Improving-the-prison-estate.pdf [accessed 09.11.21]

48. B. Tufft, 'Chris Grayling spends £72,000 of taxpayers' money to defend "unlawful" prison book ban', *Independent*, 10 January 2015. Available at: https://www.independent.co.uk/news/uk/politics/chris-grayling-spends-ps72-000-taxpayers-money-defend-unlawful-prison-book-ban-9969937.html [accessed: 09.11.21]

49. Howard League for Penal Reform, 'Breaking Point: Understaffing and overcrowding in prisons – research briefing', 2014. Available at: https://howardleague.org/wp-content/uploads/2016/03/Breaking-point-10.07.2014.pdf [accessed: 09.11.21]

50. M. Bulman and J. Di Paolo, 'Exodus of experienced prison staff "putting public at risk" as 80,000 years of experience lost since 2010', *Independent*, 30 May 2019. Available at: https://www.independent.co.uk/news/uk/home-news/prison-officers-experience-exodus-loss-jails-crisis-justice-governor-moj-a8929421.html [accessed: 09.11.21]

51. Howard League for Penal Reform, 'Breaking Point'.

52. B. Dodman, 'As France releases thousands, can Covid-19 end chronic prison overcrowding?', France 24, 27 April 2020. Available at: https://www.france24.com/en/20200427-as-france-releases-thousands-can-covid-19-end-chronic-prison-overcrowding [accessed: 10.11.21]

53. L. So et al., 'Dying Inside: The Hidden Crisis in America's Jails, Part Three', Reuters, 28 October 2020. Available at: https://www.reuters.com/investigates/special-report/usa-jails-release/ [accessed: 10.11.21]

54. J. Grierson, 'Coronavirus: only 55 prisoners freed early in England and Wales', *Guardian*, 12 May 2020. Available at: https://www.theguardian.com/society/2020/may/12/coronavirus-only-55-prisoners-early-release-england-wales [accessed: 10.11.21]

3. How to Build a Criminal – Institutionalisation

1. K. Williams et al., Ministry of Justice, 'Prisoners' childhood and family backgrounds: Results from the Surveying Prisoner Crime Reduction (SPCR) longitudinal cohort study of prisoners', March 2012, p. 8. Available at: https://assets.publishing.service.gov.uk/government/uploads/system/uploads/attachment_data/file/278837/prisoners-childhood-family-backgrounds.pdf [accessed: 10.11.21]

2. Ministry of Justice, 'Safety in Custody Statistics, England and Wales: Deaths in Prison Custody to June 2021 Assaults and Self-harm to March 2021', 29 July 2021. Available at: https://assets.publishing.service.gov.uk/government/uploads/system/uploads/attachment_data/file/1006537/safety-in-custody-q1-2021.pdf [accessed: 10.11.21]

3. Her Majesty's Inspectorate of Probation, 2 February 2021. Available at: https://www.justiceinspectorates.gov.uk/hmiprobation/research/the-evidence-base-probation/specific-areas-of-delivery/accommodation/ [accessed: 10.11.21]

4. But What About 'The Paedos'? – Sex Offenders

1. H. Christodoulou, 'PAEDO NEXT DOOR: Record number of sex offenders and violent criminals living across UK as number on streets DOUBLES to 82,000 in a decade', *Sun*, 20 November 2019. Available at: https://www.thesun.co.uk/news/10387120/sex-offenders-criminals-free-uk/ [accessed: 10.11.21]

2. C.A. Harper, 'Examining the Link between Media Representations and Attitudes towards Sexual Offenders using a Dual-Process Framework', September 2016. Available at: https://www.researchgate.net/publication/315772320_Examining_the_Link_between_Media_Representations_and_Attitudes_towards_Sexual_Offenders_using_a_Dual-Process_Framework [accessed: 10.12.21]

3. T. Wells, 'SCARRED: Paedo who raped girl, 13, needed plastic surgery after being attacked within seconds of arriving at jail', *Sun*, 30 April 2021. Available at: https://www.thesun.co.uk/news/14809954/paedo-plastic-surgery-after-brutal-jail-attack/ [accessed: 10.11.21]

4. Ministry of Justice, 'Offender Management Statistics Bulletin, England and Wales – Quarterly: October to December 2018, and Annual (calendar year) 2018; Prison population: 31 March 2019', 25 April 2019, p. 3. Available at: https://assets.publishing.service.gov.uk/government/uploads/system/uploads/attachment_data/file/805271/offender-management-statistics-quarterly-q4-2018.pdf [accessed: 10.11.21]

5. Office for National Statistics, 'Sexual offences prevalence and trends, England and Wales: year ending March 2020', 18 March 2021. Available at: https://www.ons.gov.uk/peoplepopulationandcommunity/crimeandjustice/articles/sexualoffencesprevalenceandtrendsenglandandwales/yearendingmarch2020 [accessed: 29.11.21]

6. Ibid.

7. L. Kelly et al., 'A Gap or a Chasm? Attrition in reported rape cases', Home Office Research Study 293 (London: Home Office Research, Development and Statistics Directorate, 2005), p. 5. Available at: https://www.researchgate.net/publication/238713283_Home_Office_Research_Study_293_A_gap_or_a_chasm_Attrition_in_reported_rape_cases/link/00b7d52a09b4935e0e000000/download [accessed: 29.11.21]

8. A. Mews, et al. (2017), 'Impact evaluation of the prison-based Core Sex Offender Treatment Programme', Ministry of Justice. Available at: https://assets.publishing.service.gov.uk/government/uploads/system/uploads/attachment_data/file/623876/sotp-report-web-.pdf [accessed: 10.11.21]

9. A.R. Beech and T. Ward (2004), 'The integration of etiology and risk in sexual offenders: A theoretical framework', *Aggression and Violent Behavior*, vol. 10, iss. 1, pp. 31–63. Available at: https://doi.org/10.1016/j.avb.2003.08.002 [accessed: 10.11.21]

10. H.A. Bedau, The American Civil Liberties Union (2012), 'The Case Against the Death Penalty'. Available at: https://www.aclu.org/other/case-against-death-penalty [accessed: 10.11.21]

11. Ibid.

12. P.M. Yates (2013), 'Treatment of Sexual Offenders: Research, Best Practices, and Emerging Models', *International Journal of Behavioral Consultation and Therapy*, vol.8, no.3–4. Available at: https://psycnet.apa.org/fulltext/2014-12592-016.pdf [accessed: 10.11.21]

13. See, for example, L.S. Grossman et al. (1999), 'Are sex offenders treatable? A research overview', *Psychiatric Services*, vol. 50, iss. 3, pp. 349–361. Available at: https://psycnet.apa.org/record/1999-10583-001 [accessed: 10.11.21]

14. Yates, 'Treatment of Sexual Offenders', p. 89.

15. Ibid.

16. Mews et al., 'Impact evaluation of the prison-based Core Sex Offender Treatment Programme'.

17. Ibid.

18. Yates, 'Treatment of Sexual Offenders', p. 91.

19. D.A. Andrews and J. Bonta (2010) quoted in Yates, 'Treatment of Sexual Offenders', p. 90. Available at: https://psycnet.apa.org/fulltext/2014-12592-016.pdf [accessed: 10.11.21]

20. B. Winder et al. (2020), 'UK National Evaluation of Big Lottery Funded Circles of Support and Accountability'. Available at: https://www.circles-uk.org.uk/images/documents/SOCAMRU_BL_final_report_1_April_2020_v82.pdf [accessed: 10.11.21]

21. J.W. Burrell and P. Laskey (2017), 'Attitudes Towards Sexual Offenders Returning to Live in the Community', *Journal of Applied Psychology and Social Science,* vol. 3, iss. 2, pp. 52–69. Available at http://insight.cumbria.ac.uk/id/eprint/3651/1/Burrell_AttitudesTowards.pdf [accessed: 10.11.21]

22. Ibid.

23. A number of studies across areas in the UK and Canada are available at https://www.circles-uk.org.uk/resources/research-journal-articles [accessed: 29.11.21]

24. Harper, 'Examining the Link between Media Representations and

Attitudes towards Sexual Offenders using a Dual-Process Framework'.

25. G.M. Willis and R. Grace (2009), 'Assessment of Community Reintegration Planning for Sex Offenders: Poor Planning Predicts Recidivism', *Criminal Justice and Behaviour*, 36(5), pp. 494–512 Available at: https://www.researchgate.net/publication/247744860_Assessment_of_Community_Reintegration_Planning_for_Sex_OffendersPoor_Planning_Predicts_Recidivism/link/58db788145851578dff9570f/download [accessed: 29.11.21]

26. Harper, 'Examining the Link between Media Representations and Attitudes towards Sexual Offenders using a Dual-Process Framework'.

5. Looking at Life – Murderers

1. Prison Reform Trust, 'Prison: the facts', summer 2019. Available at: http://www.prisonreformtrust.org.uk/Portals/0/Documents/Bromley%20Briefings/Prison%20the%20facts%20Summer%202019.pdf [accessed: 11.11.21]

2. Ibid.

6. Tried to Fund a Place in Rehab – Substance Misuse

1. Prison Reform Trust, 'Prison: the facts', summer 2019. Available at: http://www.prisonreformtrust.org.uk/Portals/0/Documents/Bromley%20Briefings/Prison%20the%20facts%20Summer%202019.pdf [accessed: 11.11.21]

2. R. Stewart (2019), 'Reducing the use of short prison sentences in favour of a smarter approach', Revolving Doors Agency. Available at: http://www.revolving-doors.org.uk/file/2347/download?token=e9wtT41q [accessed: 11.11.21]

3. Prison Reform Trust, 'Prison: the facts'.

4. Clinks, 'Clinks Briefing: Sentencing in England and Wales', February 2020, p. 6. Available at: https://www.clinks.org/sites/default/files/2020-02/Clinks%20Sentencing%20Briefing_Feb20_FINAL%20%281%29.PDF [accessed: 11.11.21]

5. Ministry of Justice, 'Economic and social costs of reoffending – Analytical report', 2019. Available at: https://assets.publishing.service.gov.uk/government/uploads/system/uploads/attachment_data/file/814650/economic-social-costs-reoffending.pdf [accessed 08.11.21]

6. Criminal Justice and Courts Bill, 'Fact sheet: Drug testing in prisons', https://assets.publishing.service.gov.uk/government/uploads/system/uploads/attachment_data/file/322190/fact-sheet-drug-testing-in-prisons.

pdf [accessed: 29.11.21]

7. F. Perraudin, 'Proportion of UK prisoners with drug problem doubles in five years – study', *Guardian*, 20 January 2020. Available at: https://www.theguardian.com/society/2020/jan/20/proportion-of-uk-prisoners-with-drug-problem-doubles-in-five-years-study [accessed: 11.11.21]

8. Ministry of Justice, 'Prisons Data'. Available at: https://data.justice.gov.uk/prisons [accessed: 07.12.21]

9. A. Hagan and R. Hardwick (2017), 'Behind Bars: The Truth about Drugs in Prisons', *Forensic Research & Criminology International Journal*, vol. 3, iss. 5. Available at: https://www.semanticscholar.org/paper/Behind-Bars%3A-The-Truth-about-Drugs-in-Prisons-O%E2%80%99Hagan-Hardwick/48d3be8e42d1a568f700af5ad773bba928dc095a#citing-papers [accessed: 10-12.21]

10. A. Walker, 'Two-thirds of homeless ex-prisoners reoffend within a year', *Guardian*, 12 August 2019. Available at: https://www.theguardian.com/society/2019/aug/12/two-thirds-of-homeless-ex-prisoners-reoffend-within-a-year [accessed: 29.11.21]

11. See, for example, UK Rehab, 'How much does addiction rehab cost?'. Available at: https://www.uk-rehab.com/treatment-rehab/how-much-does-addiction-rehab-cost/ [accessed: 11.11.21]

12. Prison Reform Trust, 'Prison: the facts'.

13. Walker, 'Two-thirds of homeless ex-prisoners reoffend within a year'.

14. Stewart, 'Reducing the use of short prison sentences in favour of a smarter approach'.

15. Transform Drug Policy Foundation, 'In Portugal: Setting the Record Straight', 13 May 2021. Available at: https://transformdrugs.org/blog/drug-decriminalisation-in-portugal-setting-the-record-straight [accessed: 11.11.21]

7. Containment and Confinement – Violence

1. Ministry of Justice, 'Safety in Custody Statistics Bulletin, England and Wales, Deaths in prison custody to March 2017, Assaults and Self-Harm to December 2016', 27 April 2017. Available at: https://assets.publishing.service.gov.uk/government/uploads/system/uploads/attachment_data/file/611187/safety-in-custody-statistics-q4-2016.pdf [accessed: 11.11.21]

2. Prison Reform Trust, 'Advice and Information Service: Regime and Time out of cell', November 2020. Available at: http://www.prisonreformtrust.org.uk/Portals/0/Documents/Prisoner%20Information%20Pages/15%20Regime%20info%20sheet.pdf [accessed: 11.11.21]

3. Howard League for Penal Reform, 'Breaking Point: Understaffing and overcrowding in prisons – research briefing', 2014. Available at: https://howardleague.org/wp-content/uploads/2016/03/Breaking-point-10.07.2014.pdf [accessed: 11.11.21]

4. Prison Reform Trust, 'Prison Rules and Adjudications', January 2019. Available at: http://www.prisonreformtrust.org.uk/Portals/0/Documents/ Prisoner%20Information%20Pages/23%20Prison%20Rules%20 and%20Adjudications.pdf [accessed: 11.11.21]

5. United Nations Office on Drugs and Crime, 'Assessing Compliance with the Nelson Mandela Rules: A Checklist for Internal Inspection Mechanisms', 2018. Available at: https://doi.org/10.18356/f1d2658e-en [accessed: 11.11.21]

6. C.S. Briggs et al. (2003), 'The Effect of Supermaximum Security Prisons on Aggregate Levels of Institutional Violence', *Criminology*, vol. 41, iss. 4, pp. 1341–76. Available at: https://doi.org/10.1111/j.1745-9125.2003. tb01022.x [accessed 11.11.21] See also, for example, K. Weir (2012), 'Alone, in "the hole": Psychologists probe the mental health effects of solitary confinement', *Monitor on Psychology*, vol. 43, iss. 5, pp. 54–6. Available at: https://www.apa.org/monitor/2012/05/solitary [accessed 29.11.21]. See also S. Dingfelder, (2012), 'Psychologist testifies about the dangers of solitary confinement', *Monitor on Psychology*, vol. 43, iss. 9, p. 10. Available at: https://www.apa.org/monitor/2012/10/solitary [accessed 29.11.21]

7. S. Shalev and K. Edgar, Prison Reform Trust, 'Deep Custody: Segregation Units and Close Supervision Centres in England and Wales', December 2015. Available at: http://www.prisonreformtrust.org.uk/Portals/0/ Documents/deep_custody_111215.pdf [accessed: 11.11.21]

8. There's Not Always a Mess Net to Catch You – Mental Health

1. M. Bulman and J. Di Paolo, 'Exodus of experienced prison staff "putting public at risk" as 80,000 years of experience lost since 2010', *Independent*, 30 May 2019. Available at: https://www.independent. co.uk/news/uk/home-news/prison-officers-experience-exodus-loss-jails-crisis-justice-governor-moj-a8929421.html [accessed: 12.11.21]

2. M. Bulman, 'Third of prison officers who quit leave within a year of starting, figures show', *Independent*, 30 August 2018. Available at: https://www.independent.co.uk/news/uk/home-news/uk-prison-jail-crisis-officers-quit-violence-harassment-a8507951.html   [accessed: 12.11.21]

3. 'How Norway Turns Criminals into Good Neighbours', *BBC News*, 7 July 2019. Available at: https://www.bbc.com/news/stories-4888584[accessed: 09.02.2022]

4. M. Bhuller et al. (2019), 'Policies to Reintegrate Former Inmates into the Labor Force', The Aspen Institute. Available at: https://www.aspeninstitute.org/longform/expanding-economic-opportunity-for-more-americans/policies-to-reintegrate-former-inmates-into-the-labor-force/ [accessed: 12.11.21]

5. Ibid.

6. Statista, 'Incarceration rate in selected European Countries in 2020', May 2021. Available at: https://www.statista.com/statistics/957501/incarceration-rate-in-europe/ [accessed: 12.11.21]

7. Howard League for Penal Reform, '2016 becomes worst year ever recorded for suicides in prisons', 28 November 2016. Available at: https://howardleague.org/news/suicidesinprison2016/, [accessed: 12.11.21]

8. Ministry of Justice, 'Safety in Custody Statistics Bulletin, England and Wales, Deaths in prison custody to December 2016, Assaults and Self-Harm to September 2016', revised 1 March 2017. Available at: https://assets.publishing.service.gov.uk/government/uploads/system/uploads/attachment_data/file/595797/safety-in-custody-quarterly-bulletin.pdf [accessed: 12.11.21]

9. Ministry of Justice, 'Safety in Custody Statistics, England and Wales: Deaths in Prison Custody to March 2021, Assaults and Self-harm to December 2020', 29 April 2021. Available at: https://www.gov.uk/government/statistics/safety-in-custody-quarterly-update-to-december-2020/safety-in-custody-statistics-england-and-wales-deaths-in-prison-custody-to-march-2021-assaults-and-self-harm-to-december-2020#self-harm-12-months-to-december-2020 [accessed: 29.11.21]

10. Prison Reform Trust, 'Prison: the facts', summer 2019. Available at: http://www.prisonreformtrust.org.uk/Portals/0/Documents/Bromley%20Briefings/Prison%20the%20facts%20Summer%202019.pdf [accessed: 12.11.21]

11. T. Burki (2017), 'Crisis in UK Prison Mental Health', *The Lancet Psychiatry* vol. 4, iss. 12, p. 904. Available at: https://www.thelancet.com/journals/lanpsy/article/PIIS2215-0366(17)30446-7/fulltext [accessed: 29.11.21]

12. G. Kinman and A. Clements, 'Survey of Work-Related Wellbeing', August 2020, p. 5. Available at: https://www.poauk.org.uk/media/1888/poa-survey-of-work-related-wellbeing-1.pdf [accessed: 12.11.21]

13. Ibid.

14. Ibid.

15. Ibid.

9. *In Loco Parentis* – Care to Custody

1. House of Lords Select Committee on Adoption Legislation, 'Adoption: Post-Legislative Scrutiny – Second Report of Session 2012–13', 6 March 2013. Available at: https://publications.parliament.uk/pa/ld201213/ldse-lect/ldadopt/127/12702.htm [accessed: 12.11.21]

2. E. Busby, 'Sure Start: Thousands of children end up in hospital because of cuts to support centres, study finds', *Independent*, 4 June 2019. Available at: https://www.independent.co.uk/news/uk/home-news/sure-start-children-centres-hospital-visits-injuries-ifs-closures-early-ye-ars-a8942336.html Accessed on 29/11/2021

3. K. Williams et al., Ministry of Justice, 'Prisoners' childhood and family backgrounds: Results from the Surveying Prisoner Crime Reduction (SPCR) longitudinal cohort study of prisoners', March 2012. Available at: https://assets.publishing.service.gov.uk/government/uploads/system/uploads/attachment_data/file/278837/prisoners-childhood-family-backgrounds.pdf [accessed: 12.11.21]

4. Ibid.

5. Ibid., p. 8.

6. Ibid.

7. Ofsted, 'Main findings: local authority and children's homes in England inspections and outcomes autumn 2020', figure 3, updated 20 January 2021. Available at: https://www.gov.uk/government/statistics/local-authority-and-childrens-homes-in-england-inspections-and-outcomes-autumn-2020/main-findings-local-authority-and-childrens-homes-in-england-inspections-and-outcomes-autumn-2020 [accessed: 12.11.21]

8. M. Narey and M. Owers, 'Foster Care in England: A Review for the Department for Education', February 2018, p. 14. Available at: https://assets.publishing.service.gov.uk/government/uploads/system/uploads/attachment_data/file/679320/Foster_Care_in_England_Review.pdf [accessed: 10.12.21]

9. National Audit Office, 'Children in care', Department for Education, 27 November 2014, p.9. Available at: https://www.nao.org.uk/wp-content/uploads/2014/11/Children-in-care1.pdf [accessed: 12.11.21]

10. Department for Education, 'Children's homes data pack', December

2014. Available at: https://assets.publishing.service.gov.uk/government/uploads/system/uploads/attachment_data/file/388701/Childrens_Homes_data_pack_Dec_2014.pdf [accessed: 12.11.21]

11. C. Carter, 'How cuts are affecting social care performance: what the data says', Community Care, 11 November 2019. Available at: https://www.communitycare.co.uk/2019/11/11/making-social-care-priority/ [accessed: 12.11.21]

12. Ibid.

13. P. Butler, 'Sure Start programme saved the NHS millions of pounds, study finds', Guardian, 4 June 2019. Available at: https://www.theguardian.com/society/2019/jun/04/sure-start-saved-nhs-millions [accessed: 12.11.21]

14. Ibid.

15. H. Westwater, 'Child poverty in the UK: The definitions, details, causes, and consequences', The Big Issue, 19 May 2021. Available at: https://www.bigissue.com/latest/child-poverty-in-the-uk-the-definitions-details-causes-and-consequences/#:~:text=How%20many%20children%20are%20living,in%20the%20median%20UK%20income [accessed: 12.11.21]

16. S. Murphy, 'Free school meals: the Tory MPs defending refusal to support campaign', Guardian, 25 October 2020. Available at: https://www.theguardian.com/education/2020/oct/25/free-school-meals-uk-marcus-rashford-conservative-mps-defend-ministers-refusal-to-u-turn [accessed: 12.11.21]

10. Can't Drive a Lambo Around the Exercise Yard – Gangs, Youths and Race

1. The Lammy Review, 'An independent review into the treatment of, and outcomes for Black, Asian and Minority Ethnic individuals in the criminal justice system', 8 September 2017, p. 5. Available at: https://www.gov.uk/government/publications/lammy-review-final-report [accessed: 29.11.21]

2. Ibid., p. 48. Available at: https://www.gov.uk/government/publications/lammy-review-final-report [accessed: 29.11.21]

3. J. Sanburn, 'Chicago Shootings and Murders Surged in 2015', Time, 2 January 2016. Available at: https://time.com/4165576/chicago-murders-shootings-rise-2015/ [accessed: 09.02.2022]

4. The Lammy Review, 'An independent review into the treatment of, and outcomes for Black, Asian and Minority Ethnic individuals in the

criminal justice system', p. 6.

5. Ibid.

6. Ibid.

7. T. Parsons, 'London riots', *Mirror*, 10 August 2011. Available at: https://www.mirror.co.uk/news/uk-news/london-riots-tony-parsons-on-the-warped-146710 [accessed: 09.02.2022]

8. D. Starkey, 'UK Riots', *Telegraph*, 19 August 2011. Available at: https://www.telegraph.co.uk/news/uknews/law-and-order/8711621/UK-riots-Its-not-about-criminality-and-cuts-its-about-culture...-and-this-is-only-the-beginning.html [accessed: 09.02.2022]

9. The Lammy Review, 'An independent review into the treatment of, and outcomes for Black, Asian and Minority Ethnic individuals in the Criminal Justice System', 8 September 2017, p. 3.

10. R. Ramesh, 'More black people jailed in England and Wales proportionally than in US', *Guardian*, 11 October 2010. Available at: https://www.theguardian.com/society/2010/oct/11/black-prison-population-increase-england [accessed: 12.11.21]

11. The Lammy Review, 'An independent review into the treatment of, and outcomes for Black, Asian and Minority Ethnic individuals in the Criminal Justice System', p. 48.

12. V. Dodd, 'Black people nine times more likely to face stop and search than white people', *Guardian*, 27 October 2020. Available at: https://www.theguardian.com/uk-news/2020/oct/27/black-people-nine-times-more-likely-to-face-stop-and-search-than-white-people [accessed: 12.11.21]

13. Ibid.

14. M. Alexander and C. West, *The New Jim Crow: Mass Incarceration in the Age of Colorblindness*, revised edition (New York: New Press, 2012).

15. The Lammy Review, 'An independent review into the treatment of, and outcomes for Black, Asian and Minority Ethnic individuals in the Criminal Justice System', p. 10.

16. Ibid., p. 53.

17. Ibid., p. 8.

11. When Life Means Life – Imprisonment for Public Protection

1. J. Beard, 'Sentences of Imprisonment for Public Protection', 6 June 2019, p. 4. Available at: https://researchbriefings.files.parliament.uk/documents/SN06086/SN06086.pdf [accessed: 29.11.21]

2. Dr K. Edgar et al., 'No life, no freedom, no future', 2020. Available at: http://www.prisonreformtrust.org.uk/Portals/0/Documents/no%20 freedom_final_web.pdf [accessed: 29.11.21]

3. The Parole Board. Available at: https://www.gov.uk/government/ organisations/parole-board/about [accessed 13.11.21]

4. Ibid.

5. Edgar et al., 'No life, no freedom, no future'.

6. Conway, Z., 'David Blunkett "regrets injustices" of indeterminate sentences', *BBC News*, 13 March 2014. Available at: https://www.bbc.com/ news/uk-26561380 [accessed: 13.11.21]

7. The Howard League for Penal Reform, 'The never-ending story: Indeterminate sentencing and the prison regime – Research briefing', 2013. Available at: https://howardleague.org/wp-content/uploads/2016/05/ never-ending-story-IPP.pdf [accessed: 13.11.21]

8. Ibid.

9. Edgar, et al., 'No life, no freedom, no future'.

10. Ministry of Justice, 'Offender Management Statistics Bulletin, England and Wales, Quarterly: January to March 2021'. Available at: https://assets.publishing.service.gov.uk/government/uploads/system/ uploads/attachment_data/file/1006733/OMSQ_Q1_2021_Bulletin_v1_ for_upload.pdf [accessed: 10.12.21]

12. Freedom's Just Another Word for Nothing Left to Lose – Remand

1. Fair Trials, 'Pre-trial detention – Impact'. Available at: https://www. fairtrials.org/campaign/pre-trial-detention#impact [accessed: 13.11.21]

2. The Howard League for Penal Reform, 'Revealed: The wasted millions spent on needless remand', 18 August 2014. Available at: https:// howardleague.org/news/needlessremand/ [accessed: 13.11.21]

3. Prison Reform Trust, 'Innocent Until Proven Guilty: Tackling the Overuse of Custodial Remand', October 2011. Available at: http:// www.prisonreformtrust.org.uk/Portals/0/Documents/Remand%20Briefing%20FINAL.PDF [accessed: 13.11.21]

4. The Howard League for Penal Reform, 'Revealed'.

5. Prison Reform Trust, 'Innocent Until Proven Guilty'.

6. National Information Centre on Children of Offenders (NICCO). Available at: https://www.nicco.org.uk/ [accessed: 13.11.21]

7. J. Murray, et al. (2009), 'Effects of parental imprisonment on child antisocial behaviour and mental health: a systematic review', *Campbell Systematic Reviews*, vol. 5, iss. 1, pp. 1–105. Available at: https://doi.

org/10.4073/csr.2009.4 [accessed: 13.11.21]

8. Ibid.

9. A. Nesmith and E. Ruhland (2008), 'Children of incarcerated parents: Challenges and resiliency, in their own words', *Children and Youth Services Review*, vol. 30, iss. 10, pp. 1119–30. Available at: https://doi.org/10.1016/j.childyouth.2008.02.006 [accessed: 13.11.21]

10. The Howard League for Penal Reform, 'Revealed'.

11. Statista, 'Cost per Prisoner England and Wales 2020'. Available at: https://www.statista.com/statistics/1202172/cost-per-prisoner-england-and-wales/ [accessed: 27.05.21]

12. The Howard League for Penal Reform, 'Revealed'.

13. B. Quinn, 'Third of remand prisoners in England being held beyond legal time limit for trials', *Guardian*, 17 March 2021. Available at: https://www.theguardian.com/uk-news/2021/mar/17/third-of-remand-prisoners-in-england-being-held-beyond-legal-time-limit-for-trials [accessed: 13.11.21]

14. Ibid.

15. L. Dearden, 'Number of prisoners held without trial up by almost a third because of coronavirus court delays', *Independent*, 30 October 2020. Available at: https://www.independent.co.uk/news/uk/crime/coronavirus-court-backlog-prisoners-remand-custody-delays-guilty-pleas-b1429667.html [accessed: 13.11.21]

16. Ibid.

17. M. Bulman, 'Prisoners three times more likely to die from Covid than the general population, research suggests', *Independent*, 17 March 2021. Available at: https://www.independent.co.uk/news/uk/home-news/prisoners-covid-death-rates-ucl-b1818078.html [accessed: 13.11.21]

13. There but for the Grace of God, Go I – Homelessness

1. J. Elgot, 'Thousands of ex-prisoners likely to be sleeping rough', *Guardian*, 13 August 2018. Available at: https://www.theguardian.com/society/2018/aug/13/thousands-of-ex-prisoners-likely-to-be-sleeping-rough [accessed: 13.11.21]

2. Ibid.

3. Ministry of Justice, 'Offender Management Statistics Bulletin, England and Wales – Quarterly: April to June 2016; with Prison Population as at 30 September 2016', 27 October 2016. Available at: https://assets.publishing.service.gov.uk/government/uploads/system/uploads/attachment_data/file/562955/OMSQ_Bulletin.pdf [accessed: 13.11.21]

4. The Royal British Legion, 'Literature Review: UK veterans and the criminal justice system', n.d., p. 7. Available at: https://www.britishlegion.org.uk/docs/default-source/campaigns-policy-and-research/litrev_uk_vets_crim_justice.pdf?sfvrsn=6e0c84bf_2 [accessed: 13.11.21]

5. Prison Reform Trust, 'Prison: the facts', summer 2019. Available at: http://www.prisonreformtrust.org.uk/Portals/0/Documents/Bromley%20Briefings/Prison%20the%20facts%20Summer%202019.pdf [accessed: 13.11.21]

6. M. Bulman, 'Hundreds of homeless people pushed back onto the streets of London during first lockdown "due to lack of support"', *Independent,* 12 January 2021. Available at: https://www.independent.co.uk/news/uk/home-news/homeless-rough-sleepers-hotels-london-b1785437.html [accessed: 10.12.21]

7. J. Grierson, 'Over 1,000 prison leavers left homeless amid pandemic, MoJ figures show', *Guardian,* 15 June 2020. Available at: https://www.theguardian.com/society/2020/jun/15/over-1000-prison-leavers-left-homeless-amid-pandemic-moj-figures-show [accessed: 13.11.21]

8. A. Gentleman, 'Hotels used to house rough sleepers during pandemic return to business', *Guardian,* 18 June 2020. Available at: https://www.theguardian.com/society/2020/jun/18/hotels-used-to-house-rough-sleepers-during-pandemic-return-to-business [accessed: 13.11.21]

14. Time Served – Release

1. Ministry of Justice, 'Offender Management Statistics Bulletin, England and Wales – Quarterly: January to March 2019; Prison population: 30 June 2019', 25 July 2019. Available at: https://assets.publishing.service.gov.uk/government/uploads/system/uploads/attachment_data/file/820160/omsq-2019-q1.pdf [accessed: 13.11.21]

15. Permission to Leave the Net? – Suicide

1. The Howard League for Penal Reform, 'Analysis of deaths in custody in England and Wales 2016', 16 May 2017. Available at: https://howardleague.org/wp-content/uploads/2017/05/updated-final-Analysis-of-deaths-in-custody-in-England-and-Wales-2016.pdf [accessed: 14.11.21]

2. A. Travis, 'Number of prison deaths linked to new psychoactive drugs rises to 79', *Guardian,* 11 July 2017. Available at: https://www.theguardian.com/society/2017/jul/11/prison-deaths-linked-new-psychoactive-substances-rising-rapidly-watchdog [accessed: 14.11.21]

3. S. Blewett, 'Thousands of prison officers just decided to go on strike',

Independent, 15 November 2016. Available at: https://www.independ-ent.co.uk/news/uk/home-news/thousands-prison-officers-just-decided-go-strike-a7418016.html [accessed: 14.11.21]

16. A Change Is Gonna Come . . .

1. A. Travis, 'High court orders prison officers to end protest and go back to work', *Guardian*, 15 November 2016. Available at: https://www.theguardian.com/society/2016/nov/15/uk-prison-officers-stage-protest-over-health-and-safety-fears [accessed: 14.11.21]

2. N. Clark, 'Unnecessary and unlawful', *Sun*, 15 November 2016. Available at: https://www.thesun.co.uk/news/2189367/justice-secretary-liz-truss-slams-prison-officers-for-strike-action-that-halted-jo-cox-murder-trial-saying-it-will-only-make-jails-more-dangerous/ [accessed: 29.11.21]

3. J. Grierson, 'Birmingham prison riot "should have been stopped sooner"', *Guardian*, 20 August 2018. Available at: https://www.theguardian.com/society/2018/aug/20/birmingham-prison-riot-should-have-been-stopped-sooner [accessed: 14.11.21]

4. 'HMP The Mount: No charges over two-day prison riot', *BBC News*, 16 November 2017. Available at: https://www.bbc.com/news/uk-england-beds-bucks-herts-41983069 [accessed: 14.11.21]

5. E. Lake and T. De La Mare, 'SWALESIDE IS BURNING: HMP Swaleside prison riot as 60 inmates take control of wing and set fires', *Sun*, 22 December 2016. Available at: https://www.thesun.co.uk/news/2463202/riot-breaks-out-at-prison-as-60-inmates-take-control/

6. Prison Officer Recruitment, Vol. 639: debated Tuesday 24 April 2018. Available at: https://hansard.parliament.uk/commons/2018-04-24/debates/094F7C52-C5A2-4FE3-97F2-A5EB9D242595/PrisonOfficerRe-cruitment [accessed: 14.11.21]

7. Ministry of Justice, 'National Offender Management Service (NOMS) Annual Workforce Statistics Bulletin', 31 March 2017. Available at: https://assets.publishing.service.gov.uk/government/uploads/system/uploads/attachment_data/file/614684/noms-annual-workforce-statistics-march-2017.pdf [accessed: 29.11.21]

8. Ministry of Justice, 'Safety in Custody Statistics, England and Wales: Deaths in Prison Custody to March 2020, Assaults and Self-harm to December 2019', 30 April 2020. Available at: https://assets.publishing.service.gov.uk/government/uploads/system/uploads/attachment_data/file/893374/safety-in-custody-q4-2019.pdf [accessed: 14.11.21]

9. The Howard League for Penal Reform, 'Analysis of deaths in custody

in England and Wales 2016', 16 May 2017. Available at: https://how-ardleague.org/wp-content/uploads/2017/05/updated-final-Analysis-of-deaths-in-custody-in-England-and-Wales-2016.pdf [accessed: 14.11.21]

10. Ministry of Justice, 'Safety in Custody Statistics, England and Wales'.

11. Independent Monitoring Board, 'Annual Report of the Independent Monitoring Board at HMP Coldingley: For reporting year 1 August 2019 – 31 July 2020', September 2020. Available at: https://s3-eu-west-2.amazonaws.com/imb-prod-storage-1ocod6bqkyovo/uploads/2020/09/AR-Coldingley-2019-20-for-circulation.pdf [accessed: 14.11.21]

12. M. Savage, 'Coronavirus: the possible long-term mental health impacts', *BBC Worklife*, 29 October 2020. Available at: https://www.bbc.com/worklife/article/20201021-coronavirus-the-possible-long-term-mental-health-impacts [accessed: 14.11.21]

13. L. Holmes, 'Drinking during lockdown: headline findings', Alcohol Change UK, April 2020. Available at: https://alcoholchange.org.uk/blog/2020/covid19-drinking-during-lockdown-headline-findings [accessed: 14.11.21]

14. 'Coronavirus: Iran temporarily frees 54,000 prisoners to combat spread', *BBC News*, 3 March 2020. Available at: https://www.bbc.com/news/world-middle-east-51723398 [accessed: 14.11.21]

15. J. Grierson, 'Early-release scheme for prisoners in England and Wales to end', *Guardian*, 19 August 2020 Available at: https://www.theguardian.com/society/2020/aug/19/prisons-inspector-england-wales-warns-of-mental-health-problems-from-severe-coronavirus-restrictions [accessed: 29.11.21]

16. B. Quinn, 'Third of remand prisoners in England being held beyond legal time limit for trials', *Guardian*, 17 March 2021. Available at: https://www.theguardian.com/uk-news/2021/mar/17/third-of-remand-prisoners-in-england-being-held-beyond-legal-time-limit-for-trials [accessed: 14.11.21]

17. J. Bennetto, 'Lord Woolf attacks jails' "cancer of overcrowding"', *Independent*, 30 October 2002. Available at: https://www.independent.co.uk/news/uk/crime/lord-woolf-attacks-jails-cancer-of-overcrowding-141557.html [accessed: 14.11.21]

18. E. Allison, 'The Strangeways riot: 20 years on', *Guardian*, 31 March 2010. Available at: https://www.theguardian.com/society/2010/mar/31/strangeways-riot-20-years-on [accessed: 29.11.21]

19. J. Grierson, 'Over 1,000 prison leavers left homeless amid pandemic, MoJ figures show', *Guardian*, 15 June 2020. Available at: https://www.

theguardian.com/society/2020/jun/15/over-1000-prison-leavers-left-homeless-amid-pandemic-moj-figures-show [accessed: 14.11.21]

20. C. Jayanetti, '70,000 households in UK made homeless during pandemic', *Guardian*, 9 January 2021. Available at: https://www.theguardian.com/society/2021/jan/09/70000-households-in-uk-made-homeless-during-pandemic [accessed: 14.11.21]

21. M. Bulman, 'England and Wales spend more on prisons than all of Europe except Russia', *Independent*, 8 April 2021. Available at: https://www.independent.co.uk/news/uk/home-news/prison-spending-england-wales-europe-russia-b1828396.html [accessed: 08.11.21]; Prison Reform Trust, 'Prison: the facts', summer 2019, p. 4. Available at: http://www.prisonreformtrust.org.uk/Portals/0/Documents/Bromley%20Briefings/Prison%20the%20facts%20Summer%202019.pdf [accessed: 08.11.21]

22. K. Williams et al., Ministry of Justice, 'Prisoners' childhood and family backgrounds: Results from the Surveying Prisoner Crime Reduction (SPCR) longitudinal cohort study of prisoners', March 2012, p. 8. Available at: https://assets.publishing.service.gov.uk/government/uploads/system/uploads/attachment_data/file/278837/prisoners-childhood-family-backgrounds.pdf [accessed: 08/12/21]

23. B. Quinn, 'Third of remand prisoners in England being held beyond legal time limit for trials', *Guardian*, 17 March 2021. Available at: https://www.theguardian.com/uk-news/2021/mar/17/third-of-remand-prisoners-in-england-being-held-beyond-legal-time-limit-for-trials [accessed: 13.11.21]

24. See, for example, Children in Poverty Action Group, 'Child Poverty Facts and Figures', update March 2021. Available at: https://cpag.org.uk/child-poverty/child-poverty-facts-and-figures [accessed: 08.11.21]

ACKNOWLEDGEMENTS

One of my earliest memories is of sitting in a pushchair with a placard balanced on my lap, protesting some injustice in the world. This book could never have happened without an upbringing that taught me the importance of compassion, the importance of fighting for a fairer society, the importance of speaking out for those who are ignored, or forgotten. To my mum, who made me who I am, then read and reread every single draft of this book, from the scrappy first pages to the final version. This is the woman who helped me learn how to channel this constant, fizzing energy inside, by telling me to go out and change the world. I've not yet succeeded, but I promise I'll keep trying.

To the woman who raised me, and then the women who continue to raise me.

To my aunties, Cath, Jacinta, Loretta, Ann. Such bold, brave women. You have shown me just how important it is to have a strong support network. Working in prison taught me never to take that for granted. It's rare and precious. Most of the men I worked with didn't know what it felt like to have even one person on their team. Having you all at my back is a priceless superpower.

Thank you to my sisters for life, Claire, Joanne and Lynsey. Thank you for the rock-solid love I feel in my bones. A love that makes me feel safe wherever I am in the world and whatever I do. I could not have done this, any of this, without you all. Thank you, Shell, for proving that friendships forged in adulthood can be just as strong as childhood bonds. Your belief in me, in this project, has never faltered and I wish I told you more often just how much your strength and kindness inspire me. All four of you bring out the best in me, make me want to try harder and be better.

Thank you, Ash. You have helped me to find the confidence to do the really scary stuff. Not scary like walking the landings, but scary like finding my voice and believing I needed to get this book out into the world. Thank you for listening to me read each chapter out loud again and again, filling your lockdown with prison stories. Thank you for sharing my dream of leaving this world a better place than we found it. Thank you for supporting me as I try my best to do that. Your goodness is endless.

Thank you to the friends who held me together while I worked in prison and stayed close even when I left the city and then the country. Thank you for reminding me what normal life was after I'd spent the day in the chaos of the job. Your friendships mean more to me than any of you will ever know.

Gracie, thank you (among the million other things) for your unshakeable belief in me and this book. Thank you for introducing me to Alina. Thank you, Alina, for taking the time and effort to read, critique and pass on the manuscript. A kindness that was neither expected nor necessary but is the sole reason this book became what it is. Matilda, your effort and support has been phenomenal! Thank you so much, Jamie, for seeing the potential and then gently guiding this book towards what it is today. Your support has been invaluable in shaping the story. Karla, thank you for somehow finding the time for reading, rereading, feedback and comments. Your enthusiasm for the book from day one has been a serious support.

Thank you to the colleagues who I worked alongside in the madness. Thank you to the friends who are still working inside. I don't know how you do it, but you are the very best sort of people. My respect for you is infinite.

Finally, thank you to the men whose stories I have told. I hope you'll understand why I've taken your words and histories and written your truths. I hope that sharing some of what you have been through will start to change the debate, the conversation and, finally, change the world. I felt like a failure when I left prison, when it got too much. I felt like I'd let you all down. I hope this goes some way to showing that I never gave up on you.

ORION CREDITS

Trapeze would like to thank everyone at Orion who worked on the publication of *Criminal*.

Agent
Matilda Forbes-Watson

Editor
Jamie Coleman

Copy-editor
Claire Dean

Proofreader
Ian Allen

Editorial Management
Jo Whitford
Jane Hughes
Charlie Panayiotou
Tamara Morriss
Claire Boyle

Publicity
Leanne Oliver

Audio
Paul Stark
Jake Alderson
Georgina Cutler

Contracts
Anne Goddard
Ellie Bowker
Humayra Ahmed

Design
Nick Shah
Charlotte Abrams-Simpson
Joanna Ridley
Helen Ewing

Operations
Sharon Willis

Marketing
Tom Noble

Sales

Jen Wilson
Victoria Laws
Esther Waters
Frances Doyle
Ben Goddard
Jack Hallam
Anna Egelstaff
Inês Figueira
Barbara Ronan
Andrew Hally
Dominic Smith
Deborah Deyong
Lauren Buck
Maggy Park
Linda McGregor
Sinead White
Jemimah James
Rachael Jones
Jack Dennison
Nigel Andrews
Ian Williamson
Julia Benson
Declan Kyle
Robert Mackenzie
Megan Smith
Charlotte Clay
Rebecca Cobbold

Finance

Nick Gibson
Jasdip Nandra
Elizabeth Beaumont
Ibukun Ademefun
Afeera Ahmed
Sue Baker
Tom Costello

Inventory

Jo Jacobs
Dan Stevens

Production

Katie Horrocks
Fiona McIntosh

Rights

Susan Howe
Krystyna Kujawinska
Jessica Purdue
Ayesha Kinley
Louise Henderson

ABOUT THE AUTHOR

Angela Kirwin grew up in Manchester and qualified with an MSc in social work. For over ten years in the social care sector, she worked with hundreds of people with criminal convictions both inside prison and out in the community. Her work on substance misuse and mental health was praised in Her Majesty's Prison Inspections and she went on to secure a Research Fellowship from the Winston Churchill Memorial Trust to investigate the criminal justice systems of America and Norway. She has lectured at the University of Bristol on the topics of substance misuse, mental health, homelessness and trauma-informed care. She left the prison estate in 2016.